P9-DHQ-236

Praise for *Goshawk Squadron*

'A bleak and savage book, full of the terror of warfare and shot through with grim humour; a sort of First-World-War *Catch 22*.'　　　　　　　Nicholas Lezard, *Guardian*

'One of the most powerful indictments of war I have ever read . . . quietly savage, funny and heart-breaking . . . A book which must once and for all explode the myth of honourable warfare.'　　　　　　　*Sunday Telegraph*

'An uproarious, fast-moving and relentless cynical tale of the war in the air over France in 1918.'　*The Times* (London)

'A terrific impact . . . *Goshawk Squadron* has the authoritative ring of a little classic on the subject of war.'　*Observer*

'Shocking, but by no means insensitive, this novel of Derek Robinson's is a remarkable story of war in the air.'

Peter Townsend

Praise for Derek Robinson

'Robinson . . . should be mentioned in the same breath as Mailer, Ballard or Heller.'　　　　　　　*Express*

'Bleak, black humour, intelligence, moral depth and high adventure.'　　　　　　　*Independent*

'Robinson writes with tireless enthusiasm which never sacrifices detail to pace, or vice versa . . . terrific.'　*Observer*

DEREK ROBINSON is a policeman's son from a council estate who crossed the class barrier by going to Cambridge, where he got a degree in history and learned to write badly. A stint in advertising in London and New York changed that; then – after producing a couple of unpublishable stories – he finally got it right when, in 1971, *Goshawk Squadron* was shortlisted for the Booker Prize. Two further novels of the Royal Flying Corps followed: *War Story* and *Hornet's Sting*. His equally acclaimed trilogy of World War Two novels are *Piece of Cake, A Good Clean Fight* and *Damned Good Show*. His other novels include *The Eldorado Network* and *Artillery of Lies*.

Derek Robinson has also published non-fiction on a variety of themes, from the laws of rugby to the nuclear tests on Christmas Island in the 1950s. His most recent book is *Invasion, 1940*, a revisionist history of the Battle of Britain, also published by Constable & Robinson. He lives in Bristol.

Goshawk Squadron

DEREK ROBINSON

CARROLL & GRAF PUBLISHERS
New York

Carroll & Graf Publishers
An imprint of Avalon Publishing Group, Inc.
245 West 17th Street
New York
NY 10011–5300
www.carrollandgraf.com

AVALON
publishing group incorporated

First published in the UK by William Heinemann Ltd 1971

This paperback edition published in the UK
by Robinson, an imprint of Constable & Robinson Ltd 2005

First Carroll & Graf edition 2005

Copyright © Derek Robinson 1971, 2005

All rights reserved. No part of this publication
may be reproduced in any form or by any means
without the prior permission of the publisher.

ISBN-13: 978-0-78671-595-4
ISBN-10: 0-7867-1595-2

Printed and bound in the EU

For Sheila

Force 1: Light Air

Smoke drifts, but vane and sock unmoved

January 15th, 1918, was a cold, sparkling, sunny day. Not much happened in the Great War that day. As usual, about two thousand men (of the millions along the Western Front) died; some because they stuck their heads up too high and got shot; some because they got their feet wet too often and caught pneumonia; many by accident; and a steady few by their own hand. It was one thousand two hundred and sixty days since Britain and Germany had declared war. Not that anyone was counting.

Pont St Martin was an isolated airfield, far behind the front lines. At 11.45 AM Goshawk Squadron, RFC, was preparing to land there for the first time. Twelve SE5a biplanes – squared-off machines with wings like box kites and tails like weathervanes – were spaced out in line-astern, easing down in a wide sweep towards the field, which was still white with frost under the baby-blue sky.

In the middle of the field, Stanley Woolley sat in a deck-chair and watched them. At twenty-three he was young for a major and old for a pilot. His face looked wrong for either; bad-tempered and stony, heavy-lidded, with a miserable complexion. The newspapers had tried retouching his photograph but it wasn't any better, and in any case they couldn't retouch Woolley himself. The last journalist to try to get an interview had started by asking if his men had a pet nickname for him; Woolley had kicked him painfully up the arse. There was no story for the newspapers in Woolley. He was a veteran, he was successful, he had led Goshawk Squadron for over a year, and still they could do nothing with him. They felt badly let down by Woolley.

Coffee was stewing on a coke brazier beside the deckchair, and Woolley refilled his mug, using his cap as a potholder. The adjutant, Woodruffe, stood on the other side of the brazier. Captain Woodruffe had the face of a man who pays his bills on time and believes what his country's leaders say in the newspapers. He had paid one bill in person: there were no fingers on his left hand. He gripped his clip-board between the scarred thumb and the neatly carpentered palm.

'Nearly forgot to ask, sir,' he said. 'Did you have a good leave?'

The planes tightened their sinking circle and Woolley looked through his binoculars at the number on the fuselage of the first machine. 'Seven,' he said.

Woodruffe consulted his list. 'Rogers.'

'Ah. Bloody Rogers, I hate the bastard.' Woolley fiddled with the focus. 'Is that the same plane he broke a month ago?'

Woodruffe thought. 'Yes.'

'Well, it's still broken. I can see loose wires flapping behind his undercarriage. Who's his mechanic?'

'I don't know.'

'Hemsley. I'll kick his arse. Couldn't mend an empty bird-cage.'

They watched Rogers approach, his engine cackling softly as he floated in.

'If one wire's bust, he's bound to bust another,' Woolley said.

Rogers came over the hedge at about fifty feet. He stretched his neck and searched the ground in front, trying to select a flat piece. The frost had sprayed everything a uniform silver, and the cold, bright sunshine washed away all shadow. Rogers pulled his head back in.

They watched him sail down, and heard the tiny bursts of

2

power he used to keep the heavy nose up and let the tail sink. The wheels touched and spun and gradually accepted the weight. They raced hard for about thirty feet and hit a ridge of frozen earth. Woolley and the adjutant clearly heard the *pang!* of snapping piano-wire, then the wheel-legs hastily folded up. The plane stumbled and sprawled like a tripped runner. Its wooden propeller battered at the iron turf and splintered to a stub. Rogers grabbed the cockpit rim. The adjutant took a pace forward.

Woolley said, 'I told you so.'

The plane racketed along on its belly. The bottom wing scraped and ripped its fabric on the stiff weeds and chunks of grass, making the plane zig and zag. Eventually it skidded into a wide, slow curve and stopped.

Men began running. Woolley raised his binoculars and watched Rogers unstrap himself and climb out. 'Stop them, Woody,' he said.

Woodruffe swung a handbell vigorously. The men stopped and looked. '*Go back*,' the adjutant bawled. '*Go back.*'

Woolley rested his neck on the top of the deckchair. 'It's better where it is. Now the others know where not to come in. Besides, I don't want a lot of people running across the field, it distracts me. Who's next?' He looked in the sky. 'Three.'

'Three . . . Finlayson.'

'Ah. Bloody Finlayson. I hate that bastard.' He studied Finlayson's approach. 'How long has he been out of hospital?'

'About a week.'

'Hurt his neck, didn't he?'

'Well, he hurt almost everything – left foot, hip, ribs, tail, right arm, scalp. And his neck, yes. He burned himself, too.'

'Huh.' Woolley prodded the red-hot coke with his swagger-stick. 'If his neck won't work I don't want him.' Finlayson drifted down and landed impeccably. 'Any fool can fly forwards,' Woolley said. 'Question is, can he look backwards?' Finlayson taxied off to the far end of the field. Woolley raised his binoculars. 'Ten.'

3

'Ten . . . O'Shea.'

'Ah. Bloody O'Shea. I hate that bastard.'

The adjutant looked at his list. 'You've never even met him.'

'What's his name?'

'O'Shea. He only joined us yesterday. Came straight from that new flying school on Salisbury Plain.'

'Ah. Right. A replacement. A bloody Irish replacement. My God, is he going to land in the next field or the next bloody *arrondissement*?' O'Shea made a violent correction to bring himself back on the approach.

Woodruffe glanced cautiously at Woolley. 'I don't suppose you remember,' he said, 'but O'Shea was quite famous in 1913. His father's portrait of him was in the Royal Academy Exhibition.' Woolley grunted. O'Shea had almost stalled, had dropped twenty feet, and now his engine was bellowing at full power. Woolley lowered his binoculars and lay back. They watched O'Shea's high-speed approach. 'He was the most extraordinarily beautiful child,' Woodruffe said. O'Shea skimmed the hedge at about a hundred miles an hour.

'He must go round again,' Woolley said firmly.

'It was quite a shock, meeting him,' Woodruffe said.

'He *must* go round again.'

The biplane bored across the field, making hurried dips and passes at the ground without ever touching. Woolley turned his head to watch it race by. At last O'Shea got the plane down. The wheels raced furiously, jittering at the endless jolts, but the tail would not drop. 'Throw out the anchor!' Woolley murmured sadly. He twisted still farther to follow the action.

The aircraft did not slow down. It was flying with its wheels on the ground, and soon one of the wheels broke off and fled away, bouncing hugely. 'Now he must go round again,' Woolley said finally, as O'Shea climbed by perhaps five feet. But the aircraft levelled out and flew on. Woolley's neck-sinews were stretched, his Adam's apple bulging, his eyeballs swivelled to their limit. Still O'Shea flew on. The deckchair tipped and fell. 'Balls,' Woolley said. He knelt on the crisp white grass and watched O'Shea approach the edge of the field. Trees lined the hedgerow; O'Shea seemed to plan on steering through a gap between two of them.

From that distance the outer branches looked frail and spindly with winter, but they hooked the wings right off the biplane and held them hanging in the trees like stiff and dirty washing. There was a muffled crash as the fuselage fell into the next field, and then silence.

Woolley gave the adjutant his field-glasses. 'Take a shufti,' he said. He straightened the deckchair and brushed the frost off his knees.

'Right side up,' Woodruffe said. 'No sign of fire. Should be all right, shouldn't he? Provided he had his straps done up.'

Woolley settled himself. 'Who's next? Looks like . . . four.'

Reluctantly the adjutant lowered the binoculars. 'Four is Richards. Another replacement.'

'Ah. Bloody Richards. I hate that bastard.'

The biplane wobbled out of the sky as if blindfolded, groping for earth. When it came within twenty feet of the ground it dropped too fast, and bounced. It kangarooed halfway across the field, with Woolley loudly counting the hops, before Richards made it stick and ran it harmlessly to a halt.

'They've got him out,' Woodruffe said, from behind the field-glasses.

'Who?'

'O'Shea.'

'What for? Should've left him there. Irish clod.'

'They're helping him into the field.' He lowered the glasses. 'He seems to be all right.' A wing fell out of a tree.

'That's a hell of an improvement, then. Here comes nine.'

'Nine . . . Dickinson.'

'Ah. Bloody Dickinson. I hate that bastard.'

Rogers came up, rubbing his right elbow. 'Hullo, sir,' he said. He saluted, wincing. 'Good to have you back, sir. Did you have a good leave? This place is worse than the last one, isn't it? Bumps everywhere. Hope we're not going to stay here.'

Dickinson side-slipped delicately, and Woolley allowed his eyelids to droop and frame the scene with gauzy, golden softness: the lovely balance of the plane as it settled, like an owl, mature and masterful and so controlled that it seemed lazy, only half-thinking what to do next. The instant of contact: the firm, square kiss. Then Dickinson rolled home, his left wheel squeaking. Just a man in a patched and obsolescent aeroplane. Woolley raised the binoculars again.

'Who was that up the tree?' Rogers asked.

'*Six*,' Woolley announced loudly.

'Six is . . . Gabriel. He's another replacement. Came from the school in Kent.'

'Ah. Bloody Gabriel. I hate that bastard.'

'Gabriel,' said Rogers. 'I wonder if his brother kept wicket for Essex before the war. J. T. W. Gabriel. I think he was killed on the Somme.'

'Who wasn't?' the adjutant asked.

'Not a great wicket-keeper, mind you,' Rogers said. 'Good enough for Essex, though.'

They watched Gabriel make a long, conscientious descent. Even from that distance, they could see his head sticking far above the cockpit.

'Does he have to stand up to fly?' Woolley asked.

'He's six foot three, sir,' Rogers said. 'Perfect build for a fast bowler. Big feet, really enormous feet. And hands, too. Perfect.'

'I hate the bastard,' Woolley said. Gabriel resolutely drove his machine down the invisible road. Woolley closed one eye and held up his charred swagger-stick so that Gabriel appeared to be sliding down it. 'I want you to kick your mechanic up the arse,' he said.

Rogers waited. 'Yes, sir?' he said.

'Take a good swing,' Woolley said. 'Wear boots.'

'Yes, sir.'

Gabriel landed solidly in someone else's wheel marks and

6

motored briskly, the tail-skid bouncing high on the ruts and the whole plane vibrating with the power he gave the engine.

Woolley looked away, massaging his face. 'What the hell have you lot been doing while I've been away?' he asked.

'We've been in reserve,' Rogers said. 'On two-hour stand-by, most of the time. As it happened, they hardly ever needed us.'

'No training? No work? What about all these replacements? Why haven't you brought them up to scratch?'

'Because we were on reserve, on stand-by,' Rogers explained. 'You can't do proper training on stand-by, sir, can you? Beside, the weather's been bad and there was a lot of work to be done on the machines. And in any case, I gave people as much local leave as I could.' Woolley grunted. 'They had it due,' Rogers pointed out.

'It's done them no good, has it? Find out if O'Shea's fit to fly.'

'Was that O'Shea over there?'

'Yes,' the adjutant said. 'Throttle stuck, probably. He came in far too fast, anyway. It reminded me of what's-his-name, last month.'

'Wintle,' Rogers suggested.

'Wintle? No, no. Began with a B. Burroughs . . .? *Morris*. The ginger moustache.'

'Morris didn't have a moustache, he had a spaniel.'

'Who's *two*?' Woolley demanded loudly.

'Two is . . . Delaforce. Another replacement.'

'Hate the bastard,' Woolley muttered.

'Anyway, I don't think Morris had a stuck throttle,' Rogers said. 'Wasn't he a jammed control line? Or am I thinking of Spencer?'

'Woody!' said Woolley suddenly. 'What are you going to do about Delaport? He's gone absent without leave.'

The adjutant looked at his list. 'Dela*force*,' he said. 'I can still hear him.' He stood on his toes and tried to see into the next field. 'What's he doing over there?'

'AWOL,' Woolley said. 'I want him court-martialled.

That's not his aeroplane, he's got no right to keep it. Who does he think he is? Morris? Spencer? Wintle? George V? Court-martial the bastard.'

They listened to the flat, invisible roar of Delaforce's machine. Suddenly the plane heaved itself over the hedge, panicking a flock of birds. Most escaped, some bounced off the wings and fell broken, and a couple got sucked into the arc of the propeller, which snapped, slinging chunks of wood about like a drunken juggler. The engine, workless now, screamed hysterically and then died. 'Charge Delaport,' Woolley said in the silence, 'with cruelty to animals.' The aircraft glided shakily towards an early landing; the tail-skid fell with a shuddering thud.

'I'm not sure that that's a military offence, is it, sir?' Rogers asked brightly. Woolley turned his pitted face on him and said: 'This whole war is a military offence. And for an offence of this size there is never enough offensiveness to go around, so we must not waste it on the birds, who shit impartially on either side.' He spoke flatly and stonily, as he always did, forcing Rogers to stand up and be active. 'Have you kicked Hemsley up the arse yet?' he demanded.

'No, sir.'

'Then *go now*.'

Rogers went away, making a face at Dickinson as he passed him. Dickinson came up and saluted. 'Good morning, sir. I hope you had a good leave.'

Woolley got out of his deckchair and turned away from Dickinson. He prodded the brazier with his swagger-stick until sparks glittered in the cold air. 'Everyone wants to know if I had a good leave,' he said. 'So you can tell everyone that I went on leave to bury my brother. He had TB. He was a cripple. Curly golden hair, laughing blue eyes, and he'd just won a scholarship to the Royal Academy of Needlework. His mother doted on him, and the only reason he died was the doctors were drunk.'

He glanced at a plane that was landing. 'Lambert?' The adjutant nodded. 'That only leaves the old sweats, then.

Church, Dangerfield, Mackenzie and Killion. Let's go and eat.' He sniffed the smoking tip of his swagger-stick while Woodruffe folded the deckchair.

The adjutant got the deckchair under his right arm and his papers under his left arm, and looked unhappily at Woolley, who was motionless, staring at nothing through bleak, over-worked eyes that blinked when the smoke came too near.

'Not Mackenzie,' Woodruffe said, quite clearly.

Woolley let his head drop. Out of the corner of his eye he watched Church touch down. Then he looked the other way. 'Did I say Mackenzie?' he asked.

'We have no Mackenzie flying with us. The other pilot is Kimberley. Not Mackenzie.'

'Not Mackenzie,' Woolley murmured. He kept his head down and smiled a crooked, guilty smile. 'Certainly not Mackenzie. *Never* Mackenzie. Never.' He turned and rammed his swagger-stick into the heart of the brazier and set off at a run. Halfway across the field he leaped high, took off his cap, and hurled it spinning from him. '*Never!*' he shouted. '*Never!*' All around the perimeter faces turned to look.

'Why did he go home, Woody?' Dickinson asked. 'Was it really family trouble?'

'Nobody knows. I think probably the quacks made him go.' They were walking across the field, the stiff grass crunching. 'That's only my guess, but I think they gave him a choice. Either three weeks' rest, or grounded for good.'

'He doesn't look as if he's had three weeks' rest,' Dickinson said. 'He looks bloody awful, poor bastard.'

Woodruffe glanced across curiously. 'You sound sorry for him,' he said. 'You should know better than that by now. If you're going to feel sorry for anyone, save it for yourself.'

Dickinson remembered the adjutant's hand, and took the deckchair from him. 'Who's Mackenzie, anyway?'

'One of the many,' Woodruffe said. 'Just one of the many.' He stooped to pick up Woolley's cap. 'Three weeks' leave seems to have done him more harm than good, doesn't it?'

Force 2: Light Breeze

Vane sets to wind; sock begins to fill

Woolley sat in his tent and cleaned his boots. Outside, the sky was a hard, remote grey: an ancient metal bowl placed over the world. The fields were still frozen and rutted, but a team of horses was hauling a heavy roller up and down the landing-ground. The squadron lived in tents in a corner of the field and did not like it, but nobody said so to Woolley. It was hard to tell whether he liked it or not. As usual, he seemed to dislike everything.

Apart from his cot, his canvas chair, and a folding canvas washstand, there was no furniture in his tent. Woolley kept his belongings in a tin chest, and the clothes which he wasn't wearing hung from the tent-pole. The only other item was a large piano-accordion which lay on the ground, unbuttoned and sprawling. It managed to look both stunted and bloated at the same time.

Woolley ate as he worked: beside him were a quart jar of pickled onions, half a wheel of cheese and a French loaf, plus a case of bottled Guinness. He was a messy eater, and when a pickled onion got away he left it where it fell, down among the crusts and the indented rind. He paid more attention to his boots (they were his flying-boots), lavishing dubbin on their skins and working out all the stiffness. When a young man appeared in the doorway he ignored him.

The visitor saluted and said: 'Lieutenant Richards, sir.'

Woolley spat on the toecap of his boot and rubbed the gob in. Without looking up, he examined what part of Lieutenant Richards came within his vision; immaculate breeches, impeccable puttees, elegant boots. 'How old are you?' he demanded.

'Nearly twenty, sir.'

Woolley drank some Guinness and pushed his belt down while he belched. He looked at Richards and caught the tailend of a faint distaste vanishing across his face. 'Nearly twenty,' he said flatly. 'Too young to think and too old to listen. I suppose you are valiant, dashing, chivalrous, gallant and plucky?'

Richards flushed, but held his gaze. 'I should hope to be all those, at least in part,' he said, 'sir.'

Woolley let the bottle of Guinness fall, and stretched out in his chair. He looked long at Richards, but Richards was a well-made, handsome fellow accustomed to having people looking at him; so he said nothing. Then he realized that Woolley, although still looking at him, was not thinking of him. 'Sir?' he said politely. Woolley blinked.

'Why did you join the bloody old RFC, Richards?'

'Well, sir, I was in the cavalry – 21st Lancers – and frankly it was getting rather dreary. I mean, we never seemed to go into action. So after a while it occurred to me that this wasn't going to be a good cavalry war at all. It's all those trenches, you see, sir. First there's ours, then there's theirs, and nothing in between but shell-holes. Hopeless riding country. So it occurred to me, sir, that you chaps in aeroplanes were having rather a better time of it. Sort of cavalry of the air, that kind of thing. So I decided to have a stab at that, sir. And here I am.'

'Here you are.'

'Yes, sir.'

Woolley went back to his flying-boots. 'And what are you going to do next?'

'Next, sir? Well, anything you say, sir. Go up and sort of start shooting down Germans, I hope.'

11

'Why?'

'Why, sir?' Richard stared curiously. 'Well, to help win the war, I suppose.'

'How?'

'How?' Richards felt his right hand start to tremble. He held his breeches between his fingers. Woolley, with his gamekeeper's manners and his trade-unionist voice, upset him. 'Well . . . in the obvious way, sir, I suppose. By killing Germans. Sir.'

'One at a time?'

Richards said nothing.

'That's the way they come, up there. One plane, one German.' Woolley's voice was flat as slate. 'If you're lucky you might get a two-seater and double your victory effort. Were you thinking of going after two-seaters especially, Richards?'

Miserably, Richards muttered: 'No, sir.' Even the drill sergeants had never spoken to him with such drab contempt.

'No. Albert Ball only got forty-four, you know. Guynemer only got fifty-three. Even God Almighty himself, Mr Richthofen, has only got sixty-odd.' Woolley stopped work, and stared at Richards anxiously. 'That last one is on the *other* side, you know. *He* shoots at *us*.'

'Yes, sir.'

'Good.' Work resumed. 'Are you as good as Ball, Richards? Are you as good as – say – Bishop? Who is still, astonishingly, with us?'

'I doubt it, sir. I shouldn't think so.'

'No. The way you landed yesterday, kangarooing that poor old aeroplane in bloody great *leaps* and *bounds*, I don't think you're fit to wipe Bishop's bottom. Are you, Richards?'

'No, sir. Probably not.'

'Not what?'

'Not . . . fit to – to wipe Mr Bishop's bottom, sir.' Richards' father owned a length of Curzon Street, a chunk of Yorkshire, and the warm respect of all mankind. He had raised his son in a tradition of service and self-sacrifice,

12

meaning command over others. Now Woolley's coarse assessment bewildered Richards. His fingers curled with revulsion at the thought. His common sense told him that Woolley was merely using a figure of speech, but the man's face, his attitude – like a professional gambler living on fools' money – reduced everything to a stony unpleasantness. Richards was accustomed to finding at least a little pleasure in everything. Woolley upset him. The man had gone back to his blasted boots. He was spitting on them again.

'If you really want to kill more Germans than Ball, or Bishop, or . . . or even *me*,' Woolley spread his arms in a humility which humiliated only Richards, 'well, that can certainly be arranged. If that's what you want, I'll put you in a machine-gun battalion on the most active part of the Front we can find, and with luck the Hun will attack and you can kill scores of them. People have been known to kill hundreds with one machine gun, Richards. I myself have seen it done. You sit behind your machine gun, and the enemy climb out of their trenches and advance. Some may run, but most walk. The mud, you see, and the shell-holes, and the wire. They walk towards you, and you shoot your machine gun at them. It's on a sort of swivel-thing, and you swing it from side to side. You don't aim, not in this war. The enemy walks into your line of fire, you see, so you just keep on scything away at them. That's what it's called, "scything". If you do it properly they fall down in rows, hundreds and hundreds at a time. Sixty thousand in one hour, I think that was the record, but of course somebody may have beaten that, I couldn't say, I don't read the papers. That was *their* machine guns, of course, and we supplied the sixty thousand, but the principle is exactly the same. So if you do really honestly want to kill more Germans than any other pilot in the RFC, I can have you transferred. Yes or no?'

'No, sir,' Richards said huskily. Tears of shame and fury pressed at his eyes. He had never met anyone so utterly despicable and seedy and rotten and not worth fighting for in his whole life.

'You don't think you would contribute towards victory behind a machine gun in the trenches, killing hundreds of Germans.'

Richards said nothing.

'It's not a very valiant way to fight, I agree. Nothing dashing, chivalrous, gallant or plucky about it.' Woolley guzzled more Guinness. 'What do you want to do?'

Richards clenched his teeth and forced his head to stay up. He kept tasting something hot and foul in the back of his throat. This was what he imagined rape felt like. He found that he was shaking his head. 'I don't know, sir,' he said.

'Then thank God, because that's the first sensible thing you've said! You don't know a bloody thing, lad. You're like a Boy Scout on a new bicycle. The first Hun you met would cut you in half without even taking the sausage sandwich out of his mouth. You know nothing – *nothing*. So what are you going to do?'

'Going to learn, sir.'

'How?'

'I expect . . . you'll teach me, sir.'

Woolley finished his boots and pulled them on. 'Wear plenty of warm woollies,' he said. 'It's cold up there.'

At twelve thousand feet Richards could no longer feel his feet. The passive misery of freezing in the cockpit overlaid all memories of Woolley's tent. It was wearying just to sit there and keep flexing every muscle, and climb and climb and climb, with the engine clattering ahead and the wires whistling all around . . .

Abruptly he realized that Woolley was blaring at him on a klaxon horn fitted to his cockpit. Richards raised an arm stiffly, and Woolley waved him back to line-astern position.

The instant Richards was ready Woolley began the lesson. First, simple banks and turns and easy dives; then faster banks, and tighter turns, and steeper dives. As soon as Richards straightened out from one manoeuvre Woolley led him into another. The pressure increased. When Woolley fell away in a side-slip, it was sharper and deeper than Richards thought safe; but Richards followed as closely as his icy feet and sweating hands allowed.

Woolley dropped into a dive, let Richards join him and pointed to the right. He flattened the dive and threw the plane into a tight right-hand turn, skidding its wings across the thin air. Richards tried to follow and missed by a mile. His turn was soft at the start, and when he tried to compress it the correction was violent, and the aircraft lurched into a sideways waddle. He lost speed, the controls were sluggish, the engine bellowed resentfully. Cursing and sweating, rigid and heavy handed, he laboriously straightened up.

Woolley charged him from the right, above and a fraction behind, klaxon blaring like a maniac. He drove in so hard that to Richards' shocked eyes all that could be seen was the head-on profile, violently magnifying itself until with a sickening, diminishing howl Woolley lifted and skimmed over Richards' cockpit, and droned away.

Richards sucked breath into his lungs. He felt disgraced. *If that had been a German*, he thought, *I should be dead.*

Woolley came back and flew alongside and looked at him. He signalled Richards to get back into line-astern. For the next ten minutes they flew in ever-tighter circles, first one way, then the next, until Richards expected the plane to come to pieces under the grinding strain of chasing its own tail.

By now the blood was back in his feet, his body was wet to the neck, and his nerves sensed every vibration of the machine as if it were a live thing. He realized that its limits were his limits, its abilities his abilities. This he had never felt when driving a tubby Avro 504 over Salisbury Plain. This was a different life.

Woolley broke off the tail-chasing and they practised Immelmann turns: diving into a loop and rolling out of the top of it to emerge right-side up. Richards was so slow that Woolley completed a second Immelmann and dived over him as he came out of his first. They did Immelmanns for a quarter of an hour.

By now Richards was very tired. The manual labour of working the controls, the wasted tension of uncertainty, the draining fatigue of concentration, left him limp. He wanted nothing more than to sit in a soft chair in a quiet room with a good cup of tea.

Next Woolley led him in ten minutes' miscellaneous spinning. At the end of it Richards' hands were trembling inside his gloves, his forearms were stiff with effort, and he had been sick over the floor.

Woolley turned for home and Richards trailed behind him, lamb-like. He had to brace himself with one hand on the rim of the cockpit in order to hold the controls steady. His feet slithered on the freezing vomit.

Woolley changed his mind and took them back up to eight thousand feet, where he led Richards in a series of power dives. Each time, he made the dive a little steeper, held it a little longer, until Richards saw the French fields held up like a backdrop before him, and heard the wing-roots creak and felt the fuselage judder under the rising speed. He watched Woolley out of the corner of his eye and saw the tearing air pressure begin to bend the wing-tips back; and he repeated the same stableboys' obscenity over and over again until Woolley smoothly pulled out and sent the SE soaring up the other side of the invisible hill until it lost its impetus and lazily toppled forward into level flight.

Richards followed, shakily, and at a thousand feet Woolley led him over the edge again, only this time the plunge was vertical. Richards clenched the stick in both hands as if it were a tiller in a storm. The air shrieked; he could see hedges and trees and things moving. He was acutely conscious of a harmless skim of oil, drifting back on the top of his engine cowling.

There was a field with a haystack in it, dead ahead, and he made a tiny, pointless adjustment to miss the haystack. At five hundred feet a strip of fabric ripped off his lower wing with a bang and cracked itself to shreds. He was aware of a small satisfaction: this would be the end of Woolley, too. Then Woolley eased his nose up and carved a long, luxurious curve that left them racing across the countryside at twice treetop height. Woolley gave Richards a couple of minutes to recover his breath, his vision and what was left of his nerve, and then hooted on the klaxon. They went down low and hedge-hopped all the way home. The first Richards knew about their landing-ground was when they jumped over some trees and he saw the planes parked around the edge of the airfield.

Woolley met him as he got out of the cockpit. The bulky coat and helmet made Woolley's face look even thinner. A smear of oil darkened his patchy complexion, and where the goggles had been his eyes looked raw.

'What did you see in the sky?' Woolley asked.

Richards stumbled and hung on to the wing. He shook his head.

'You didn't see anything in the sky?'

Richards tried to make his mouth work but the muscles had locked.

'You must be bloody blind, then. I counted sixteen aircraft, and I wasn't even looking.' Richards blinked at Woolley's boots and tried to stop his head trembling. 'What did you see on the ground? Anything worth reporting, if you'd been an enemy pilot?'

Richards forced himself to look up. His ears roared with the negative bellow of silence and the uncertain surge of blood; the landing-ground felt unsteady, as if it might tilt and fall away without warning. *Had* he seen anything on the ground? Only a haystack. Only a haystack. 'I . . . didn't have much time to look,' he said.

'You had all the damn time there was,' Woolley told him. 'You didn't see the French camp at Conty? We flew around it long enough. No tanks on the road from Beauvais to Breteuil? No artillery on railway trucks near Poix?'

'No, sir.' Richards' lips were rubbery. Speaking was a monstrous effort. He wanted only to be allowed to go away and never have to say another word to anyone, ever.

17

'If you didn't *see* anything, what the hell were you doing up there? You obviously weren't paying much attention to flying the aeroplane. Joan of Arc in full armour could have flown better than you did. And don't go up in those boots again, they're too poncy. Get something thick and heavy, and wear plenty of socks. You had cold feet up there, didn't you? Bloody tramping on that poor bastard rudder bar. You can't make it go by kicking it, you know.'

Woolley left him and ambled over to the cockpit. For a moment Richards was afraid he might look inside, but he only patted the fuselage and spat on the hot exhaust pipe, which sizzled. 'Poor old cow,' he said. 'Who's your mechanic?'

'Fairbrother,' Richards said.

'Get him now, tell him to fix that fabric and everything else, and refuel. Then find Rogers and Lambert and practise close-formation stuff. They'll explain.' He ambled off.

When he was thirty yards away he looked back. Richards was wiping his face with a handkerchief. Woolley put his hands on his hips. Richards dropped the handkerchief and lurched away from the aeroplane. 'Fairbrother!' he shouted weakly. 'Corporal Fairbrother!' A man came running.

Rogers had a car. That evening he and Lambert took Richards, Gabriel and the adjutant into the nearest town, which was Montigny. Rogers and Lambert had flown together for several weeks; they talked easily and treated Woodruffe almost as an equal. Richards was very tired. He made himself comfortable in the back and left everything to the others. Gabriel was not tired; he sat forward and paid attention to the conversation, but did not join in. He was tall and gave the impression that he could have been taller, for his frame was strongly boned and his head bulged powerfully, like an intelligent swede.

'How did you get this car, Dudley?' Woodruffe asked.

'Hugo gave it to me.'

'Hugo couldn't afford a car like this.'

'No, he won it. He and another chap were attached to one of those odds-and-sods squadrons, you know, Dutchmen and Americans from the Foreign Legion, and Japs, and Canadians on the run, and a few Portuguese. Well, one day a Portuguese lost his wings in a power-drive. I think he'd caught fire and he was trying to blow it out, or something. So they all drew lots and Hugo got the chap's car.'

'Yes, but how did *you* get it?' Woodruffe asked.

'Well, Hugo got shot up, and his last words were, "Give Dudley my car." So I took it.'

'I don't believe that for a minute,' Woodruffe said. 'Hugo couldn't stand you. He said you talked too much.'

'No, no. It wasn't that. He never forgave me because of school. I got elected captain of cricket when he was only made secretary, that was all. Hugo was a bad loser, you see. He got frightfully emotional about the Germans, you know, when his brother was blown up. He was just the same at school – couldn't bear to lose.'

'Unlike our froggy friends,' Lambert said, 'who make a career of it.'

'They fired at me again last week, you know,' Rogers said. 'Twice. And they *must* have known. Perfect visibility.'

'Of course they knew,' Lambert said. He had a restless, brooding face that had been born looking battered; now, twenty-one years later, it was lined and pouched. Between the creases the skin was white, and even slightly freckled, but the face retained all the baggy reluctance of infancy. 'Of course they knew. They got a damn sight nearer hitting you than any poor Fokker.'

'I saw a great big château this morning,' Rogers said. 'Only a couple of miles from our field, too. Make a perfect place for us to live, and the lawns are big enough to land on. I went down and tried it, actually, and had a quick look-around. No one's living there, Woody. We could move in tomorrow. Honest.'

'The old man would never agree,' the adjutant said.

'How can you tell? He might.'

'Ask him, if you think there's a chance,' Woodruffe said.

'Not likely. You ask him.'

'I'm happy in my tent, thank you.'

'You're scared of him,' Lambert accused.

The adjutant did not answer. Gabriel glanced at him. Woodruffe was thinking. He said: 'I honestly don't expect to be afraid of any man who isn't actually trying to kill me, ever again. I was very scared in the trenches, scared of the Minniewerfers and the whizzbangs and the jack joneses, but the men who fired them . . . no. They were too far away.'

They drove in silence for a while.

'The only man who *really* frightened me,' Woodruffe said, 'was a colonel. He believed that the best time to attack was 1 PM because that was when the Germans would be eating lunch. He said he got the idea quite suddenly one day when *he* was eating lunch at brigade HQ. He said he looked up and saw everyone with his Sam Browne off, spooning soup, and he realized how horribly vulnerable they all were. So he went around trying to get up a surprise attack – no artillery barrage – precisely at one in the afternoon. Just over the top, cut our wire, cross the shell-holes, cut their wire, and capture the enemy trenches. Now *that* man frightened me.'

Gabriel cleared his throat. 'Did he ever do it?' he asked.

'Yes, after I was posted, I heard that he did. He was one of the first killed, in fact. He led the attack, you see, because he really *believed* in it. He was *so* enthusiastic, he kept on and on, until he bored everyone so much, they finally let him try.'

'I wonder if the Germans do take lunch at one o'clock,' Rogers mused.

'Events seemed to indicate not,' Woodruffe said.

Montigny, when they reached it, was dark. This part of France was within range of German bombers, and no street lights were lit. They drove through thickening traffic to the main square.

Only one restaurant was open. It was full of smoke and soldiers. Everyone seemed sober, but they made a great deal of noise, and many smoked cigars. Nobody saluted

Woodruffe, although his captain's insignia was clearly visible. 'They must be Americans,' Lambert said. He stopped a passing soldier and examined his badges. 'They *are* Americans,' he said. 'Goddam right,' the soldier told him.

They waited for a table. Woodruffe said: 'If these aren't all gym instructors, or drill NCOs, then they're physically the finest-looking infantry I've ever seen. They don't even know the *meaning* of defeat.'

'I didn't know it had any meaning,' Lambert said. 'I thought it was just policy.'

They were hungry now, and the healthy, muscular confidence of the American troops both impressed them and depressed them. Eventually a table emptied and they sat down. Waiters – all old men – hurried past, until Rogers seized one by the elbow. 'Menu, menu!' he shouted.

'Nussing,' the waiter said automatically. 'All gone. No food, no wine. *Les Americains ont tout mangé.*' He tugged his arm.

'*Mais nous sommes pilotes*,' Woodruffe said.

'No you're bloody not,' Lambert told him.

'*Avions*,' said Rogers. '*Aviateurs. Contre le Boche, n'est-ce pas?* Bleriot. Vrooom! Acka-acka-acka!' He released the man to use both hands for his impression of aerial combat, and the waiter scuttled off. 'Soup!' Rogers bawled. The waiter waved and kept going.

'Think we'll get anything?' Gabriel said.

'My God, I'm hungry,' Richards said. He was awake again, and alert.

'You had a busy afternoon, didn't you?' Woodruffe asked sympathetically.

'Up for three hours,' Richards said. 'Half that time was with Major Woolley, too.'

'That counts double, at least,' Rogers remarked. 'The old man flies every minute as if it were his last.'

'And one day it will be,' Lambert said, 'and God help hell, then.'

'One sees what you mean,' Richards said. 'He has a

forceful manner. Not a man to tolerate differences of opinion.'

'Blunt,' said Woodruffe. 'Blunt and bloody, like a well-used bludgeon.'

'Really, they ought to bring us some food,' Richards said. All around them waiters were clearing away the debris of large meals. A different waiter came by, and Richards grabbed him. 'Look here, you simply must bring us some food,' he insisted.

'*Pas moi, pas moi,*' the waiter gabbled. '*Il faut demander au—*' He put his foot against the chair and dragged his skinny arm against Richards' grip. 'We must keep him,' Lambert said, 'as a hostage.' The waiter stamped his puny foot. 'Ah, the famous French offensive spirit!' Woodruffe exclaimed. The waiter burst into tears. After a while he sat on Gabriel's knee, still crying, still held by Richards.

The first waiter came back with three bowls of soup and three pieces of bread.

'*Plus?*' Rogers asked. 'Two *plus?*' The waiter said nothing, but put the bowls on the table. Lambert seized him. '*Pas assez!*' he shouted. The waiter had a fit of coughing and ended up on his knees, choking and spitting. The second waiter watched miserably. 'My God!' Rogers said. 'Is this what we're fighting for?'

Gabriel tasted the soup and pushed it away. 'Cold,' he said. Woodruffe yawned and rested his head on his arms. Rogers, who was smoking, began using his cigarette to singe the white hairs on the backs of the second waiter's hands. The second waiter watched, fascinated. After a while he developed hiccups. Several waiters had gathered and were watching from a safe distance.

'One begins to wonder,' Richards said, 'whether there *is* in fact any more food.'

'Ex-cuse *me*,' said an American. 'Can we have our wader back? He gets the cawfee, see.' The man was brawny; he seemed to be an officer: he wore a tie and two revolvers. 'The hiccupy one,' he said.

22

'Nearly finished,' Rogers said. He singed the last of the hairs and polished the wrist with his cuff. 'There you are. Give it a rub with an oily rag and it'll last for years.'

'Thanks. What's goin' on here, anyway?'

'We are on hunger strike,' Woodruffe said. 'We have sworn not to eat until they bring us food. The fast is entering its ninth day. As you can see, my comrades are in a sorry state.'

' "Sorry" is not the word,' Lambert said. 'We are almost sickeningly apologetic. What if we die here? Who will pay the cover charge?'

'You want some grub, is that it?' the American asked.

'Yes,' said Rogers, quickly and firmly.

'Whyncha say so? *Ay-Meel!*' he shouted. '*Ay-Meel!* See, we own this dump . . .' The head waiter arrived. 'Ay-Meel, these friends of mine want a big, long dinner, with lots of good booze. Okay? Toot Sweet, see, goddamn hungry, got it?' The head waiter hurried off. 'You get any trouble, just ask for me. Name's Chuck Martin.'

'How do you do. I'm Woodruffe.' They shook hands. 'I must say that we are all greatly obliged to you, Mr Martin.'

'Chuck. Real pleasure meeting you all. Enjoy your meal, now. Stop by and see us again, you hear?' He led the hiccuping waiter away.

Waiters converged, laid a fresh cloth and place settings, a big plate of *hors d'oeuvres*, fresh rolls and butter, and two carafes of wine. 'You asked what we were fighting for,' Lambert said to Rogers. 'Whatever it is, the Americans seem to have cornered the market.'

As the meal got under way they began to relax once more. Woodruffe asked Gabriel what he did before he joined the RFC. He was obviously too old to have come straight from school.

'I was a theological student,' Gabriel said. 'I wanted to enter the Ministry.'

'I knew a cricket Blue who became a parson,' Rogers remarked. 'They let him play, too. Say what you like about

23

the Church of England they know the value of a good off-break bowler.'

'I was going to be a Baptist minister.'

'You wouldn't have liked that,' Rogers said. 'They won't even let you read the sports pages, did you know? They're not keen on alcohol, either. And they're definitely discouraging about sex. In fact the only thing they positively approve of is praying.'

'And total immersion,' Woodruffe said.

'In that case they should put all the Baptists in the trenches,' Lambert said. 'From all reports they'd find it an ideal existence.'

'Pardon my vulgar curiosity,' Woodruffe said, 'but what made you want to be a Baptist minister? Were you . . . inspired, or . . . or . . . I mean, did you hear The Call, so to speak?'

Gabriel laughed. It was the first time they had heard him laugh, and there was little humour in it. The function of Gabriel's laugh was to preface a point of interest.

'It wasn't like that at all; quite the opposite. The reason I entered theological college was sheer snobbery, to prove that I really was better than everyone else. You see, ever since I was sixteen I'd been doing slum missionary work.'

'My dear chap!' said Richards. He topped up Gabriel's glass.

'Where?' asked Woodruffe.

'Sheffield.'

'A *dreadful* place,' Rogers said. 'I couldn't stand *living* in a place like that.' He drank deeply.

'Couldn't your people go somewhere else?' Richards asked. 'It does seem awfully bad luck having to grow up in a place like Sheffield.'

'You could have moved to Harrogate,' Rogers said, 'or Scarborough. Or even York. Why live in Sheffield?'

'It was unavoidable,' Gabriel said. 'My parents were slum missionaries, too.'

'Oh, I say, look here!' Richards protested. 'But how utterly beastly for you.'

24

'They still are,' Gabriel said calmly. 'And doing magnificent work, too.'

Richards was deeply moved. 'My dear fellow,' he said. 'I had *no idea*. Not the slightest idea.'

'Well, why shouldn't Gabriel's parents be slum missionaries?' Woodruffe demanded impatiently. 'Why not?'

'Somebody's got to look after Sheffield,' Lambert said. 'Important source of steel. That's where they make the penknives for the generals to sharpen their pencils so they can draw red lines on maps. The war wouldn't last five minutes without Sheffield.'

'I think we should all be jolly grateful to Mr and Mrs Gabriel for going round sobering up the slums of Sheffield so that the disgusting steelworkers have a cool head and a steady hand for making generals' penknives,' Woodruffe said, 'and I ask you to drink to that.'

'More wine!' Richards called, but a waiter was already topping up their glasses. They drank to Mr and Mrs Gabriel.

'Let's look on the bright side,' Richards said. 'Old Gabriel got away from the beastly Baptists, after all. Isn't that what matters?'

'Oh, absolutely,' Woodruffe said. 'Tell us how you did it, Gabriel. Can one buy oneself out, or . . .'

'I had a Vision,' Gabriel said. 'I was attending a lecture on Redemption, Faith and Freedom, and God spoke to me. He said it was all a lot of balls, the whole course at this Baptist College. I glanced up, and He was cleaning the windows.' Gabriel forked a small potato and looked candidly at their several faces. 'Please don't think I dramatize or exaggerate,' he said, 'because that is *exactly* what happened.'

'You say that He . . . that He was . . . uh . . . cleaning the windows,' Woodruffe said uncomfortably. 'I don't suppose . . . What I mean is, there's not the slightest chance that—'

'The raiment was quite distinctive,' Gabriel said. 'Also the beard.'

'Quite so, quite so.' Woodruffe nodded strenuously. 'Just a thought.'

'*What* was it you said He said?' Rogers asked.

'The exact words were: "This is all a lot of balls",' Gabriel said, 'delivered in a firm, but not angry, tone of voice. It left no doubt in my mind as to what to do.'

'What *did* you do?' Lambert asked.

'I joined the RFC.'

'Hmm.' Woodruffe chewed thoughtfully. 'And do you feel that you are nearer your God here than you were in Sheffield?'

'Really, Woody!' Lambert exclaimed. 'What a question to ask.'

'Oh,' Woodruffe said. 'Ah. Sorry.'

The meal burbled on. Lambert ordered brandy and cigars, forgot that he had ordered them, and ordered them again. Only Gabriel remained more or less expressionless. Woodruffe sprawled and studied the man's inscrutable marble bust of a head. He felt a desire to walk around behind it and suddenly bawl '*Gas attack!*' in its left ear. It was not natural for a man to drink and yet look so sober, especially when his normal appearance was so depressingly competent and controlled.

'I say,' Richards said to Rogers, 'did you really mean what you said about the French firing on you last week?'

'Last week and every week. They never miss a chance.'

'But I thought there were signals, and no-firing zones, and things. Can't you pop off a Very light and shut them up, or something? I mean, suppose they were to hit you . . . think how awful that would be.'

Rogers smiled, and swirled his brandy about.

'I mean to say, a joke's a joke,' Richards said.

'Oh, well.' Rogers lit Woodruffe's cigar, and then his own. Richards blinked uneasily.

'If I were a French gunner I'd fire at everything that flew within range,' Lambert said.

'But what possible good would that do, if it was a British plane?' Richards demanded. 'I mean, be serious for a minute.'

'It would make *me* feel better,' Lambert said, as if that ended everything.

Richards stared from Lambert to Rogers. 'Well, you chaps surprise me,' he said. 'If any blasted French gunner started popping off at me, I'd soon go down and put fifty rounds behind his left ear for him.'

'Which would prove that he was right all the time,' Woodruffe said.

'Certainly not. How can anyone expect—'

'Oh, tish and tosh,' Rogers said easily. 'Look, the frogs have had an awful war. Inconceivably horrible, tragic, appalling, *wasteful* war. Not much worse than ours, maybe, except that it's their country, so they *feel* worse.' Richards glowered, red and resentful. 'Don't look like that, old chap, it's true. All they want is to be left alone. If anybody disturbs them they shoo him away. Bang-bang, go home, whoever you are. Don't you see, they don't want to win the war – *they want the war to end.*'

'Not the same thing at all,' Woodruffe said, yawning.

'But we're Allies, we're helping them,' Richards protested.

'Extremely dubious, that,' Lambert said. 'The frog is our natural enemy. We should be fighting *him*, only God got the history books wrong.'

'Well . . .' Richards shrugged, too disgusted to speak.

'I know, old chap,' Rogers said. '*Ce n'est pas magnifique, mais c'est la guerre.*'

'Well, all right then, how do they think they're ever going to end the war like that?'

'Ahah,' said Woodruffe, 'they don't. We're going to end it for them, us and these well-fed Americans. The French don't want to fight the Germans any more.'

'But they don't mind shooting down a few of our planes.'

'Look,' Lambert said, filling the glasses. 'You know the answer, don't you?'

'Don't fly over the French lines,' Gabriel said promptly.

There was a pause.

'I'm sorry, but that's simply not good enough,' Richards said. He was still angry.

'Nothing ever is, when you get right down to it,' Lambert said.

'Except, perhaps, this wine,' Woodruffe said, 'which we should now finish up and toddle off home . . . Waiter, the bill . . . *L'addition* . . . Good God,' he said. 'This looks like the balance sheet of a small yet vigorous company. I can't pay that. Dudley, you have young eyes: show me where the decimal point falls.'

'There,' said Rogers.

'How awful! . . . Did we really eat all that? I suppose we must have done. Turn out your pockets, everyone.'

They piled their scruffy French banknotes on the tablecloth and weighed them down with battered coins. Woodruffe sorted through the heap and kept a running total. The others lay back and finished the wine.

'I think this will just be enough,' Woodruffe said, 'to cover the tip. Dudley, how much is that car of yours worth?'

'I'm not walking home,' Lambert said.

'I have a fairly valuable pocket-watch,' Richards suggested.

'No, no, dear boy, what we need here is more in the nature of a small jeweller's shop,' Woodruffe said. 'But the offer is appreciated.'

'Do you think they would take a cheque?' Rogers asked.

'Only if they're a great deal more gullible than they look.'

Rogers produced a cheque-book bound in quarto with pale green Moroccan leather and secured with a gold clip. When he opened it, a gilt-embossed crest glinted dully on handmade cream paper. 'Suppose it were a cheque from . . .' he peered at the printing '. . . Dom Antonio da Terceira e Silva, Count of Vila Real Maior, drawn on the House of Rothschild in London? Might that make a difference?'

'Where the deuce did you get that?' Richards asked.

'Found it in the car . . . Worth trying, d'you think?'

'By all means,' Woodruffe said. 'The gold leaf alone should pay for the wine. Wouldn't it be as well for one of us to impersonate this count thingummy? Who speaks Spanish?'

'I have a little Swiss-Romande,' Gabriel said.

'I think this is Portuguese,' Rogers said. 'It belonged to a Portuguese.'

'Well, you know some Portuguese,' Lambert encouraged him.

'Only a very little.'

'So use it sparingly. Give him the bill, Woody.'

'*Obrigado*,' murmured Rogers. He filled in a cheque, using a florid hand, and touched up the capitals with generous filigree. He took a swig of wine, dashed off a long signature, proudly angled, and tossed the cheque to Lambert, '*Obrigado*,' he said.

Lambert signalled the head waiter and handed him the cheque, indicating Rogers. '*Merci, m'sieu*,' the head waiter said. '*Obrigado*,' Rogers replied. He stood up. The others followed. Waiters hobbled over to remove chairs and help with coats. When all were ready, Rogers held up a hand for silence. He wore his greatcoat like a cloak; in his right hand was a glass of brandy. He saluted all present. '*Obrigado*,' he told the waiters. He drank down the brandy, handed the glass to Lambert and indicated the fireplace. Lambert hurled the glass into it. The waiters cheered weakly, and turned hastily to the stack of money as Rogers led the party to the door.

Here the head waiter was waiting for them with a smile of deep misery. Bowing, holding the cheque carefully by its edges, he began a speech of profound regret and lamentable necessity. Rogers took a medal from his pocket and pinned it on the man's lapel. '*Obrigado*,' he said, and went out. Lambert shook the head waiter's hand. Woodruffe shook his hand and embraced him. Richards saluted him. Gabriel brushed the scurf off his shoulders. Then they were out in the street.

Chuck Martin came up to them as they were getting into the car. 'Enjoy the meal?' he asked.

'Excellent,' Rogers said. 'Thanks very much. Any time you're near Pont St Martin, drop in and we'll take you for a flight. Just ask for Goshawk Squadron, RFC.'

'I'll do that.'

* * *

29

They drove home at high speed in bright moonlight. The car was warm and comfortable; the road was straight and empty; and Rogers bowled along the crown at an exhilarating pace. 'So the cheque-book was in this car?' Lambert asked.

'In one of the pockets. I found it yesterday. Jolly handy, what?'

'Did you find the medal here, too?' asked Gabriel.

'Certainly not! That was my medal. Some Belgian general was going around awarding medals to any unit with twenty-five per cent casualties in one week, so we qualified. I was the only one at home when he called.'

'No, you weren't. I was in,' Woodruffe said.

'Were you, Woody? Well, he fancied me, that's all. You can have the next one.'

'I'd sooner have the car.'

'No, I need the car. We shall be starting cricket soon, and some form of transport will be essential.'

'There won't be any more cricket when the war ends,' Gabriel said flatly. Rogers looked around in surprise. 'What on earth makes you say that?' he asked.

'It's true. You haven't been home as recently as Richards and I. The whole world's changing. People aren't going to put up with the old 1914 standards any more. They've sacrificed too much for that. They want a real say in their future. They want better lives, better jobs, better homes. There won't be room for longwinded rituals like cricket.'

'What absolute bloody nonsense!' Rogers swerved indignantly. 'Of course there will be cricket, what the blazes d'you think we're fighting for, the whole purpose of the entire operation is to get back to a world where chaps like you and me can play as much cricket as we want to. Besides—'

'We can't "get back" to any world. That's gone for ever. We can only get forward. The leisured class has had its day.'

'What rot! The only reason we're going to win this war is that we've got some decent sportsmen in command, and the Huns have got a lot of Prussian pig-stickers. Look at old M. N. T. Matthews, captain in the Grenadier Guards, finest

30

opening bat Sussex ever had, killed leading his men over the top at Mons! Look at Martin Stanhope, captained Oxford, *brilliant* slip-fielder, absolutely brilliant, died of wounds after the Somme! What did they die for, if not for the country they loved? Eh? Answer me that!'

'It's already been decided,' Gabriel said. 'This war has killed cricket.'

'Poppycock! There will *always* be cricket, because cricket makes men, just as men make cricket. You can't—'

'Look out!' shouted Woodruffe.

Rogers jerked around just as the front wheels ran off the road and hit the frozen ruts of the verge. For five terrifying seconds he fought the car's determination to bounce into the ditch; and then they were back on the road, running smoothly again. 'Bloody French roads!' Rogers said. 'Bloody Portuguese cars! Everybody all right?'

'Slow down, God damn you, and watch where you're going,' Woodruffe said thickly. He had hit his nose on the windscreen, and it was pouring blood.

'For Christ's sake, Dudley,' Lambert said. 'What's your bloody hurry?' He had been thrown sideways against a door, and was massaging a bruised ear.

They drove in silence the rest of the way to Pont St Martin. Rogers kept to a safe speed. 'Anyway,' he said as the camp came in sight, 'I bet you anything you like we'll all still be playing cricket after the war's over.' Nobody argued.

Force 3: Gentle Breeze

Leaves rustle; wind extends light flag

At eight thousand feet the top of the cloud was flattened and slightly tattered, like spume beaten white on a heaving sea. The sun shone up here, having nothing to stop it, and Woolley flew low across the endless expanse, his wheels ripping casually through ridges and humps. Behind and on either side flew Gabriel and the third replacement pilot, Delaforce, his SE5a patched up with a new propeller to replace the one which had smashed itself against the panicking birds.

Woolley waved them in closer. He was flying towards the sun, and the glare off the cloud was painful. Gabriel moved his wing-tip behind Woolley's, almost opposite his rudder. Delaforce twitched about, his position never steady. Woolley lost speed fractionally so that the others found themselves of necessity creeping in; then, when he decided they were close enough, he took them down in a dive.

Delaforce's first feeling was relief that they were going home. They had been flying for two hours, and the nervous excitement made him very hungry; he had been sick shortly before take-off, also from excitement, and now his stomach insisted on food.

Woolley had led them around this stupendous universe of sky as if it were an estate which he had poached all his life. He showed them passing aircraft, often pointing them out seconds before these tiny flecks became visible to them. He stalked planes through the naked sky, placing his own aircraft where the sun and the angle made them least visible, and closing in with endless, painstaking patience; until the quarry lay below, as shining-innocent and unaware as trout in a clear pool.

Then, when Woolley had made Gabriel and Delaforce understand how all things moved towards a favourable conjunction – height, sun, distance, angle of attack, drift of wind – he would take them right up to that perfect instant and drop on the droning French Nieuport or British two-seater RE8 or whatever it was, in a lethal gathering pounce that could have only one ending; except that he cut it short after a hundred feet and curled away to do it all over again somewhere else. It was fascinating and exhilarating and draining, and Delaforce wanted urgently to get some good food inside himself so that he could go up and do it all again.

Now they plunged through the first layer of cloud into a grey cavern where wisps and flecks floated up like bits of broken barricades. Woolley deepened the dive and waved Gabriel and Delaforce in closer. The brittle clatter of engines merged into a hoarse roar. Each aeroplane spoke its individual strains and pressures: loose fabric drummed furiously, struts wheezed or ticked, wires whistled. Delaforce sensed a steadily mounting throb which possessed his entire machine: it shivered his limbs. The flimsy obstacles grew bigger, and Woolley started swinging over or under each puffball; or sometimes he banked left and careered round it only to bank right and skid past another. Each decision he delayed until the very end, like a skier gauging the last inch he needed to whip round a rock.

The canyon narrowed, the barricading cloudlets grew, and still Woolley swept on down, skidding and skedaddling like a lunatic. Gabriel and Delaforce hung on, losing him a little more at every turn, but rarely clipping an obstacle, either. The dirty, blank wall at the bottom rushed up, and its grey face began to reveal cracks and hollows. Woolley flew right into it.

Delaforce hunched his shoulders as he smacked into the woolly gloom. At once all sense of speed dissolved, and then all sense of altitude or direction. He was going forward; that was all. The gloom slipped past, muffling his engine and burying his comrades. There was literally nothing he could do. He even closed his eyes and listened to the soft howl of the slipstream. Then he was out in the clear, hard open again, and Woolley was wheeling the dive into a long, slow cork-screw to the right, where a funnel of sky pushed a hole through the murk. He spiralled down the walls of this funnel, losing speed with each turn and flattening the coils until the three aircraft were lazily chasing their trails over a bank of cloud as firm as blancmange. Delaforce laughed aloud at the sheer pleasure of it.

Without warning, Woolley switched off his engine and let the plane slip sideways into the cloud. This caught Gabriel and Delaforce by surprise: he had told them to follow him, but they didn't expect this. They flew another circuit. Dela-force cut his engine and let the plane drop. Gabriel went round once more and followed him.

Delaforce came out of the cloud about three hundred feet above the ground. After the empty oceans, this seemed frighteningly close and definite. He grabbed the plane out of its side-slip and thrust it into a shallow dive. Then he saw that it was the airfield underneath. Down there on his left was Woolley, drifting in for the touchdown. Delaforce felt stupid: what was he doing up here? Hastily he side-slipped again. It never occurred to him to re-start his engine. Woolley hadn't. Delaforce landed as near to the old man as he could. Gabriel came in about twenty seconds later.

Delaforce undid his straps. He stretched his legs and arms, and filled his lungs. He put his head back and rubbed his eyes, and luxuriated in doing absolutely nothing for the first time in two hours. Woolley said: 'Get your fat arse out of there.' He turned and walked over to Gabriel's machine and spat on the hot exhaust. Gabriel, climbing down, looked at him like a private tutor meeting a difficult child for the first time.

'You piss-proud ponce,' Woolley said. 'You drive that miserable sodding aeroplane around as if you're mowing the bleeding lawn. You *drive* it, you cruel bastard. You get your great horny hands on it and you *drive* it, you son of a bitch. Jesus, I'd hate to be the first woman you climb on top of.'

Gabriel listened carefully. 'In what respects did you find my technique faulty?' he asked.

Woolley stared with a kind of weary disgust. 'Your bloody technique is word-perfect,' he said bitterly. 'It's just that you're sterile, frigid and impotent. You treat this aircraft as if it owes you money.'

Gabriel stood stiffly. 'Yes, sir,' he said.

'Take off your gloves,' Woolley ordered. 'Roll up your sleeve.'

Gabriel did these actions with a semi-medical air. Woolley took his wrist and felt the pulse. After a moment he let go. 'Does flying bore you?' he asked.

'No, sir.'

'Doesn't excite you, does it? I don't suppose you ever get scared up there.'

'One tries to keep a clear head, sir.'

'Good Christ . . . Don't you ever lose your temper, you bloody fillet?'

'As I said, sir, one tries to stay in control of oneself.'

'*Prick!*' Woolley swung his right leg, heavily booted, and swept Gabriel's legs from under him. Gabriel landed hard on his rump, on the frozen ground. Tears of pain came to his eyes. Woolley advanced on him, delivering short, jabbing kicks. Gabriel rolled away, but Woolley went after him, so Gabriel had to roll faster. 'You craven little sod!' Woolley bawled. 'Haven't you got any balls at all?' His boots thudded into Gabriel's ribs. Gabriel grappled, seeking to smother, but Woolley was too strong: the kicks hurt more and more. 'Fool! Infant! Coward! Lawnmower!' Woolley shouted. 'Gutless bloody lawnmower!' He hounded Gabriel, going after the vulnerable parts of his body.

At last Gabriel lurched to his knees and grabbed Woolley's legs. Woolley pounded him about the head with his fists. Gabriel roared and tried to butt Woolley in the gut. They fell, rolled and punched, and came apart. Gabriel drew back his boot to lash out – and stopped.

Woolley, on his hands and knees, was watching him, looking into his eyes, searching. Gabriel stared back and hated him. Their breath gasped harshly in the cold air. 'Did you keep a cool head then, lawnmower?' Woolley panted. 'Were you in bloody control of yourself then? That's what you've got to do up there. Turn into a bloody assassin! Kill! Understand, you bastard Boy Scout? *Kill*. Only a maniac would do this job, and you're too sane by half. You madden up, lawnmower, before some madman beats you to it, or I'll kill you myself. Understand? Understand?'

Woolley got up. Delaforce was open-mouthed, wide-eyed. 'As for you,' Woolley said stonily, 'you're putting your gallant little heart and soul into it, aren't you? Start using your tiny brain too, or you'll end up with your lights all over the cockpit floor.'

He trudged off to the marquee where the pilots ate their meals.

Half the squadron was eating lunch when Woolley went in. Dangerfield was reading a letter, Church was staring into space, Lambert was nursing a headache, and Kimberley and Killion were arguing.

'But there's millions of things that have nothing to do with sex,' Kimberley insisted. He was a farmer's son from Derbyshire: sturdy, sceptical, with the rapid, almost stuttering speech of his region. 'Coal mines, for instance. Nothing sexy about them, is there? Or . . . or wood.' He rapped on the table. 'Or anything around here. Flying. What's flying got to do with sex?'

'Starting with coal mines,' Killion said. He was twenty; a slightly built, intense-looking man who could have been a very young schoolmaster or a very old schoolboy. In fact, he had failed his exams after a year as a medical student in a London hospital, and joined the RFC the same day, on impulse. 'Here we have man creating, as it were, an opening in Mother Earth. What does he do then? He explores it, testing its limits. Goodness gracious, Kimberley, coal mining is practically an act of rape! You *force an entrance*, my dear chap, in order to reach the *source of all power*. Honestly, I blush at your innocence, I do really.'

'I went pot-holing once,' Lambert said. 'I never thought of it like that. Awfully mucky down there.'

'That,' said Killion, 'only goes to show how much you have idealized and disinfected the act of penetration. If anything, I should say that you were in a worse condition than Kimberley. He has his eyes shut, but you are facing in the wrong direction.'

'You haven't done wood,' Woolley grunted.

'Wood? You seriously ask me to explain the sexuality of wood?' Killion looked at them. Dangerfield stopped reading his letter. 'Wood is what trees consist of. Have you never *looked* at a tree?' He stood his knife on end. 'Have you never appreciated the thrusting trunk . . .?'

'God, Killion, you've a mind like . . . like a . . .' Kimberley gave up.

'Like a choirboy,' Killion said. 'Pure and sensitive and ready for anything.'

'Do flying,' said Lambert. Dangerfield went back to his letter.

'I'll do flying,' Woolley said. He slouched on the table, one hand rubbing his chest, the other forking stew into his thin-lipped mouth. Lambert studied him and saw that it wasn't really the skin that was grubby; it was the cast of the face that was sour. Woolley's expression could never be washed clean.

Woolley pushed his plate away and took a bottle of Guinness from his pocket. 'Why is flying like sex?' Gabriel and Delaforce came in and stopped. 'Because you get on top and batter away with your weapon until you've won.'

'Then you both go limp,' Killion said. Gabriel and Dela-force sat down.

'That's no good,' Lambert complained. 'On that basis you couldn't shoot down two planes in five minutes.'

'Well, can you?' Killion asked.

'Me? No. But other people have.'

'Sex maniacs,' Woolley suggested.

'*You* have,' Lambert said.

Woolley said nothing. He drank from the bottle and looked at Kimberley. Kimberley looked at a tent-pole. Dangerfield finished reading his letter and put it away. 'I seem to have inherited a farm,' he said.

'What luck!' Kimberley cried. 'Where?'

'Somewhere in Cumberland. It belonged to a cousin. He got shot by a sniper last month and it seems I'm the next in line.'

'Wonderful! Congratulations. Cumberland – that's probably sheep. Do you know the place? How big is it?'

'Not the slightest idea.' Dangerfield took out a pocket mirror and scissors, and trimmed his neat black moustache. 'I shall sell it, anyway. Sell and be thankful.'

'Church!' Woolley called. 'Church, have you had any lunch?'

Church looked up and smiled. His smile turned the corners of his mouth down, as if in self-deprecation. He had been leaning back, arms folded and head down, studying the grass beyond his feet; an attractively ugly little man, well muscled like an amateur jockey. First he smiled at Gabriel, who looked at Woolley. Church then smiled at Woolley and cocked his head a fraction.

'What will you do with the money?' Lambert asked Dangerfield.

'Go to dances, of course. What else is there to do with money?'

'*Well* . . .' Kimberley was appalled. 'I knew you were keen on dancing and all that, but to throw away a good farm for the sake of slithering about some stuffy dance-floor—'

Church got up. Dangerfield, who was next to him, feigned surprise. 'With me?' he said, lisping. 'You want to dance with little me?' Church stood awkwardly, trying to keep his smile steady, and gripped the back of his chair. Dangerfield rose, managing to make his neat figure look almost voluptuous. He took Church by the arms and led him into a hopeless waltz. Chairs went down, mess-waiters grabbed other chairs before Dangerfield could steer Church into them. Near the entrance to the tent Church ducked free and trotted out. He stumbled and fell, and took his time over getting up, and stood swaying. Woolley, his elbow on the table and his head propped against his hand, saw this and said nothing.

Rogers came in, swinging a cricket bat. 'Ah, there you are, sir,' he said. 'There's someone to see you. An enormous American. Chap we met last night.'

'Nothing to do with me,' Woolley said firmly. 'Shove him on to Woody.'

'I have, sir. *He* wants to see you, too.'

'What about?'

'More pilots, I think.'

Woolley finished his Guinness and got up. 'See me in ten minutes,' he told Delaforce. He went out. Delaforce tried to appear normal but he was so excited he could hardly eat.

Rogers glanced at the food on the table and moved away. 'Funny, I don't feel very hungry,' he said. He played an imaginary shot with his cricket bat. Kimberley watched.

'Find something sexual in cricket, Killion,' he challenged.

Killion glanced at Rogers, who was now holding the bat low and facing an imaginary bowler. 'Observe how the handle seems to emerge from the groin,' he said. 'Then look at the remarkable length of the bat. Did you ever see such boasting?'

'What nonsense,' Rogers said angrily. 'Utter nonsense. If that's all you know about cricket, Killion, it's no wonder you failed your exams.'

'Medicine's loss,' Killion said, 'is aviation's gain.'

'That's what I like about you, Killion,' Lambert said. 'You quit while you were still behind, and it shows.'

Woolley found the adjutant in his tent, drinking Scotch with a truly enormous American.

'Sir, this is Mr Martin, of the United States Army. He was extremely kind to us last night in Montigny.'

'How do you do?' Woolley shook hands. 'I don't understand your American ranks.'

'Stameetcha. That's all right, Major. Just call me Chuck.'

'Dudley promised our friend a flight,' Woodruffe said.

'Dudley's a bloody fool,' Woolley told him. 'I'm sorry you've had a wasted journey. My squadron only flies SE5as, and they're all single-seat planes.'

'Oh, well,' said Martin. 'Give me enough Scotch and I'll fly home anyway.' The adjutant topped up his glass.

'If I could have a word with you, sir,' he said. They went outside.

'Bad news, I'm afraid,' Woodruffe said. 'O'Shea died in hospital last night. There must have been some hidden brain damage, they think.'

Woolley scratched his face and looked in his finger-nails. 'Who?' he asked.

'O'Shea. You know, yesterday morning. He went through those trees.'

'I thought you were going to get them chopped down.'

'I am, as soon as—'

'Was that aircraft a complete write-off?'

'No,' Woodruffe said miserably. 'Just the wings. The wings were smashed.'

'Oh.' Woolley lost interest.

'I wondered if you intended to write to O'Shea's parents,' the adjutant said.

'Have they written to me?'

Woodruffe set his teeth. 'No, sir. But—'

'The hell with them. What d'you say his name was?'

'O'Shea.'

'Never heard of him. Useless goddam pilot, too. Have you got a replacement yet?'

'I wanted to ask you about that. D'you think I should get two?'

'What for?'

'Well . . . in anticipation, so to speak.'

Woolley stared at him stonily. 'Good idea,' he said. 'Get three.'

Delaforce came over. Woolley went to meet him. 'I'm starting you on combat practice,' he said. 'Draw a Very pistol, take off and climb to five thousand feet. I'm going to fly to Montdidier and back. If you can surprise me and shoot a flare so that it falls within fifty feet of my plane, I'll give you a medal. Understand?'

Delaforce couldn't speak for joy. He nodded, saluted, and sprinted away to Stores, to get his pistol. He hadn't felt so wonderful since he got elected Head Boy at school, last year.

After he had flown around for an hour, Delaforce had a sick feeling that Woolley had played a joke on him.

It was not his first misgiving. After twenty minutes Delaforce had developed a sudden doubt about the destination which Woolley had named. Was it Grandvilliers, or was it Montdidier? Perhaps he was patrolling the wrong piece of sky.

Five minutes later Delaforce had convinced himself he was in the right place. Five minutes after that, he began to wonder if the wind had blown him off Woolley's route. He had flown a consistent box pattern, with a slight overlap on one side to compensate for wind-drift. Maybe the wind was stronger than he thought.

Or weaker.

Delaforce thrust the stick forward. He came out of cloud at about eight hundred feet and immediately recognized landmarks. He was a mile or so off course, not enough to make any difference if he kept his eyes open. He climbed hard and won back the mile of drift. It took a long time to reach five thousand feet again. By the time he'd made it, Delaforce was worrying whether Woolley might have gone overhead while he was down below.

From then on, he searched the sky in both directions. Because he wasn't tall enough to get a good look over the side of the cockpit he flew at a slight angle, one wing dipped. This made one buttock stiff and numb. He reversed his flight pattern and rested on the other cheek. It too became stiff and numb. The other merely stayed numb.

Then Delaforce began to suspect a joke. Woolley thought him too cocksure . . . Or maybe this was some kind of squadron initiation . . . If so, it was a feeble rite. And passive jokes didn't sound like Woolley's way of doing things. Then maybe Woolley's plane had given trouble. An important visitor. A phone call.

An SE5a came out of a cloud about a thousand feet below him and a mile behind, heading for Montdidier.

Delaforce swung hard away and climbed, presenting as small an outline as possible. Viewed from either end, an SE was skimpy: just a barrel with thin wings and fins. If he could hide quickly and lie in wait, he could dive on Woolley from above and behind – the hardest angle for a defending pilot to turn his head. Delaforce bounced excitedly in his seat.

He flew behind a bank of cloud and throttled back to just above stalling speed. Woolley had been a mile behind, so he would take well over a minute to catch up. Delaforce loaded the Very pistol.

After a minute and a quarter he couldn't wait. 'Right, chaps?' he asked himself. He dropped one wing in a steep side-slip. When he cleared the cloud he was diving almost vertically.

Woolley wasn't there.

Delaforce pulled up quickly and went into a searching circle, looking everywhere. The sky lay bare for two thousand feet below. Delaforce felt cheated. A flicker of black on grey, no more than a wandering eyelash, caught his attention. Half a mile away and climbing straight at him was Woolley's

SE. He'd been seen. Delaforce opened the throttle and roared around in a hard-climbing turn.

Crimson fire bloomed on his right and seemed to leap towards him, trailing smoke, before it curled sharply and dropped away out of sight under his tailplane. He was so astonished that he first looked backwards, trying to see what it was; then down, suspecting anti-aircraft fire; and then – too late – up. An SE5a hurtled over the top wing and curved up and away in a celebratory loop, at the top of which it half-rolled and flew complacently on.

It couldn't be Woolley; Woolley was still climbing. It looked like Gabriel. How humiliating, to be scored against by Gabriel! The memory of that hot-red flare made Delaforce flinch and sweat. He must have been blind.

What mattered now was to get Woolley. That mattered more than ever.

Delaforce flew into cloud and turned back towards where he had last seen Woolley. He flew straight and level through the murk while he counted to twenty, and then eased up into daylight.

Gabriel was off to one side, cruising around, so that was all right. Delaforce took out the Very pistol again, and slipped down the side of the cloud, eyes wide open.

Woolley, exasperatingly, was now a thousand feet below, and flying the opposite way. So perhaps he'd already been to Montdidier after all. For the second time, Delaforce pushed the stick forward and leaned the aeroplane into a dive. The whistling of air became a screaming; the clatter of the engine a bellow. As Woolley's machine came into view through the shimmering arc of the propeller, Delaforce concentrated on nursing the controls towards a precise intersection. There would be only one chance. If he fluffed this, Woolley would never let him get close enough again.

At five hundred feet range he raised the Very pistol and thumbed the safety-catch back. He held his angle, letting Woolley pull away just a bit. He would fire the flare dead ahead and over the top of his own propeller when he was about four lengths away, and then drop behind him. The flare should fall under Woolley's wing. Three hundred feet.

A sound like tearing canvas made Delaforce grab at the stick: was his SE breaking up? Again the angry crackle. It wasn't his plane. He was being machine-gunned.

Delaforce twisted violently and saw flames spurting from the gun mounted high over the upper wing of yet another SE5a, diving behind him, fifty feet to one side. The pilot signalled, pointing forward. Delaforce recognized him. *That* was Woolley.

He jerked round to see his target looming up fast but now off to one side. Angrily he corrected, bullying his plane over, kicking it for his mistakes, and fired; the flare trailed badly wide: not within a hundred feet; a miss. He pulled out of the dive. Woolley flashed past him, heading for home. Instinctively, Delaforce climbed. Making height gave him something to do: a substitute for success, or competence, or something.

At six thousand feet he found Gabriel, fell in alongside him and fired a shot from his Very pistol. The flare actually went between the wheels and Gabriel dived away in a great hurry. Delaforce took little comfort in the achievement. He had flown very stupidly. He wondered who had been flying the plane which he had missed. Richards, probably.

Woolley was waiting for them when they landed. 'A right old cock-up you all made of that,' he said. 'Not one of you got near me, and I could have pissed into your cockpits, all three of you, one after the other, and drowned you, which you might say is a wonderful way to go, but it's still a bloody awful waste of government money. What did you think you were doing at five thousand feet?' he asked Delaforce.

'Sir, I was patrolling,' Delaforce said. 'That was what you said. I was waiting for you. To intercept you, sir.'

'Who told you to piss about at five thousand? I told you to *get up there*. What you did after that was up to you. You could have come back here and got me as I took off. You could have got me over Montdidier. You could have hung around and sneaked up on me as I came in to land. Come to that, you could have walloped one past my nose while I was still on the ground. Couldn't you, you mental pygmy?'

'Yes, sir,' Delaforce said, white and blinking.

'But you didn't, did you? You did exactly what you *thought I wanted* you to do.' He turned to Richards. 'I said five thousand feet, so you all flew at five thousand feet, for ever. Combat practice, you horseman, is practice for combat. It's not sodding pistols at dawn. Just now, I was your enemy. En-em-y.' Woolley screwed up his face and shut his eyes and took a little stamping, circular walk. 'Oh Christ, what words do you understand? You wouldn't know an enemy if he bit you in the arse, you'd think he was a great big affectionate dog . . .' He heaved a deep breath. 'An enemy,' he declared, speaking with tremendous clarity, 'is a man . . . who is trying . . . to kill you . . . before you can . . . see . . . him.' Woolley stared hard at Gabriel. 'Has anybody ever tried to kill you, lawnmower?'

'Only drunkards,' Gabriel replied.

'Why did they fail?'

'I suppose I saw them coming.'

'You didn't see *me* coming, this afternoon.'

'No, sir.'

'Why not?'

'I'm afraid I was concentrating too much on Delaforce. Besides, I didn't expect you.'

'Why not? You expected to attack him, but you weren't prepared to be attacked yourself?'

Gabriel said nothing.

'When nothing happened after an hour, sir,' Richards said, 'I rather assumed that combat practice had fallen through, you see, so I went home. That was when I was . . . well, *dived upon*.'

'Do you expect the enemy to stop fighting when you stop fighting?' Woolley asked.

Richards said nothing.

'Every second you are in the air,' Woolley said, 'someone is trying to kill you. If he does it properly you will never know. *You* must look for *him*, because he's always there.' He stared at them, and his black, pouchy eyes were full of anger at their stupid humanitarianism. 'God damn it,' he said, 'you're murderers turned loose against murderers! Some will come at you head-on with an axe. But the ones that *think*, the good ones, the professionals – they hide behind a tree and stick you through the ribs from behind. They are up there *now*. They go up every day and murder nice chaps like you,' Woolley made *nice chap* sound like a genetic defect.

Gabriel studied him thoughtfully. 'Speaking for myself, sir,' he said, 'I feel sure that I could have given a better account of myself if I had been aware of the true circumstances.'

Woolley licked his narrow lips. When he spoke, it was in a harsh whisper. 'There are no true circumstances in this war,' he said. 'There is only what happens.'

'Well, exactly.'

'No, not *exactly*,' Woolley said, 'there is no *exactly*, God blast you! You want me to tell you the rules of this tennis-club, don't you, and I am trying to make you see that the first rule is to stop looking for any bloody rules. Up there you will live among murderers and victims. Now make up your decent, law-abiding little minds which you want to be.'

Delaforce felt sick. All the excitement of the hunt had turned sour; Woolley made it seem squalid and callous, vicious and cold. Delaforce desperately wanted to rescue something from this shabby summary. 'I can see now, sir,' he said, 'that I could have gone after you when you were taking off, but I suppose I didn't think of that at the time because I sort of wanted it to be more of a fair fight, you see.'

Woolley grabbed him by the lapels and slammed him hard against the side of Gabriel's plane. His twitching face was thrust so close that Delaforce could smell the Guinness on his breath. 'You will never use that word again,' Woolley said thickly. 'That is a filthy, obscene, disgusting word and I will not have it used by any man on my squadron. That word disgusts me.'

46

He let go and turned round and walked away. Outside the adjutant's tent he saw Woodruffe and Chuck Martin. They were still drinking whisky. Woolley went over and took Woodruffe's glass and sipped the Scotch. 'Mr Martin has been telling me about America, sir,' the adjutant said. 'It seems that he has done quite a bit of flying himself.'

'I was an instructor, see,' Martin said. 'They wouldn't release me to come over here and fly. So I faked a bum eardrum and transferred to the infantry.' He swilled the Scotch around in his glass and patted a little arc of grass flat with an enormous foot. 'What are the chances of getting transferred to your outfit, Major?' he asked, not looking up.

Woolley hunched his shoulders. He had a sudden, vivid memory of sitting alone in the empty, late-afternoon sunshine on the top of a Welsh mountain, and watching the rabbits hop about the slopes far below. He felt his skin cringe at this treachery, and forced himself to look up at the hulking American. The man had a hard, almost brutal look; not the look of a willing victim. 'Do you think you can fly one of these?' he asked.

Martin glanced at the SEs, wrinkled his brown brow, and pretended to weigh the matter up. 'I think I can,' he said softly.

'No parachutes, you know.'

'I know.'

'We've got a spare plane sir,' Woodruffe said. 'O'Shea's machine – they've replaced it.' Woolley saw that the adjutant was every man's friend today.

'Take that up if you like,' he said. 'After that I'll see.' He went inside the tent. Rogers was sitting, reading an old newspaper. 'Hullo, sir,' he said. 'I've found a most comfortable château near here, completely empty. It would make a perfect home for the squadron. Honestly.'

'Bugger off,' Woolley said.

'Jolly good, sir.'

Woolley cranked the adjutant's telephone and asked for the military hospital at Abbeville. While they were getting the number he sat and looked at the stains on the canvas walls. Once he shuddered like a man entering a fever; the rest of the time his pessimistic face remained slack and empty.

An aircraft started up, and the noise made the field telephone resonate. Woolley ignored it. The roar receded; swelled and deepened; and slowly turned brittle as it climbed away. Woolley yawned. The telephone rang and he answered it. There was a long pause at the other end, at the military hospital in Abbeville. The noise of the aeroplane gradually returned, then rapidly enlarged to a thunder as it flew low overhead. Woolley pressed the receiver hard against his ear.

The radiating shock-waves of the explosion sent little tremors up the legs of the camp chair. Men were shouting and running. Far away a woman's voice spoke. 'Hullo, bitch,' he said, 'I need you. I need you now.'

Force 4: Moderate Breeze

Raises dust and loose paper;
small branches are moved

Woolley flew Goshawk Squadron all day, every day, whenever the weather allowed.

As well as individual flying skills, he drilled them in the routines for reconnaissance, escort duty, balloon attacks, low-level infantry support, and artillery observation. Everything was done intensively; there were no easy days. He never congratulated; he frequently denounced. Not to be damned by Woolley was as near to praise as anyone would ever get. He demanded tight formation flying, so there was a constant risk of collision, which meant that everyone was living on his nerves. 'Flying with the old man,' Rogers said one day, 'is like living with a maniac. You know that the instant you take your eye off him, he'll kill you. I find it both exhilarating and debilitating.'

'Like opium,' Lambert said.

'Exactly.'

Their eyes became permanently red-stained and grey-pouched; most people lost weight. Everyone complained to Woodruffe about something: the food, the tents, the lack of hot water. Those who sweated a lot began to smell, because it was impossible to bathe regularly. Killion became withdrawn. When he tried to speak a stammer confused him, so he said little. Dangerfield's face developed a nervous twitch; Kimberley chewed his nails; Lambert couldn't get to sleep at night and couldn't wake up in the morning.

It was not a happy squadron. They resented the way Woolley treated them and secretly longed to see him humbled, but one of the infuriating things about him was his impregnable social life. There was no way of retaliating against Woolley, because his off-duty life was without manners or morals. He was scruffy, ill-shaven, contemptuous of any courtesy or human warmth, and apparently indifferent to personalities. Since there was nothing anybody could find attractive about Woolley, there was nothing anyone could hurt. The squadron, unable to hate him, and deprived of Germans to hate, fell back on hating itself. Woolley watched this with his usual remote indifference.

He drank considerably, mostly Guinness, which more and more became a food for him. Many pilots were drinking a fair bit, and a good few started at breakfast. This included Richards and Delaforce. On their third day with the squadron, Richards had approached Delaforce and asked him if he didn't find that one of the difficulties of flying was that the aircraft tended to stay up rather too long.

'I don't quite follow you,' Delaforce said. Richards looked away.

'One finds,' he said, 'that flying seems to accelerate one's bodily functions to an embarrassing degree, sometimes. One wishes that there were some . . . er . . . device for . . . well, for coping.'

'I know,' said Delaforce. 'I barely landed in time this morning.'

'Yesterday,' Richards said, 'I didn't.'

They went to Lambert for advice. 'It's probably only nerves,' Delaforce said, 'but there's no denying that it reduces one's efficiency.'

'It's not nerves, it's castor oil,' Lambert said. 'All these SEs run on castor oil, it's the only stuff that'll lubricate the innards without going treacly at height. You're getting the fumes.'

'Good God,' said Richards. 'Can one build up a tolerance to it?'

'Not that I know of.'

'But look here,' Delaforce said, 'I shan't last five minutes at this rate. I nearly crashed this morning.'

'It's not only dangerous,' Richards said, 'it's unhealthy.'

'Booze is a first-rate antidote,' Lambert said. 'Drink hearty before you take off. On long flights, carry a spare bottle and top up the system regularly.'

'*Alcohol?*' exclaimed Delaforce.

'Booze. Plum brandy works fast, but it's really a matter of taste. The important thing is to stun the bowels before they can go into action.'

'Yes, but look here,' Richards said. 'I haven't *got* any liquor. And I haven't got any money, either.'

'See Woody,' Lambert advised. 'He'll give you a chit for Stores. Best thing is to get a crate of what you fancy.'

The adjutant signed the chits without comment. 'Does this go on the mess account?' Richards asked.

'Good Lord, no. This is squadron equipment. We get it with the engine parts and the petrol and so on.'

'Extraordinary . . . Doesn't anyone query it?'

'I've never known anyone query anything the old man wants. Mind you, I enter it as lubricant, same as the castor oil. I can recommend the rum,' Woodruffe added. 'It tastes unusually well on porridge.'

The weather in January and early February helped Woolley. There was plenty of cloud, which he welcomed for his aerial stalking exercises, but little rain and no high wind. Showers or mist sometimes soaked the grass and made it slippery; then Woolley always started with half an hour of circuits-and-bumps, until the squadron felt it could land on a melting glacier. There were accidents: broken wheels, broken propellers, broken noses. But, as the adjutant pointed out to Kimberley when he came in grumbling after an unusually dramatic skid, the day might come when he would have to go

51

up or come down in a cloudburst, and dry weather landings would be no help then. Kimberley chewed a corned-beef sandwich. 'Listen,' he said at last, 'I don't care if it *is* good training, the old man's not thinking of that . . . All right, he *is*, but . . . he'll not be satisfied until somebody catches a packet, that's all.'

'He wants to get the squadron match-fit for when we go back into the Line,' Woodruffe said.

'I tell you he'll not be satisfied until somebody touches wing-tips. Or does a ground-loop on a wet field. Or dives their wings off. He'll not be satisfied until he's gone too far.' Kimberley's hand was trembling: Kimberley, the stolid ploughboy.

The adjutant watched the sulky faces of the pilots as they sat around the mess tent, and decided to talk to Woolley. He found him in his tent, dubbining his flying-boots.

'I thought you ought to know,' Woodruffe said, 'some of the chaps feel you're pushing them a bit hard.'

'How many pilots have died through cold feet, Woody? I wonder. I killed a German last year who had on dress-uniform jack-boots. I pulled them off him: no socks. Too tight for socks, I suppose. Fifteen thousand feet, and no socks. He looked lovely, though, even without his head. Lovely shine.'

'The squadron does look a thought weary, sir. Have you any plans for leave? Perhaps a long weekend soon?'

Woolley dug a gob of dubbin and spread it thickly over the leather. 'Going too far,' he said. 'Somebody thinks I'm going too far. How far is the war going, Woody? Is the war going too far?'

'I don't know. It already has, I suppose.'

'This year it will go further. This year will be the worst of all.'

'I don't see how it can be any worse than last year. Passchendaele was about as bad as anything could be. Three hundred thousand killed and injured. Nothing gained.'

'Magnificent stalemate. A two-way siege. We besiege them while they besiege us. What farce.'

Woodruffe resented Woolley's tone; after all, Woodruffe had left a set of fingers in the trenches. 'It's the best that a dozen generals can think of. What else can they do?'

Woolley shrugged. 'Somebody had better think of something soon. When spring comes the Germans will attack.'

'Perhaps we shall attack, too.'

Woolley looked at him mockingly.

'Well, we have to attack before we can win, don't we?' Woodruffe cried.

'What a patriot you are, Woody. Chin up, grin like the devil, and everything's bound to come out right in the end.'

'I've had more experience of bloody war than you have. I'm twenty-eight.'

'You should have been shot. If wars were fought so that the old got killed before the young, the survivors would damn soon cut things short.'

'You seem to be doing your best to make sure that nobody in *this* squadron has a chance to grow old.'

'Of course they won't.' Woolley spat into his dubbin. 'They'll all be dead in a year.'

'That's an absurd way to think.'

'They'll all be dead in six months, then.'

'I don't see how you can possibly lead the squadron if that's what you really believe.'

'I don't. I personally believe there won't be one of them left alive by the end of April.'

Woodruffe got up to go. He was angrier than he could explain or understand. 'One expects casualties . . .' he mumbled.

'The trouble with pilots is that they are civilized, rational human beings,' Woolley said. 'They have been brought up, trained, educated, stuffed to bursting with *never going too far*. In a few weeks they're going to get chucked into the most horrible fucking slaughterhouse this war has ever seen.'

'You can't be sure of that.'

'Oh, shut up. And when this bloodbath starts, if we don't fight like animals, we'll lose. The difference between man and animals is that animals never worry about going too far, they just kill.'

'These men can kill,' Woodruffe grunted.

'When they try to kill *me*,' Woolley said, 'I'll believe you.'

Next day it rained heavily. Richards sloshed over to the mess tent for breakfast, skirting the pools that would not drain into the hard ground. The sky was as grey as the Atlantic it came from.

Rogers was pacing out distances inside the mess tent. 'I thought we might play some indoor cricket,' he announced. 'Get up two teams – the over-twenty-ones against the under-twenty-ones, or something. I've got an old tennis-ball. Everybody bats, everybody bowls. It's jolly good exercise. Sharpens the reflexes.'

Lambert said: 'I intend to spend today getting drunk.' He was eating fried bread and drinking gin.

'Well, you can do that too. I mean, I think we should organize something. There's not going to be any flying to-day.'

'It may be nothing more than a belt of rain,' Gabriel said. 'It could have passed by noon.'

They looked at him with dislike. Gabriel was the only pilot who didn't drink in the morning. Apparently the engine fumes did not distress him. Dangerfield, who made frequent trips to the latrine, was impressed by Gabriel's continence. 'Gabriel keeps a very tight ass-hole,' he once said. 'I admire that. It's a sign of strong character. Those sort of people don't give much away.'

'But who would want what Gabriel doesn't give away?' Lambert had asked.

Now, Gabriel's remark met with such a silence that he felt obliged to support it. 'This weather blew up without warning,' he said. 'It could blow over just as quickly. Who knows?'

'I'll bet you there's no flying today,' Dickinson said. He was a smooth, well-groomed young man with the anonymous face of an actor. Only when he was gambling did it light up; the rest of the time he wore the patient, professionally vacant look of a man eternally waiting to be auditioned. But he moved well, and flew elegantly. 'I bet you a fiver there's no flying today.'

'No, no. It's too early for w-wagers,' Killion said, and got no further: his stammer jumped in. Nobody paid any attention.

Finlayson limped in. 'Somebody's plane just got blown over,' he reported.

'I'll take that bet,' Church said carefully. Nobody paid any attention to him. He put his face in his hands.

The tent began to leak. Richards put a bucket under the drips. 'It's definitely getting worse,' he said.

'All right then, I bet you there *is* flying today,' Dickinson said. He looked around, but nobody spoke. Church took a piece of toast and carefully buttered it, clutching the knife in his fist.

'This bloody French weather,' Kimberley said. 'You can't trust it.'

Church piled marmalade on his toast and spread it thickly and thoroughly. 'I'll take that bet,' he said distinctly. Again, nobody paid any attention. He put the toast back on the plate where he'd found it and got up and went out.

'It must be hell in the t-t-t-t—' began Killion.

'Trenches,' Dickinson supplied. Killion nodded.

'Oh well,' said Dangerfield. 'They shouldn't have volunteered.'

'Funny to think that people actually did volunteer in the beginning,' said Richards.

'Hilarious,' said Lambert.

Finalyson went to the door of the tent. 'Old Churchy's standing out in the rain,' he said.

'I don't think he had any breakfast again,' Kimberley said. 'Did he?'

'Don't worry about Church,' Dickinson said. 'Church is feeling no pain.'

'Why does he do it?' Gabriel asked.

'The real question is, how does he do it and still manage to fly,' Rogers said. 'But he does.'

Woolley came in, wearing a potato sack over his head and shoulders. 'Finlayson?' he said. 'I want to look at your neck.'

Finlayson stood up. 'It aches a bit, but I can turn it all right, sir,' he said. Woolley walked behind him. 'Move it,' he said.

Finlayson turned his head from side to side. 'Stop moving your shoulders,' Woolley told him. He gripped Finlayson's shoulders. 'Do it now.' Finlayson flung his head about. Woolley grunted and let go. Stuck to Finlayson's left shoulder with sticking-plaster was a piece of string. On the end was a small firecracker. 'Now look straight in front and nod,' Woolley ordered. He blew on his cigarette and lit the firecracker. 'All right,' he said.

Finlayson sat down, looking relieved. The firecracker exploded. He ducked, covering his head. It went off again. He jerked around; again it exploded, and he twisted the other way. The firework hissed and banged, and then he understood, and struggled to throw off his jacket.

'Good God all bloody mighty,' he said, watching the stub fizzle and flutter about.

Woolley was sitting astride a chair, drinking coffee. 'Slow,' he said. 'Too damn slow.'

'One of the buttons stuck,' Finlayson protested.

'Bugger the buttons, your neck is too slow. You don't turn fast enough.' He leaned across and poured coffee on the dying squib. It sighed furiously. 'No future in that,' he said. 'Dead end.'

'All right,' muttered Finlayson. 'I know.'

'You *should* know. That's what happened last time, you didn't look behind you. By rights you should be cremated. He must have been a very stupid German.'

'I'm exercising it,' Finlayson said, rubbing his neck. 'I'm having treatment for it.'

'I don't care if you have mass said for it. Get it right. From now on I'm going to carry a Guinness bottle around with me. Every time I see you I'm going to chuck it at you and shout.'

Finlayson stared at him, white-faced and hating.

'The Guinness botle is very good for the throwing. If I hit you once, you're grounded. Twice, you're posted.' Woolley finished his coffee. 'No flying today. Everybody get over to the butts. Gunnery practice.'

Half of Goshawk Squadron sat on soaking wet camp chairs and hunched their saturated shoulders against Lewis guns which hissed steadily as the rain washed their hot barrels. The rest of Goshawk Squadron was slithering about in the deepening mud of a seven-foot trench, thrusting the targets up, waving them for a few seconds, and hauling them down again.

Woolley prowled up and down behind the guns, counting the shots. 'If you aim right, five is enough,' Woolley told them from beneath his potato sack. 'If you don't, it's all wasted anyhow.' Whenever anyone shot off too many, Woolley hurled bits of mud at him. Delaforce was terribly excited, and the shuddering, air-shaking, hot-smelling thunder of the weapon often got the better of him. He hardly felt the clods thudding against his back.

The bitter wind swung veils of rain across the range, blurring the targets. The shooting was poor: only odd bullets nicked the soggy cardboard, and none smashed through the nine-inch white circle that marked the heart. The gunners' teeth chattered, their legs trembled, and their boots attracted pools of rain which seeped inside and sucked the warmth from their feet.

Down in the butts the target men crouched, splay-footed to stay upright, and sucked the water from their upper lips. Bullets cracked overhead, chasing each other like mating hornets.

Woolley rang his handbell. All firing stopped. There was a clinking of safety-catches, and the target men splashed out of the trench, to change places with the gunners. Woolley trudged down and stood looking at the targets. The rain made an oily sheen on his skin. He took a bottle of Guinness from his pocket and sucked at it until the new men arrived.

'These targets are wrong,' he said. 'Look at the hearts. When do you see a heart on your right-hand side?' They stood, shoulders bowed, like cattle in stockyards. 'When you face him, you sodding musketeers, you ratfaced gang of stinking honour . . .' The words fell cold and flat, discarded, worthless. 'But we do not face the enemy. We do not fly up to him and slap him with our glove. We shoot the bugger in the back while he's picking his nose.'

Finlayson sneezed. Woolley went towards him. 'The man you kill has his heart on your left,' he announced. 'You fire at his back, so you aim to the left. Paint a new heart on the other side.'

While they got on with it, Woolley stood above Finlayson and sucked noisily at his stout. Finlayson fumbled with the target, his eyes nervously sneaking back to Woolley's feet. After a while Woolley went away. Finlayson took a deep breath. 'I could do with a tot,' he muttered to Killion.

'*Finlayson!*' bawled Woolley. Finlayson hurled himself flat. The bottle skimmed Killion's head and skidded along the trench. By the time Finlayson got up, fingering mud from his eyes, Woolley was gone, trudging back to the dripping gunners.

They fired for another hour. Woolley squatted under his potato sack and broke wind at regular intervals, while the pilots blasted away at increasingly difficult targets. Finally a sergeant-mechanic arrived and reported to Woolley. He clanged his handbell and they all went back to camp.

The ground crews had built two box kites, eight feet by five, painted grey. Each kite-string led to the back of a truck. Behind the trucks were two canvas-topped lorries from which the canvas had been removed, leaving the metal hoops. Clamped to the hoops were three Lewis guns, mounted on swivels. The whole outfit waited on the edge of the airfield.

The pilots stood with their hands in their pockets, trying to shrink their freezing bodies inside their icy clothes, and regarded the column without enthusiasm.

'The mechanics will tow the kites,' Woolley shouted above the gusting wind. 'You lot take the lorries with the guns. One man drives, three men on the guns. Let the kites get up to about two hundred feet, then start shooting. Right, get on with it.'

Nobody moved, except the mechanics.

'Rogers, Richards, Church, Lambert.' Woolley pointed a muddy boot at one lorry. 'Gabriel, Finlayson, Killion, Mackenzie.' Three men lumbered to the other lorry. Woolley stared at the remainder. 'All right, then, *you*,' Woolley shouted at Kimberley. Engines roared. Woolley went up to the cabs. Lambert and Killion were settling behind the wheels. 'Drive backwards,' he ordered.

'Backwards?' Killion said, 'I d-d-don't know h-h-how to d-d-drive f-f-f-f-f—'

'Backwards!'

The trucks moved off, skidding on the sopping turf, and the mechanics paid out the kites. The wind grabbed them and they soared away at an angle, forced up by their forward speed. Lambert clumsily put his lorry into reverse and set off in pursuit. Killion followed, zig-zagging wildly. As they headed into the field they began to lurch and jolt: on Woolley's orders one tyre had been made flat.

The gunners clung to the hoops and tried to line up the heavy guns on a kite. As the drivers worked their speed up, and the flat tyres pounded brutally on the grass, so the zig-zagging got more violent. The guns wavered, fired wild bursts, missed hopelessly. The grey kites flitted about the grey sky like bats at dusk.

At the end of the field, the tow-trucks made wide, fast turns. On the return trip the gunners had more wind in their faces, they were half-blinded by rain, and the pounding jolt of the flat tyres made it impossible to aim steadily. Nobody hit the kites.

'Get out and change crews,' Woolley ordered. 'Change crews every lap until the kites are hit.'

After forty minutes one of the kites took a lucky burst, but it still flew. The other was intact. Briefly, the rain gave way to hail. The trucks pounded up and down, roaring in and out of their wheelmarks. It seemed impossible that so many rounds could have been sprayed into the sky to such small effect.

After an hour one of the kite-strings broke. Woolley ordered its repair. During the delay he had all the vehicles refuelled. The pilots huddled together and tried to thaw their freezing hands. Woolley sat on the only petrol drum and opened another Guinness. Finlayson edged away.

After seventy minutes the wind dropped, and Dickinson found a kite flying absolutely stiffly and steadily on his quarter. He fired with a spiralling action, blasting bullets all over the corner of the sky until he saw the kite kick. The lorry swerved, and his fire swung wide. He raked the gun back and waited, blinking the rain from his eyes. He poured in a second circular volley. The kite fell to pieces.

Lambert said: 'God help the Hun if he ever comes at us with kites. We'll murder him. Given time.'

The wind rose again and the remaining kite thrashed all over the sky. It took another twenty minutes to shoot it down. Nobody knew who hit it. They were all still blazing away when the tow-truck stopped.

Woolley stood up without a word and headed for the mess tent. The others trailed after him.

Dangerfield slouched along with masochistic slowness. 'All I've learnt today,' he said, 'is that we've been shooting at the wrong bloody target.' He was looking at Woolley's sack-clad figure, up ahead.

'Yes,' said Church, trembling.

They drank soup and chewed bread. Nobody talked. Woolley sat in the middle, impervious to the rage and resentment that stained the air. Once he looked up and caught Kimberley's eyes. Kimberley glared. He became aware that Woolley was analysing his glare, rating it, giving it marks out of ten. He looked down.

When they had finished their soup, Woolley stood up. 'Back to the butts,' he said.

Behind the trench was a mound of earth, over ten feet high. This formed the actual butts, the barrier that stopped the bullets. Woolley led the pilots up on top of it.

Below, four mechanics stood around a large, primitive see-saw, about five feet off the ground. A small wooden keg, the kind used for storing nails, sat on one end of the plank. A step ladder stood next to the other end.

'Right,' Woolley bawled.

A mechanic climbed the ladder, balanced, and jumped on to the see-saw. It crashed down, catapulting the keg up and over their heads. They watched it land on the other side of the butts. At once a group of armourers moved forward with the Lewis guns and began setting them up where the keg had landed.

'Hit the little barrels,' Woolley said, 'before they hit you.' He slid down the bank and went over to the catapult.

The pilots trooped gloomily across to the guns. 'Farce upon farce,' Lambert said. He squatted on a camp stool and leaned wearily against his gun. The rain plastered his hair over his forehead like weed on a rock. They heard a muffled crash, and the first keg soared over the butts, hung, and began tumbling down. Lambert just managed to jump side-ways before it thumped to earth and rolled behind him. 'Bugger me,' he breathed; and then the massive blast of machine-gun fire drowned his voice. Another keg was on its way, and another.

As Lambert got to his feet and wiped the muck from his hands, the first keg exploded behind him. He staggered away, his ears ringing, and was surprised to find himself unhurt. Grey smoke drifted up, acrid and chemical. Another keg went off, further down the line. A new delivery smacked into the mud less than ten feet away. Lambert woke up and ran to his gun.

Beyond the butts Woolley lit a thunderflash, dropped it inside a keg, closed the lid and stood the missile on the catapult. A mechanic stepped off the ladder and another took his place on top. The catapult righted itself. Woolley loaded it, the man jumped. Each discharge shifted the catapult's position, so that the next keg followed a different course. At intervals, over the steady chatter of gunfire, muffled explosions could be heard.

It lasted for ten minutes, until he ran out of thunderflashes. 'Keep going with the empty kegs,' he told the gasping mechanics. 'Those buggers won't know the difference, anyway.'

He walked around the end of the butts and watched the performance. The kill-rate was high: three kegs out of five were blasted in mid-air. The guns had divided themselves into two batteries, left and right. They took alternate kegs, and this extra time allowed them to aim better. One gun was not firing. A man lay stretched out behind it; as Woolley watched, a keg bounced right over him. Woolley made no move until the last keg soared over the butts and was destroyed.

The casualty turned out to be Gabriel. A keg had clipped the side of his head. 'As long as it didn't hit anything important,' Woolley said. They all stood around and watched. Gabriel groaned. 'Why don't you do something for him?' Woolley asked.

'Why don't you?' Kimberley demanded.

The armourers were unloading the guns and taking them away. 'I thought we might all go for a five-mile run after tea,' Woolley said. 'That would only leave arms-drill and community hymn singing before bed-time.' Gabriel rolled on to his side and felt his head.

'Here comes the ambulance, sir,' called an armourer.

Woolley turned. It was indeed an ambulance: a field ambulance, boldly redcrossed, lumbering down the track.

A couple of men put their arms around Gabriel and helped him up. Woolley stared at the ambulance, took a couple of paces, stopped and stared again. The ambulance blipped its klaxon. He broke into a run. As it slowed and turned, the woman driver leaned out and waved. She revved the ambulance into a U-turn, and Woolley jumped on to the running-board. She changed up and accelerated away. The men holding Gabriel put him down again.

'In bloody credible,' Lambert said.

'How long for?' Woolley shouted.

'Two days.'

'Bring any Guinness?'

'Case in the back.'

'I love you.' He leaned inside and kissed her. 'Do you love me?'

'No.'

'That's right. Killed anyone lately?'

'Three last night. Are you all right?'

'I'm all right.'

'You sounded bad, on the phone that night.'

'Nothing you can't cure.'

Her name was Margery, and she was a nurse. Woolley met her in a Belgian hospital, in the summer of 1916, after he had broken both ankles in a forced landing. Since then she had followed Goshawk Squadron up and down the Line, moving from hospital to hospital. An uncle in the War Office managed the transfers for her. At first she told him that she wanted to be near her cousin Freddy, in the Engineers. Then Freddy got blown up and drowned in a shell crater, and all the time Margery was in a hotel two hundred miles away, putting Woolley to bed, dead drunk after a promotion. That was the first time she heard him mention Mackenzie. He seemed to wake with a cry that was half a snort. 'Hah!' he said, and stared at her. 'Where's Mackenzie?'

'Go back to sleep.'

He blinked. 'I want Mackenzie,' he ordered. 'I must have Mackenzie.'

'All right,' she said.

He stared for a few more seconds and let his head fall back. Soon he was asleep. Next day he remembered nothing of it. She asked if there was a Mackenzie in his squadron, but he refused to talk about the war, which suited her.

Conversation between them had been a problem in the hospital where they first met, right up to the night when she pushed his cot into an empty room, locked the door, took off her uniform and climbed in beside him. 'I realize we have nothing in common,' she told him then.

'Not true,' he said. 'We have our lust for each other and our disgust for everyone else.' They made love, clumsily because of the plaster casts on his legs, while somewhere a patient shouted in delirium. Afterwards she walked her fingers up his ribs. 'Why is your body so dirty?' she asked.

'I was a miner,' he said. 'It got forced in.'

'That's not true. Tell me the truth.'

'Listen, I'll make you a bargain. I'll never tell the truth, if you'll never tell lies.' He was serious.

'All right. Only what good will that do?'

'It'll show us the best side of each other.'

Margery usually talked about her family, which was like Margery herself: ample and affectionate, in a critical sort of way. They expected everyone to do something, and then expected to tell them how it could be done better. They approved of her becoming a nurse and going to France, but they told her she should have done it sooner. 'You've left it awfully late,' her father told her in January 1916. Even then, at twenty, she was beginning to look matronly, and of course she had always been good with animals. Everybody else was in France, and she was afraid that if she stayed at home she might fall in love with some disabled veteran and marry him.

The first few months horrified her. Her experience of suffering had been limited to rabbits in traps. Now she spent her days amongst men with holes blown through them, and every night some died. By the time Woolley arrived in her ward she was turning into a slaughterhouse attendant: she no longer saw them as men but as damaged stock; if they screamed it was not a sign of pain but a signal to fetch a doctor. Blood was part of the job, like spilled paint to a house-painter. She could not help them, so she began to hate them for the waste they brought into the hospital. Everything was waste. Her life was waste. Normally you tried to make things better; here you tried to stop them getting worse. The waste-factory that produced these defective goods roared day and night. It was making a scrap-merchant of her.

Woolley stopped all that.

He came into the hospital with six cases of Guinness, and a shepherd's crook. He had the bottles placed under his bed, and when the ward sister tried to interfere he fended her off with the crook while he produced medical certificates, all signed by Army doctors, stating his need for regular supplies of the stuff. She rejected them. He appealed to her in several languages, including German. She ignored his appeals and began to move the cases. He placed her under arrest. She turned white and rang for a doctor. Woolley placed her under *close* arrest for mutiny. When the doctor arrived Woolley was lying on the floor, apparently semi-conscious. 'She hit me with my own stick, Doctor,' he whispered, displaying the scrapes and cuts received in his flying accident. 'I was trying to save some of the Guinness for you, but she hit me with my own stick. I – I must have passed out.'

The doctor felt his pulse, then took a bottle from the nearest case and examined it.

'He was ranting and raving at me,' the ward sister said, '*in German.*'

Woolley cringed. 'Don't let her hit me,' he pleaded. The doctor opened the bottle and sniffed it. 'All right, Sister,' he said. When she had gone he helped Woolley to his feet. 'You've got a bloody nerve,' he said.

'I paid two quid for those certificates,' Woolley said.

'They're all valid, you know. You might as well drink that now you've opened it. You don't want it to go flat.'

'It's the real thing, all right,' the doctor said. He sighed. 'All right. Keep the stuff out of sight. And I want a dozen bottles for myself.'

'Leeches,' Woolley said. 'Bleeding leeches.'

He was soon the centre of scandal and unrest. Anybody with anything juicy to report went to Woolley for an audience and a bottle of stout. He ran a sweepstake, supposedly based on the intake and discharge of patients; actually the winning number was the daily total of deaths in the hospital. He got a key to the blanket store and rented it out to randy nurses and hungry walking-wounded, many of whom he had introduced in the first place. For a sensational week he published a news-sheet which libelled everyone from the governor's wife to the assistant chaplain, including both together. He won a piano-accordion at cards and taught himself to play sea-shanties. He circulated two new rumours a day: cholera was sweeping Paris; the Kaiser was in Rome looking for a divorce; the kitchen was putting aphrodisiacs in the gravy; Lloyd George had been charged with rape; Switzerland had invaded Germany. Nurse Jenkins was pregnant. The hospital was about to be moved underground. The Czar was going to visit the wards at 10 AM next day and everyone would get a medal.

At first Margery hated him for always showing off, and for mocking others who were suffering; above all, for attacking the harsh and humourless atmosphere of her scrap-body factory. But his outrageous irreverence was a relief; eventually she had to admit to herself that she looked forward to hearing what Lieutenant Woolley had done *now*. He lifted some of the curse from that place of death. She went out of her way to pass near him, and he went out of his way to insult her. He disturbed her, because he was not handsome, he was ugly; he was not gallant, he was cynical; he was not worthwhile at all, and yet inescapably she was in love with him.

*   *   *

Woolley's tent was hot. He had spread a tarpaulin over the duckboards, and on top of it they dumped blankets from the ambulance. The door was tightly laced and a pressure lamp burned whitely. They sat, naked, and ate the food she had brought. Margery sweated slightly.

'We always do the same thing, don't we?' she said.

'Practice makes perfect,' Woolley said. 'Never change a winning team. When in doubt, remove all clothing.'

'It's not really the same thing, I suppose. Every time it's different. But it's always . . . like this.'

'Why chop and change?' Woolley said. 'Look at the dinosaurs. They were happy.'

'Happy,' Margery said. She put down her food and carefully brushed her fingers, staring at the floor. Woolley belched, and stretched. Margery sucked at the inside of her lip. 'You know that I want you,' she said steadily, still not looking at him. 'And I know that you . . . need me. What I don't understand is why . . .' But here she ran dry. Her voice had no more words. She turned to face him and he saw how her skin was shivering, the self-control leaking out of the corners of her eyes, her face breaking up. He put down the bottle and sat on his hands and waited.

'I'll never be any use to anyone else,' she wept. 'You're the only one I want to help and you won't let me get near you except . . . except . . .' Now the hair was over her eyes, the drops were splashing wetly down her breasts.

He wriggled his toes and saw a flight of aircraft peeling off, beautifully, one by one. 'Well, I haven't changed,' he said gently; only it came out curtly.

'I know.' She couldn't find a handkerchief. 'Oh *blast blast blast*.' She found it and mopped up. 'It's all right for you. You're not fat and you don't spend all day washing bloody bodies.'

'Everybody knows you're the best in the business.' He took her hand.

'I could have married cousin Freddy's best friend Gerald,' she said.

'Tell me about him.' He pulled her on top of him.

'Tell me about yours, first.'

'My cousin Freddy's best friend was Norman,' he said. 'He was deported to Liverpool for strangling Lady Mayoresses. Three, he done, in one afternoon.'

'Liar,' she said. 'Lovely liar.' They kissed.

That night, in the damp gloom of the mess tent, Goshawk Squadron got good and drunk.

'Pneumonia,' Lambert said, pouring gin. 'I ask you: what a way to go.' He sneezed.

'You noticed that he didn't bloody condescend to pull a bloody trigger himself,' Finlayson said. He was wearing red flannel around his neck to ease the pain. 'I'd like to see *him* hit one of those bloody kites. Arrogant bastard.'

'Hear, hear,' agreed Church. He was wandering around, standing in front of people and smiling. Occasionally he sneaked off to one side and had a good long suck at a silver flask.

'P-p-p-ower c-c-c-corrupts,' Killion managed.

'I wonder if we've got grounds to complain to Corps?' Dangerfield said suddenly.

'Oh, definitely,' Church said. He came over and smiled at Dangerfield.

'Tell you what,' Dickinson said, 'I bet you he does it again tomorrow. I'll give five-to-one on.'

'Oh Christ,' said Lambert. He reached for his glass and knocked it over. 'Double Christ.' He found the bottle and drank from that.

'It's not impossible,' Gabriel said. 'After all—'

'For God's sake take a drink and shut up,' Finlayson told him.

'I second that,' Church said cordially. He went over to Gabriel and smiled.

'You can't dimiss the possibility that the old man might have a plan,' Gabriel said stiffly.

'Major Woolley to you,' Rogers said.

'If you ask me, I think the fellow is certifiably loony,' Dangerfield said. 'I think he's finally cracked a cylinder.'

'Bound to happen,' Kimberley said.

'Bound to happen,' Church agreed, nodding.

'I'll lay three to one he's still sane,' Dickinson offered.

'Done,' said Woodruffe, coming in from the rain. 'Put me down for a fiver both ways.'

'You can't bet both ways on a two-horse race,' Dickinson objected.

'All right, old man. If you want to back out. Perfectly okay with me.' The adjutant squinted muzzily through the cigarette smoke. 'Look here, you chaps,' he said, 'I want to do something for you.'

'Well, you can do something for me,' Lambert said. 'You can tell that sadistic bastard to cut out bloody gunnery practice in the pouring rain.'

'Sorry,' the adjutant said. 'Not possible.'

'Useless clown,' Finlayson said.

'Tell you what I will do,' the adjutant said, 'I'll get hold of everybody's score-card and alter it so you all get full marks.'

'Bound to happen,' Church said softly.

Killion stood up and walked stiffly over to Woodruffe. 'W-w-w-what I w-w-w-want,' he said, 'is a g-g-g-girl.' He blinked seriously.

'You're sex-mad, Killion,' Dangerfield said.

'Mad,' Church endorsed.

'Tell you what,' Woodruffe said. 'Can't get you a girl, but if you get her into trouble I'll see it's all right.' Killion walked away, stony-faced.

'I know you're tight, Woody,' Finlayson said, 'but the only thing you could do for us now would be to shoot the old man. It's time he was put down. Can you do that?'

'Bound to happen,' Church said.

'Sorry,' the adjutant said. 'Can't shoot the Commanding Officer. Tell you what, though. If *you* shoot him, I'll get you off the court-martial.'

'Shooting's too good for him,' Lambert said.

Faintly, above the moaning of the wind, they heard a cracked wheezing, the unskilled sequence of chords of a sea-shanty played at half speed.

'Listen,' Finlayson said, 'the bastard's at it again. Celebrating another kill on his bloody squeeze-box.'

'That p-p-p-poor g-g-g-girl,' Killion said.

'Bound to happen,' Church murmured. He slipped out and went to his tent, got his revolver, and emptied it in the direction of Woolley's tent. Everyone ran into the rain to see what was happening; everyone except Woolley. 'By the time I got my boots on it would all be over,' he told Margery. 'I don't suppose he hit anything, anyway.' They found out next morning that he had, in fact, hit an aeroplane; but not seriously.

Force 5: Fresh Breeze

Small trees in leaf begin to sway

February was a wretched month. Woolley's training programme was grindingly hard, tent-life cold, wet and colourless, and the news from the Front depressing. One day at breakfast Richards asked Woodruffe what was going on.

'Nothing much, officially,' the adjutant said. 'All the rumours are that Jerry's been bringing his troops back from the east by the train-load. Corps think he'll try a really big push as soon as the rain stops.'

'He always does,' said Finlayson wearily. 'Spring wouldn't be the same without an offensive.'

'This will be different,' Gabriel said.

'What the hell do you know about it?' Finlayson demanded.

'I read the newspapers,' Gabriel said, unmoved. 'Presumably the Germans do, too. They know the Americans are sending troops.'

'They already have,' Rogers said, 'as we well know.'

'Only a few divisions,' Gabriel said. 'Not yet enough to stop a German assault.'

'Balls,' Finlayson said. 'In case you didn't know, an American division is twice the size of an ordinary division.'

Gabriel supped his porridge in silence.

'In any case,' Finlayson went on, 'all those Huns the Kaiser is bringing back from Russia are fagged out. They've been fighting out there for bloody years.'

'And winning,' Gabriel said.

There was a gloomy silence.

'What d'you think, Woody?' asked Rogers. 'Has the Hun got enough troops to do any damage?'

'Somebody did tell me he thought they might be a tiny bit stronger than us at the moment. I believe the figure mentioned was one and a half million in rifle strength.'

'Good Christ,' said Killion, before he could remember to stammer.

'Of course I got that from a chap in Intelligence,' Woodruffe said. 'They're always wrong.'

'What I can't understand,' Richards said, 'is why we have to wait. Why don't we hit them first?'

'It's been tried,' Lambert told him. 'Remember Passchendaele? That was our idea.'

'Passchendaele,' said Dickinson softly 'Passion Dale. There's something almost Miltonic about it. Or do I mean Bunyanesque? Ranks of valiant warriors crashing to catastrophe, with a great deal of rolling thunder and rather too much sulphur and brimstone.'

'It was pretty horrible,' said Kimberley severely.

'Don't tell *me*, chum. I was there. I flew forty-three patrols in one week.'

'Have you really been in the Corps that long?' Woodruffe asked in surprise. 'I had no idea it was *that* long.'

'Only last July,' Dickinson said.

'Still . . .' Woodruffe peered at him thoughtfully.

'If I were Jerry,' said Finlayson, 'I'd go for the French. They don't want to fight any more. Our froggy friends have had enough.'

'I say, is it really true that the French artillery had to fire on their infantry?' Delaforce asked. 'To drive them over the top?'

'Absolutely,' Finlayson said. 'They had a mutiny. The troops wouldn't leave the trenches, so the French generals laid down a barrage on them. That soon shifted them.'

'What happened afterwards?'

'Afterwards? There was no afterwards. Why d'you think they didn't want to get out of the trenches?'

'It makes me feel sick,' Rogers said. 'Physically sick.'

'Mind you, the other side has the same problem,' Dickinson said. 'I've seen the Jerries running up and down behind their men, waving pistols. It's the same for both sides.'

'What a filthy war it is,' Richards said. 'It's all so cramped. There's no room for a bit of cut and thrust, it's just . . . it's like . . . two great stupid fellows standing toe to toe and . . . *bludgeoning*.'

Woodruffe listened to all this with deepening anxiety. 'I was at Corps yesterday,' he said, 'and General Somebody was telling people how things looked, and he said we were definitely on top. He thought that one big blow would knock the Germans right out. He said there was every reason for optimism.'

'God,' Lambert said. 'I didn't know things were as bad as *that*.'

As soon as the rain stopped, Woolley had the planes warmed up. He went to the middle of the field and spread out a small tablecloth. Then he rang his handbell and waited for the pilots to assemble.

'This,' he said, 'is your life insurance policy. Read the small print carefully.' He walked across the white square. Delaforce and Richards looked at his footprints doubtfully. Church twisted his head sideways as if the writing were the wrong way round. The others stood and smoked, or twitched, or shrugged, or blinked, or nodded, or performed whatever other small compulsion their nervous systems required of them these days. Gabriel noticed how grey the hairs were on the back of Woolley's neck. Finlayson stood behind Kimberley.

'This cloth is today's target,' Woolley said. 'It makes a good target, for two reasons. First, you attack it from above. Always attack from above. When we get into action, some of you will forget that. They will be killed. Height is an advantage. Always try to fight with an advantage.' Woolley pursed his thin lips and addressed Rogers and Kimberley in particular. 'I have been described as lacking in chivalry,' he said, and his flat Midlands accent made the word sound medical. 'This is not true. I try to kill the man with the first shot. I see no point in needless pain.'

Kimberley could not tell if Woolley were serious or mocking. He looked away.

'To kill with the first shot,' Woolley went on, 'means getting close. The closer the better. Twenty-five feet, one length of the aeroplane, is a good distance. Fifty feet is the maximum. I am talking now about the first shot. Get in close and kill him before he knows it. Marksmanship is more important than flying skill. If you can kill him first, you won't need to out-fly him. If you miss, you lose the advantage of height and surprise. The enemy has a chance to out-fly you, and if he has a better machine he will probably kill you. Never give him a chance to fight on even terms if you can sneak up and kill him first. Do you all follow that?'

The wind licked at the white cloth and peeled up one corner. Woolley stood on it.

'Suppose there's a lot of them,' Gabriel said.

'Kill one or two and run away,' Woolley told him. Gabriel nodded as if that was what he expected.

'The second reason why this is a good target is that it's the same size as the vital part of the aeroplane.' Woolley turned his back on them and sat in the middle of the cloth. 'Your bullets must hit this. Never shoot at the aeroplane. A Fokker or an Albatros or a Pfalz does not bleed. You can perforate a Triplane until it looks like old net curtains, and the pilot will end up killing you and flying home.' He stood up. 'Shoot at the pilot. If you miss him you may still hit the petrol tank or the engine.'

'That's all very well,' said Finlayson sourly, 'but in a dog-fight you've got to fire at whatever presents itself.'

'It's just luck, really,' said Dickinson.

'Anyone who depends on luck is a fool and a suicide,' Woolley said. He squinted at the overcast sky. 'The sun is *there*,' he pointed. 'Come out of the sun and fire one burst of ten rounds from no higher than fifty feet. Red flag for a hit, white for a miss.'

They walked to their aircraft, which stood gently shuddering against their chocks, the engines droning in unison. Gabriel, Dangerfield and Finlayson discussed the best angle of approach.

'The flatter you come in, the longer you can take to pull out,' Dangerfield said. 'So you get a better chance to aim.'

'But you reduce the visible area of the target,' Finlayson said. 'Ideally, you should come straight down on it.'

'At fifty feet?' Gabriel asked.

'He's never made us do this before,' Dangerfield said. 'If you ask me, it's bloody dangerous.'

'That, it would seem, is half the point,' Gabriel said. 'Incidentally, taking the old man's philosophy to its logical end, I presume that one would be expected to destroy an enemy machine even if one knew that, say, the pilot were injured or out of ammunition, and therefore unable to fight back.'

'Oh, shut up,' Finlayson said.

Dickinson was the first to dive. He came out of the non-existent sun at 45 degrees and concentrated on keeping the nose pointing just below the tablecloth, remembering that the Lewis gun would fire high to clear the propeller. The wind tugged the machine one way and he nudged it back. At fifty feet he squeezed the gun lever just as another block of air shouldered into the little SE5a. The short burst made the plane tremble.

He pulled firmly back and cleared the target by twenty feet.
White flag.

Rogers was hard behind him but he undershot and came in shallowly, and only touched the Lewis lever for a second before veering away.

White flag.

Lambert learned from them both, steepened his angle, and left everything a fraction later. His plane seemed to swoop down a straight slope until an abrupt crackle signalled the moment to pull out. He levelled off about ten feet above the ground and banked as he climbed, looking back at the red flag.

The rest of the squadron, circling and watching from five hundred feet, took their turns. Each pilot wheeled out of the fictional sun, nosed down, and jockeyed his bouncing machine into a dive. The white square slowly magnified, then seemed to blossom, and there was one second when everything happened: the cockpit was shaking, the engine bellowing, the ground looming, the tablecloth leaping and dancing. Then he was swinging out of it, feeling the blood retreat from his head, sensing the ground reach up for his wheels: twisting to see the flag, before he went up and waited his turn to do it over again.

Everybody missed on the first attempt except Lambert, Church and Kimberley. On the second round half the squadron scored hits, and by the end of the third only Finlayson, Delaforce and Rogers had failed. Rogers was having trouble with his gun. Finlayson couldn't master the wind conditions. Delaforce was simply a bad shot.

On the fourth round the tablecloth was cut to ribbons, and there was a delay while the ground crew put a fresh one in its place. Everyone except Rogers and Delaforce had scored with at least part of a burst. Rogers landed to get his gun cleared, but Delaforce was by now wild with disgust; he had an almost physical appetite to see his bullets strike home. He climbed hard, hurried around the field and broke into the circling planes for another attack.

This time he could not believe the white flag. He was convinced that he had been on target. He couldn't have missed: they were wrong! He drove the plane back into the circuit and again forced them to let him through. He dropped on that maddening, tattered square of dirty white like an eagle on a lamb. He pushed the SE into a near-vertical dive and stared wide-eyed at the growing target.

Long before it was time to fire he realized that he would have to pull out or crash; below fifty feet there would be no recovering, not from this angle, not at this speed. Yet he couldn't bear failure again, with the whole squadron watching. He decided to risk a burst at long range and squeezed the trigger; nothing happened. He checked that the gun was cocked, and squeezed again. Again, nothing. The slipstream built up to a scream, and despair drugged his actions. When at last he hauled back on the stick the ground was close and rushing up. He pulled out of the dive and cleared the target area, every joint and spar in the aeroplane shuddering under the strain. He could see the horizon just above the shining disc of his propeller, and he fought to drag the leaden nose up to it. His wheels ran into the wet turf and the whole machine crumpled and fell to its knees like an animal shot in the chest. Delaforce was impaled on the control column, but by then his neck was broken anyway.

Woolley wanted to see only one thing: the ammunition drum. It was empty.

Nobody spoke to Woolley at lunch, yet everybody meant Woolley to hear. Accidentally, obliquely, the squadron had found this way of striking back. It was a feeble retaliation, but it was all they had. They spoke loudly and clearly, not interrupting each other: like actors.

'I don't see why you should be a captain when I'm only a lieutenant,' Dangerfield said to Rogers. 'I'm a much bigger bastard than you are.'

'You don't get promoted just for being a bastard, you know,' Rogers said. 'You've got to be a bloody bastard.'

'I question whether Dangerfield has the right hide for a commander, anyway,' Lambert said. 'I saw him smile yesterday. That's no good, you know.'

'I'm more fitted for command than any of you,' Kimberley said. 'I once stuck a pitchfork through a toad.'

'But did you enjoy it?' Dickinson asked.

'Of course I did. I revelled in it.'

'That cuts you out, then. Too emotional.'

'You're all wrong,' Finlayson said. 'You've got to have the right accent before you get promoted.'

'What sort of accent is that?' Gabriel asked.

Finlayson chewed his food while he thought. 'Bloody horrible,' he said at last.

'As far as I can see there's only one reason why anyone gets promoted,' said Richards, 'and that's survival. Live long enough, and up you go.'

'Yes, but why do some people live longer than others?' Dangerfield asked.

'As I already said,' Rogers told him. 'You've got to be a bloody bastard. Look at me.'

'You're not a bloody bastard,' Lambert objected. 'You're not even a filthy swine. When one gets right down to it, I doubt very much whether you're fit to be called a bad lot.'

'Oh, I say, steady on,' Rogers complained. 'Dash it all, I am a captain.'

'Plenty of much bigger bastards than you have been made captain,' Kimberley said. 'Plenty.'

'All right, then, name three,' challenged Rogers.

'You wouldn't believe me,' Kimberley said dourly. 'It would sound like a flock of sheep.' Church tittered.

'I'll tell you another reason why you won't get promoted,' Lambert addressed Dangerfield. 'You're far too clean. You wash excessively. I have evidence that you wash in excess of once per week.'

'Only in order to remain tolerable to my comrades,' Dangerfield protested. 'I don't do it for any reason of self.'

'As I said; you haven't got the right hide for command. It requires a very thick, *very dirty* hide.'

'What about b-b-b-brains?' Killion asked.

'Opinions are varied,' Dickinson said. 'Some say a commander needs no brains at all. Others say he needs a very tiny brain. Just enough to enable him to, say, count the survivors.'

'I c-could d-d-do that.'

'No, no, no. You're far too intelligent. Why, I've been told you can count up to fifty or sixty, on a good day.'

Killion nodded.

'Well, then. Besides,' Dickinson sniffed hard, 'you're not nearly filthy enough, you're only moderately dirty in parts.'

Church laughed out loud: the clear, delighted laughter of a child. Killion glanced quickly and looked away. Church was certainly dirty enough. A combination of tent-life and gin had kept Church away from soap and water for weeks. He shaved but he did not wash, and his bright, shallow smile was like the contentment of a piglet fresh from the teat.

The adjutant hurried in, carrying a small cardboard box. 'Dispose of this lot, would you, Dudley,' he said. 'I must eat or I shall collapse.' He sat down and began lunch.

'I thought we weren't going to do it like this any more,' Rogers said. 'I thought it was going to be first come, first served.' He poked about inside the box. 'Not much here, anyway,' he grumbled. 'Hardly worth bothering.'

'For God's sake stop pawing it over like some damn pawnbroker's wife,' Lambert said.

'What is it?' Richards asked. 'What's in there?'

'Hardly anything,' Rogers said. 'A few gew-gaws, a couple of knick-knacks, and a what-not.' He fished out a pair of carpet slippers. 'Anyone want these?'

'Two shillings,' offered Dickinson.

'Half-a-crown,' Lambert said.

'They're not worth half-a-crown,' Dickinson grunted.

Richards threw the slippers to Lambert. 'Sold,' he said. 'Pay Woody, and make sure he puts it in the mess account. Any offers for these hair brushes? Silver-backed. Exquisite workmanship.'

'Look here,' said Richards strongly, 'I'm not sure that I like all this.'

'Then don't bid, laddy,' Finlayson said. 'I suppose they're monogrammed?' he asked Richards.

''Fraid so – C.P.D. Suit Dickinson or Dangerfield, of course. They could always claim they were family heirlooms.'

Nobody wanted the hair brushes. Rogers put them back and took out a New Testament. 'In original wrappings,' he announced. 'Mint condition, uncut leaves.' He took it from its case and opened it. 'With a rather touching inscription in green ink,' he added. 'Any offers?'

'Damn it. I'll have that,' Richards said angrily. He looked at Gabriel. 'I'm surprised *you* don't want it.'

'I already have one,' Gabriel said.

'Do I hear a bid?' Rogers asked.

'A pound,' Richards snapped.

'Any advance?' Rogers looked around. 'Not only green ink but also excellent spelling,' he urged.

'God damn you,' Richards swore. He jumped forward, snatched the testament, and thrust it into his tunic pocket.

'Sold for a mere quid.' Rogers rummaged around and produced a silver cigar-cutter, a small framed photograph of a middle-aged couple, and a pocket-watch. Nobody wanted any of them. He then took out a small book, expensively bound in limp leather. '*Highways and Byways of Old Hampshire*,' he announced. 'The work of a clerical namesake, possibly a relative.' There were no bids. 'Are you quite sure?' he asked Richards. 'After all, you do have the beginnings of a small library . . . As you wish. That seems to be that, then.'

'Pitiful,' said Finlayson. 'Not worth the effort.'

'All right,' the adjutant said, 'you can go back to a vulgar free-for-all if you like. I don't care.'

'Half a tick,' Rogers said, 'I missed something.' He scrabbled in the bottom of the box and came up with a small piece of carved and polished wood. 'This appears to be a miniature cricket bat,' he said, 'carrying the miniature signatures of a pygmy team. Some kind of trophy or mem-ento, no doubt.' He peered at it. 'Somebody seems to have scored a hundred runs and been the hero of the school.'

'I'll take that,' Gabriel said. Lambert raised his eyebrows. 'As a keepsake,' Gabriel said.

'The chair will consider a motion,' Rogers told him. 'In other words, how much?'

'Well; five shillings.'

Rogers looked at the little bat. 'Five bob for an unbeaten century? The chair is disgusted. The chair itself will bid ten.'

'A pound.'

'Two pounds.'

'Four pounds,' Gabriel said thickly. He was sitting with his hands inside his pockets, legs crossed, shoulders hunched, watching closely as if Rogers were trying to trick him. Rogers tossed the piece of wood in the air so that it spun.

'Oh, eight pounds,' he said.

Now the squadron was alert, watching to see if Gabriel would fight. He was taken aback. 'Look here,' he said. 'You've no right . . .' Rogers flicked the bat in the air again. 'Hell and damn,' Gabriel said flatly. 'A tenner.' It was the first time anyone had heard him swear.

'Fifteen.'

Gabriel looked at Richards, but Richards said nothing. 'It's got absolutely nothing to do with you,' Gabriel told Rogers. 'You scarcely knew him. I'll give twenty pounds for it.'

'Forty,' said Rogers shortly.

'I would remind contestants that all bids are cash,' Woodruffe said, 'and if you haven't got it I shall take it out of your pay.'

Gabriel looked at the ground. His head was quivering slightly, and his breathing was jerky.

'The bid stands at forty,' Rogers said. 'Any advance on forty pounds?'

Woodruffe laid down his fork and closed his eyes.

Rogers cleared his throat. 'Going, then, for forty pounds,' he said. 'Going. Going.'

'Eighty,' said Woolley.

'*Eighty?*' Rogers asked. He pulled his hat over his eyes, over his nose, his whole face, and held it there. Then he lifted it, like a waiter taking the lid off a dish. 'Do I hear eighty pounds for this excellent example of . . . of . . .'

'You heard,' Lambert said. 'Now speak up or shut up.'

'Ninety,' Rogers said. He looked at their sceptical faces as if seeking support. He cleared his throat again and laid the little bat carefully on the table. 'Ninety pounds.'

'A hundred,' Woolley said. He was holding a bent fork and scraping at a loose fibre of wood on the table-top.

'Guineas,' Rogers said rapidly, before he could think about it.

'And twenty.'

Rogers sat nodding, and looking down the table. He reached for the bat and sent it skimming along the boards. Woolley stopped it with his fork. He picked it up and went to the door of the tent. He looked at the sky, and scratched the back of his neck with the bat. 'Gunnery practice,' he said. 'Take off in ten minutes.'

He walked over to the coke brazier where the cooks kept the food hot; and looking first at Rogers, then at Gabriel, he tucked the little bat into the bright red fire, and walked away.

A sack of empty tins lay beside each aircraft: accumulated cookhouse waste. Woolley briefed the squadron. Starting in numerical order, each plane would climb to fifteen thousand feet and empty its sack. The rest of the squadron would circle at twelve thousand. By the time the tins had fallen that far, the wind and slipstream would have blown them all over the sky. Close in to no more than twenty-five feet and fire no more than five rounds at a time.

The difficulty lay not only in hitting the tiny spinning fragments of silver but also missing the bigger objects flying all around. It had been some time now since the old pilots had been in a dog-fight, and Killion for one was sweating heavily by the time he landed. The nervous tension of dodging and ducking about a sky crowded with equally dodging and ducking planes, some firing, some looking as if they might fire at any instant, some sheering wildly away to avoid a collision; and all the time trying to grab a quick shot at a mere point of light: all this brought back the strain of combat, when you were pressed on by the excitement of chasing the enemy, pulled back by the horror of shooting a friend, and periodically shaken with fright by the thought that at any second you might be cut in two.

As soon as they had all landed, Woolley rang his handbell.

'For Christ's sake, ding bloody dong,' Finlayson growled. He joined Kimberley and they trudged across the field. 'This is the stupidest thing I've ever heard of,' he said. 'Jesus! You've got to fly right up to them before you can *see* them.'

'It's a madhouse,' Kimberley said. 'I nearly hit old Lambert just now. Miracle I didn't hit him. Miracle.'

'Maybe you did.'

'Well, he landed all right.' Kimberley looked around for him. 'As a matter of fact, I think I *did* hit him,' he said. 'In the tail.'

'Somebody hit *me* in the tail,' Finlayson said. 'There's a damn great hole in it.'

'Could have been a tin,' Kimberley suggested.

Finlayson grunted. 'Any bastard starts shooting at me, I'll do the same back at him.'

'Don't blame you,' Kimberley said, without enthusiasm. They fell silent as they got near Woolley.

He had found one of the tins, and it lay at his feet. He took his revolver from its holster and cocked it. 'Get closer,' he told them. 'Get much closer.' He kicked the tin away from him and took a snap shot. He missed. The explosion made them flinch. 'At a hundred feet,' he said, 'all you're doing is warning him that you're there.' He stopped nearer the tin and fired again, and missed. 'At fifty feet you might hit a wing, or a wheel,' he said. He bent and scooped up the tin with the barrel of the revolver, and held it high.

'Get right up close!' he cried. 'Get right up where you can put the muzzle under the back of his helmet and blow his bloody head off!' He pulled the trigger and sent the tin spinning through the air. The echoes soaked into the vastness of the windy field. 'Get close,' Woolley whispered. He holstered the weapon and walked away.

'Some bastard got too close to me,' Finlayson said. 'I got a burst through the tail.'

Woolley stopped and turned. 'That was me, Finlayson,' he said. 'I thought you knew. You were hanging back, Finlayson.'

'Fighting's one thing,' Finlayson said angrily. 'Target practice is another. I'm not going to get myself killed just because—'

'Fool!' Woolley boomed. 'Feeble fool! You can't *survive*, Finlayson. You can only *win*. If you want to *survive*, you shivering ninny, you might as well shoot off your big toe. Here, I'll do it for you.' Woolley snatched out his revolver. 'A Blighty number, that's what you want.' He pulled the trigger. The bullet missed by twelve inches. Finlayson jumped and retreated. 'What's the matter, Finlayson, don't you want to survive? I'm trying to help you survive, Finlayson!' He fired a shot over the man's head. Finlayson ran backwards. 'For God's sake, sir, have some sense,' he pleaded.

Woolley lowered his gun. 'Sense,' he said. 'Now there's a silly word to use in the middle of a war. All the sensible people are dead.'

Richards suddenly understood. Richards saw that Woolley was trying to do more than train them, and lead them, and pass on the lessons of experience: he was also struggling to turn each of them into the kind of person that he himself had become.

When Woolley instructed them in shooting the enemy in the back he was not being melodramatic, he really meant it, because Woolley was a professional. The amateurs played at fighting; they kept their scores and rejoiced in their adventures, and they were brave, good-humoured warriors. But Woolley took it seriously. He had asked the ultimate question – *What is it for?* – and got the obvious, the only answer. You flew to destroy the enemy. You did not fly to fight, but to kill. It was neither fun nor adventure nor sport. It was business.

Woolley was in business with death, while the rest of them were just playing with life. Richards suddenly saw this, and

84

he guessed how erodingly lonely the man must be. Then Woolley looked at him. All the emergent pity in Richards turned sour. You couldn't feel sorry for Woolley. You couldn't feel anything *for* him. Woolley was a man you could only feel against.

It was still an eventful afternoon. Half the squadron had a go at Woolley, popping off a couple of rounds in his general direction and then having to dive away fast when he swung towards them. Woolley patrolled the squadron and gave a brisk burst more or less behind the tail of anyone he considered to be holding back. The flying became more disciplined. Instead of hunting all over the sky, the pilots concentrated on one scatter of targets and spiralled down through them, turning tightly in order to cut down the risk of collision. Marksmanship improved. The pilots became more aware of each other, developing a slick, anticipatory sense of where and when each one would go next.

One man flew with real urgency and some venom. Finlayson followed Woolley all around the squadron, looking for a chance to get his own back. Woolley gave the squadron a lesson in evasive flying. The only times he allowed Finlayson to get a clear view of him there was always another plane lined up on the other side. Nobody – not even Finlayson – knew what would have happened if he had ever got the chance to pepper Woolley. Meanwhile he blazed away at the tumbling dots of metal with a grim obsession.

The exercise nearly ended badly. Dickinson was the last to empty his tins, and so he was the top plane when bits of wood began spitting in all directions. There was a bang; the spinning disc vanished; and the engine raced from a bellow to a scream. His propeller had gone.

At once he put the nose down and switched the engine off. The plane slid into a shallow dive. All around he could hear the toy snarl of wheeling planes. It was a sound he had never heard before: like sitting in a tall tree full of hornets. The weight of the engine tugged his nose down and he had to keep tugging it up again. He slid between two planes, Church and Killion, and saw them circle and follow him down. He stood up and pointed forward. Killion waved. The rest of the squadron was still below, plunging and climbing and chasing its tail. He side-slipped to miss three tightly spiralling planes, and found himself drifting into another cluster. Automatically he hauled back on the stick. The nose lifted sluggishly, the rush of air slowed, and the plane stalled.

Dickinson slammed the stick forward, but by then he was falling, wavering, spinning. He plunged past one plane and caught a blurred glimpse of another, wheeling towards him. He manhandled and trampled the controls: nothing answered. The other plane continued its turn, its wingspan widening. Dickinson half rose and screamed at the man but the plane lumbered on, seeming to spread itself with deliberate stupidity right across his path. Dickinson shouted his rage. At the last moment the other pilot looked up. Dickinson ducked down and screwed up his face, bracing himself against the shock, listening to the widening roar of the other engine.

The blow rattled the plane as if it had been a car bouncing through a pot-hole. Then the engine note was suddenly fading, turning light and harmless; and Dickinson felt the controls start to answer. He eased the SE out of its manic plunge and into a steady glide.

One set of wing-tips was a mess, and both wings on that side looked a bit bent back; otherwise, nothing. He looked up and saw a plane following him down; it too had a battered wing-tip. He laughed aloud. What a nonsense it all was! The difference between two dead men and two slightly bent aeroplanes was just a fraction of a second. What a joke! A couple of wires in his damaged wing snapped, slashing open the fabric. He stopped laughing.

The other plane powered alongside him: Kimberley. Dickinson waved, and Kimberley waved back, and dived away. Dickinson sailed down in slow, sweeping curves, feeling strangely innocent. It occurred to him that if this were over the Front he would be a gift for even the stupidest German pilot. It also occurred to him that if he ever found a German plane as helpless as this, Woolley would require him to destroy it.

Finlayson came over and looked at the splintered stubs of Dickinson's propeller.

'It's this bloody awful field,' he said. 'You must have nicked it when you were taking off.'

'Probably.'

'The least he could do is have it rolled. He bloody well chewed it up, him and his childish kite-flying.'

'No doubt about that.'

Finlayson walked around and looked at the damage from the other side. 'Aren't you going to do anything about it?' he asked, waving at the lumpy grass.

'I expect he knows.'

Finlayson sniffed. 'I'll make bloody sure he bloody knows,' he said, and went away.

Woolley listened to Finlayson in silence. 'You don't like the field,' he said.

'I don't see why it should be dangerously bad,' Finlayson said, 'sir.'

Woolley drained his Guinness. 'Draw a dozen spades from Stores,' he said. 'Take the pilots and flatten the field.'

'But sir, it needs to be *rolled*.'

'Hit the field,' Woolley said, 'with the spade.'

Finlayson looked at the bleak, vast meadow. 'That'll take hours,' he said.

'Better hurry,' Woolley advised.

Finlayson walked away without saluting. Woolley watched his resentful back. 'Finlayson!' he called. Finlayson half-turned, ducked under the flying bottle, slipped on the wet grass, and fell. Woolley, arms folded, watched him get up and limp away, trembling with rage.

It took the squadron all the remaining hours of daylight to clean up the airfield. They replaced hundreds of divots, flattened hundreds of bumps, filled in scores of ruts, and pounded the turf until their backs ached and their hands burned. From time to time light showers blew over, but the squadron plodded on with a mute, masochistic determination. The sound of their sodden thwacking punctuated the dusk.

When it was too dark to see, they came in, grimly satisfied. 'It's done and I hope he likes it,' Finlayson told the adjutant. 'I notice *he* never took his coat off and helped.'

'That was hardly possible,' Woodruffe said. 'He was called to Corps HQ for a conference two hours ago.'

They received the news silently, unwilling to concede that Woolley had a good reason for doing anything. 'When's he coming back?' Lambert asked.

The adjutant shrugged. 'You know Corps. It's supposed to be a very big conference.'

'Woody,' Rogers said, 'is it all right with you if we all go over to St Denis and cause a certain amount of devastation?'

'That depends,' the adjutant said. 'Will it bring the fair name of the squadron into disrepute?'

'Inevitably,' Rogers said. 'Inevitably and repeatedly.'

'In that case I'd better come with you,' Woodruffe said.

Force 6: Strong Breeze

Large branches in motion; telegraph wires 'sing'.
Umbrellas used with difficulty

S ix empty barrels stood on the main dining table of the best restaurant in St Denis. They supported two large chairs, which supported one small chair. Lambert sat in this chair and emptied his wine over Finlayson, seated far below. 'That was a Low Story,' he said. 'The chair find bloody old Finlayson guilty of telling a Low Story, the bastard.'

'All right,' Finlayson said easily, licking the drops off his upper lip. 'Tell you another. Man walking down quiet street, gets taken short—'

'Heard it!' The other pilots sprawled, bloated with food and squiffy with drink, around the table. Some of them started throwing bread at Finlayson.

'Another story, then,' Finlayson said. 'Man falls down at stag party and breaks his cock.'

'*Heard it!*' The squadron booed him.

'Christ, that's old,' Kimberley said.

'My problem,' said Finlayson, drinking, 'is I don't know any new dirty jokes.'

'Your problem is you don't know any old jokes,' Dangerfield boomed. 'Your problem is you have absolutely no sense of humour.'

'I deny that!' Finlayson cried. 'I categorically repudiate that!'

'There you are, that proves it,' Rogers declared. 'Boring and pompous.'

'Found guilty,' Lambert ruled from on high. 'Mr Woodruffe will pass sentence.'

'Relax and enjoy your problem,' the adjutant decreed.

Lambert emptied his glass over Finlayson again. 'Perhaps you'll know better next time,' he said. 'Next problem.'

'My problem is I can't see straight,' Rogers said. 'Seriously, chaps, you all look a bit squiffy to me.'

'You're boozed, Rogers,' Lambert told him.

'Who's that?' Rogers closed one eye and peered up. 'Is that God?' The bread-throwers turned their attention on Lambert. 'I always knew God was on our side,' Rogers mumbled, 'but I never knew He was so bloody ugly.'

Lambert stood up. 'Being God,' he said, 'and seeing as this is Tuesday, I shall now make water.' He began unbuttoning.

The owner of the restaurant came in. '*Non, non, messieurs!*' he pleaded. Lambert sat down. 'Good news,' he said. 'We've found someone who really has a problem.' They cheered, and threw bread at the haggard Frenchman. Lambert tried to douse him with wine. '*In nomine Patris—*' he began when the street door burst open, and Killion rushed in. 'I found them!' he shouted.

'You forgot to stutter,' Rogers said. 'Go out and come in again.'

Six sulky girls sidled through the door. 'I f-f-f-found them,' Killion bragged, 'in a b-b-b-brothel.'

The restaurant owner had turned white. '*Mon dieu!*' he gasped. '*Ah! Ça non! Quand même!*' He rushed over to Killion and shook him, spitting demands.

'I s-s-s-say,' Killion said as he rattled back and forth. 'This is f-f-f-f-u-n.' The girls slouched moodily into the room and found places to sit. 'We shall now sing one chorus of "Praise God, from Whom all Blessings Flow",' Lambert announced. Woodruffe rose and led the singing. The girls found themselves glasses and bottles and began drinking. The Frenchman slapped Killion hard on both cheeks and ran out into the

90

street. Dangerfield selected the thinnest girl and began dancing a waltz to the hymn-tune. Killion stood there hiccuping until Lambert threw wine over him; then he woke up and went to the doorway and started calling out.

The singing ended. Killion came back in. 'I found these ch-ch-chaps in the b-b-b-brothel, too,' he said. Three elderly French accordionists eased sideways through the door, smiled nervously, and played conflicting chords. 'Music!' Dangerfield shouted happily, and kissed them. '*Allez, allez!*' The eldest one wheezed uncertainly into a waltz. The others listened hard, launched themselves, and put on speed until they caught up with him. Soon all the girls were dancing. Lambert conducted them on high with an open bottle, sprinkling the couples as they passed beneath. The owner came in with a gendarme.

'*Bonjour*, gents,' Lambert called, '*vous avez une réservation?*'

The gendarme came over to the table and began a long address to Lambert, who listened politely commenting '*Peut-être*', from time to time. The restaurant owner went around the room, trying to separate the dancers. He grabbed Killion and shouted at him, spitting heavily. Killion put down his glass and used the Frenchman's necktie as a towel to mop his face.

The man trembled with rage, leaning slightly forward because of the strain on his collar. Then he slapped Killion hard on the face and took a pace back and kicked him in the groin. Killion collapsed, screaming; the music faltered, stopped, and started up again in a noisy polka. Kimberley left his girl and knocked the Frenchman down. Lambert leaned over and sprinkled wine on both bodies. 'Ashes to ashes,' he intoned. 'A tooth for a tooth.'

The gendarme hurried around the table, drawing his truncheon as he came. Dangerfield followed and, as the gendarme raised his truncheon, reached up and tugged it away from him. The gendarme whirled around and swung a punch. Dangerfield dodged; the Frenchman stumbled over

Killion and lurched into one of the girls. She kicked him on the leg and also knocked his hat off. He got away from her and looked for Dangerfield. The French girl came up behind him and kicked his backside. The gendarme saw Dangerfield and flung a chair at him.

It went through a window.

The band faltered, took a breath, and plunged into a two-step. The gendarme stood bewildered for a moment, and then ran into the street, where for some time he could be heard blowing his whistle. But he did not come back, and soon they were dancing again. Discarded clothing began to litter the floor. The band was fairly drunk, and the tunes tended to overlap now. A small crowd gathered in the street and was watching through the shattered window. Church came up from the cellar with his arms full of bottles, and handed them out to the spectators. 'Plenty more downstairs,' he assured them. 'They've been hiding it, you know. But I found it.' Killion got to his feet, kicked the groaning restaurant owner, and took a bottle from Church.

Woodruffe found Rogers, and shook his hand. 'Dudders, old boy,' he said. 'Don't you think we ought to be toddling off? Otherwise the chaps might start getting into mischief.'

'Can't go yet,' Rogers objected. 'These girls still have to be stuffed. Besides, we're not all here. Dickinson and Gabriel haven't come back.'

'Where are they?'

'Don't know. Went off on their own.'

'Damn nuisance.'

'Never mind, Woody. Relax and enjoy your problem.'

'I hope you're sober enough to drive us all home, that's all.'

Rogers studied him curiously, 'Funny thing, Woody,' he said. 'I can see your lips moving, but I can't hear what you say.'

'That's because you're absolutely stinko, Dudley.'

'I won't deny it, I am a bit squiffy.'

Dangerfield danced past and called out: 'That nasty frog is beginning to come round. He just tried to bite my ankle.'

'We ought to do something about our genial host,' the adjutant said.

'Look here, I'm coming down,' bawled Lambert. 'I've been making several very funny speeches and no bugger has laughed, so I'm coming down.'

'We could put him up there,' Rogers suggested.

'What, the high seat? Not very safe, is it?'

'Best place for him. Better tie his hands, or he might do himself an injury.'

They bound the restaurant owner, who moaned feebly and threshed about a bit; then with Lambert's aid they hoisted him to the high seat. They got down and looked at him. He swore so violently that he nearly fell off; then he froze. Then he was sick all down his front. 'Definitely the best place,' Rogers said.

Twenty minutes later the band had been augmented by violins and drums, and several new girls had joined the party. Church was making regular trips to the cellar. The girls from the brothel had taken over a small back room. Rogers found Killion and congratulated him on his work. 'Don't get left out, old chap,' he urged. He tried to slap Killion on the shoulder and missed, and ended up on the floor. 'Make sure you get your share,' he advised.

'Don't worry, D-Dudley,' Killion said. 'I h-h-h-had mine at the b-b-b-brothel. All s-s-s-six of them.'

Rogers rolled his eyes. He found himself looking up the skirts of a girl dancing by, and he rolled across the floor in an attempt to keep up with her. The dancers kicked him and trod on him until he got to his knees and crawled away.

A few minutes later the lights went out. 'Boche bombers,' said Woodruffe complacently. 'Hit the electricity works again. Now we can all go home.' He trod carefully, searching for pilots in the occasional glow of cigarettes. 'Is that you, Kimberley? The lights have all gone out. Don't you think we might get started?' Kimberley grunted as he took off his trousers. 'I am,' he said.

Woodruffe found a bottle and sat down. A couple of

minutes later a soft glow appeared in the cellar doorway. Church tip-toed into the room, carrying a biscuit-tin full of candles. He tittered nervously as he tried to see through the glare of the flames. His sweaty, unshaven face gleamed like wet chalk.

'Christ, Church, you look like the Spirit of Syphilis Yet to Come,' Lambert said. Church shook with silent mirth and dropped the tin. All the candles went out. 'Bloody good job,' someone said. 'I don't need any bloody beacons to guide my way.' Eventually a few candles were lit, the band started playing, the couples uncoupled and went off to the back room, and the party went on.

Woodruffe slouched around, looking for Rogers. He noticed that the floor was running with wine. Over in one corner Church was systematically emptying bottles. The dancers sent up a spray of froth and droplets. Woodruffe turned his head sideways and dimly saw Rogers sitting under the table, cross-legged, smoking.

'Come in out of the rain,' Rogers said. 'Bags of room in here.' Woodruffe crawled in.

'Far be it from me to play the kill-joy, Dudders,' he said. 'Is that a bottle you have there? Thanks.'

'Good party, eh?'

Woodruffe drank thoughtfully. 'Church is behind all this,' he said, pointing at the floor. 'Church is raining booze.'

'Trouble with this lot,' Rogers said, 'don't know when to stop.'

'I always said, right from the start – and you'll bear me out, Dudley – I always said it would end in tears.'

'Right.'

At that moment the police smashed down the door.

The struggle was messy. A dozen policemen rushed into the room and tried to herd everyone into the corners. One of them slipped on the sopping floor, cannoned into the table, and brought down the pyramid of barrels and chairs which still supported the restaurant owner. He fell badly, unable to use his arms to protect himself. In the excitement Church hit a policeman with a bottle. Abruptly the atmosphere changed, and the police began knocking people about.

The pilots were drunk and half-naked; they got no help from the French girls, who simply screamed and tried to get out of the window. The band, too drunk to understand, began to play the *Marseillaise*. More pilots ran out of the back room, aroused by the uproar, and joined in the fist-fight.

Only Woodruffe kept his head.

'Candles, Dudley,' he shouted in his ear. 'Put out the candles.'

They crawled from under the table and knocked over every candle they could see. Soon the room was no longer dim but gloomy. The fighting became wilder and more confused. One policeman accidentally hit another, who fell to his knees, cursing. He was evidently their leader, for most of them stopped. Woodruffe scrambled towards the splintered door and croaked: 'Everybody get out!' Nobody heard him. Rogers bellowed: '*Get out, get out, get out!*'

This started a scrambling rush to the door. Woodruffe was vaguely puzzled by the passivity of the police. One or two lashed out, but most did nothing. He held the broken door and shoved people into the street. Still nobody tried to stop them, or come after them. It was too good to be true. Perhaps the leader was too badly hurt to give orders . . .

He joined the tail-end of the rush and slammed the door behind him. The night was ten times blacker than he expected. He heard a confusion of puzzled shouts ahead and stumbled over something. His wet feet slithered on a wooden ramp which sounded hollowly underneath. Woodruffe paused, suspicious, yet too muzzy to decide.

'Get on!' rasped someone. He scrabbled up the ramp and fell over a body. Behind him the tailgate went up with a bang, and through his face he felt the vibrations of an engine. Then the truck accelerated over the cobbles into a violent right-hand turn, and the squadron found itself thrown hard against the side of the police patrol-wagon.

The truck raced along bad roads for about five miles, crashing over pot-holes and making heavy weather of the gear changes. The pilots sorted themselves out, and tried to find something to hang on to. The inside was black, dirty and deafening. Woodruffe shouted a question which even he could not hear. After that he concentrated on saving his battered skin.

The truck finally swerved off the road and jounced across pine roots before it stalled with a jerk in the middle of a little grove. The pilots cautiously relaxed their grip and let their muscles slacken. Nobody spoke. Chains rattled and pins grated. The tail-board fell with a bang. A dark figure took off a police helmet and wiped his brow. 'I think we've shaken them off,' he said. It was Dickinson.

'Can we get out, Dicky?' Woodruffe asked.

'By all means. Stretch your legs, have a smoke. I'm out of cigarettes myself. Got some snuff, though.'

Groaning and wincing, Goshawk Squadron fell clumsily on to the springy turf.

'I'll take a pinch, if I may,' Dangerfield said. 'Head seems a spot thick.'

Dickinson offered his snuff. 'You didn't get beaten up by those savage rozzers, I hope,' he said.

'To tell the truth, I'm not one hundred per cent sure whether I did or not,' Dangerfield said. 'I wasn't paying much attention.' He sniffed vigorously.

'Look here, Dicky,' Rogers said, 'what on earth are you doing wearing that ridiculous hat? And driving this filthy lorry? I take it you were driving.'

'None other. I got her up to seventy-five, too. Not bad, considering I had the handbrake on all the way.'

'So that's what that funny smell is,' Lambert said. 'I thought it was Church.'

'I keep seeing great big purple Catherine Wheels,' Dangerfield said. 'Purple with orange spots.' He sneezed hard. 'Ah, that's better,' he said damply.

'I thought we were done for,' Kimberley said. 'I thought we were all going to end up in some manky frog clink.'

'Dicky rescued us from the jaws of the Bastille,' Richards said. 'How did you do it? Damned lucky you came along when you did.'

'Actually, I'd been hanging around the street for quite some time. Those coppers had been assembling, you see, so I lurked in the shadows and watched, and when the Top Cop turned up he told them all to get in the Black Maria, then they backed it up to the front door and they all charged inside.'

'I remember that now,' Lambert said. 'They didn't even knock. I mean, we could have been doing *anything* in there.'

'I thought I ought to do something,' Dickinson said, 'but I couldn't think what. The driver was still in the cab, you see, so I couldn't let the tyres down.'

'What?' Woodruffe interrupted. 'You were going to let the tyres down?'

'That was my first idea.'

'Ah.' The adjutant opened his mouth, then closed it. 'Never mind,' he said.

'So what I did was, I got some stones and threw them at the driver.'

'Quite right,' Lambert said. 'When in doubt, always stone the police.'

'Well, it worked,' Dickinson said defensively. 'He jumped out and came galloping down the street, waving a sort of club. I remember he was an awfully big chap. Big, but not fast.'

'Like an elephant,' Kimberley suggested.

'Elephants are bloody swift,' Finlayson declared. 'I'd like to see you out-run an elephant.'

'Shut up,' Woodruffe said.

'Well, I nipped down a little alley. There was a doorway on one side, so I got in there. I still had a stone in my hand, and the moment the bobby turned into the alley I threw this stone up the other end. He thought it was me, and he put on a bit of a spurt, and as he went by I tripped him up.'

'With your foot?' Rogers asked.

'Well, yes. I mean, it was all I had.'

'Just trying to get the picture, old boy.'

'Walking sticks are best,' Kimberley said. 'Walking sticks are bloody lethal.'

'Shut up,' Woodruffe said. 'So down he went.'

'Oh, rather. He came the most appalling cropper. I think he knocked himself out, or something. Anyway, I removed his belt and pulled his trousers down and tied the legs in a knot, just to make sure. Then I came back, just as you chaps were pouring out. Fortunately the engine was still running.'

'Remarkable, Dicky,' the adjutant said. 'I honestly never thought you had it in you. First-class performance.'

'It did come off rather well, didn't it? That bit about throwing the stone up the alley to make him rush off after it, I got that from a detective story. The business with the trousers was my idea. I must admit – Good God, what's that dreadful noise?'

They turned towards a choking, bubbling death-rattle. 'It's only Church being sick,' Finlayson said. 'D'you think you could drive a little slower for the rest of the way, Dicky? My arse is raw.'

'Now that I've got the handbrake off,' Dickinson said, 'I think it'll be less of a struggle. I suppose we *can* go back now?'

'Why ever not?' Dangerfield asked in surprise.

'Well, everybody *did* get out? You are all here?'

A simple count answered that question. Killion was missing.

A minority was in favour of abandoning Killion and going home, but the others were persuaded by Rogers. 'Killion got hold of the whores *and* the band,' he pointed out. 'Whatever you think about Killion, you must admit that it was a damn good band.'

They got into the truck and Dickinson drove cautiously back towards St Denis. When they were still two miles away his headlights caught a half-naked figure trying to scramble through a hedge. He pulled up alongside. 'B-b-b-b-bugger off, you w-w-w-w-wogs,' Killion called. 'Ooooh!' he added with feeling as a bramble raked his shoulder.

'Killion, it's us.' Dickinson got down and held back the prickly branches while Killion blundered out, his lips trip-hammering away at the opening consonants of all the swear words he knew. It turned out that Killion had been in the cellar when the police came, and he escaped through a trap-door into the street. As he was wearing only trousers and shoes he knew that he would soon be picked up in the town, so he got away through alleys and into the country. It was sheer luck that he had chosen the same road as the truck.

'Now, perhaps, we can all go home,' said Finlayson.

'N-n-n-n-no, not y-y-y-y-yet.' Killion shook his head emphatically.

'Who the hell else?'

'G-g-g-g—'

'Gabriel,' said Rogers disgustedly. 'I'd completely forgotten about Gabriel. Where the devil is *he*?'

'I know,' said Killion.

Dickinson stopped outside a Catholic church on the outskirts of St Denis. Killion and Woodruffe were in the cab with him. 'Are you sure?' he asked. Killion nodded. 'He s-s-said he'd b-b-b-be here.'

Woodruffe said: 'I can see a little light. See? In the corner of that high window.'

They walked through the churchyard. It was bitterly cold, and Killion wore Dickinson's tunic. Dickinson, in shirt sleeves, shuddered. Faintly they heard music.

The church door was not locked. Woodruffe pushed it open, and the organized moan of pleading chords reached out to them with a smell of cold masonry and dusty matting and faintly clinging incense. They walked in, feeling their way along the matting: the church was even darker than the night. From the middle they could see, by the limited and spherical aura of two candles, Gabriel's large and lumpy head, up on

99

high beyond the choir-stalls, outlined against the soaring stalagmites of organ pipes. He leaned slightly to the right, and a high trickle of icy notes began to feel its way towards them.

'Has he been up to this all night?' Dickinson whispered. Again Killion nodded.

Woodruffe took a deep breath. 'He really does have a problem,' he said; but he too spoke softly. 'All the same, we can't stay here.'

They stood, feeling the groan of Gabriel's chords vibrate through their teeth, and tasting the pure crystal of his wandering notes. At last, when there was a brief pause, Woodruffe cleared his throat.

Gabriel turned his head and stared. He was utterly calm, waiting for the interrupter to explain himself.

'We're going back now,' Woodruffe called. 'If you want to come with us.' His voice resounded and redounded, searching into every cold corner.

Gabriel looked sharply in their direction. Then he took his hands from the organ and looked all over the keyboards as if to make quite sure that all the keys and stops were there. He snorted quietly: an unemotional noise; a punctuation mark. He pinched out one candle and took the other to light his way down.

Nobody spoke on the way back to the truck.

'Now can we *please* go bloody home?' Finlayson said.

'I think we might,' Dickinson said, yawning.

'You do know, of course, that you're pointing in the wrong direction,' Gabriel stated.

Woodruffe stared. 'You mean *that's* the way back to camp? Back through the town?'

'Unless you want to make a fifty-mile detour.'

'We can't just drive back through the middle of St Denis,' Rogers said. 'They'll lynch us.'

'I'm not so sure,' Richards said. 'It's the last thing they'd expect, you know. Besides, I don't fancy going fifty miles the wrong way at this time of night.'

'Church has just been sick again,' Finlayson said, 'partly over me.'

'You're absolutely sure, Gabriel?' Dickinson asked.

Gabriel gave him a short, flat look. 'Yes,' he said.

'All right,' Dickinson said. 'Only you don't know what's been going on.'

'Let's get started, for God's sake,' Kimberley growled. 'I don't care if I sleep in camp or the Bastille. There's damn-all to choose between them, anyway.'

They got into the truck and drove gingerly through the town. They had to pass the restaurant in order to reach the right road; but as it happened nobody even looked at them. The restaurant was on fire.

'Not a happy day for our genial host,' Lambert said. They scrambled to the back to see the fire brigade squirting water on the flames. 'He must be feeling pretty discouraged.'

'I expect he did it for the insurance,' Dangerfield said. 'Some chaps are like that, you know. Completely irresponsible.' They turned a corner, and the scene vanished. Almost immediately the truck came to a stop. 'Police,' guessed Finlayson. 'Now we're for it.' But it was Woodruffe who came around from the cab.

'You can drive me home, Dudley,' he said. 'We've found your car.'

'Haven't got a car,' Rogers said. 'Have I?'

'Well, you drove it here. You might as well drive it back.'

'I can't,' said Rogers. 'I'm too squiffy.'

'But you must. It's got your cheque-book in it, and we still haven't paid for tonight's meal.'

'All right.' Rogers got down. The truck rumbled away. With some difficulty he got the car to start and drove slowly along the middle of the road. He gripped the wheel tightly and held his face quite close to the windscreen. They were in top gear, but still moving slowly.

'We'll never get home at this rate, Dudley,' Woodruffe said.

'These hills are a lot steeper than they look,' Rogers said. 'It'll be all right when we go down the other side.'

After a few minutes Woodruffe said: 'You've got your foot on the brake, Dudley.' Rogers released it, and the limousine bounded forwards. He relaxed and sat back. 'Dickinson has the same trouble, sometimes,' he said.

A few miles later, Rogers asked what Gabriel had been doing in the church.

'Playing the organ. Rather well, too.'

'You mean he played the bloody organ all night?'

'Yes.'

Rogers frowned. 'Odd thing to do.'

'Yes.'

'Sounds as if friend Gabriel has a bit of a problem.'

'Perhaps. On the other hand, he seems to be able to relax and enjoy it.'

They caught up with the truck and followed it back to camp. It was four in the morning when they arrived, and the place was alive with men taking down tents and loading stores and checking supplies. Woodruffe jumped out of the car in a panic and looked for Woolley.

He found him sitting in his canvas chair beside a brazier, drinking Guinness with the chief armourer. Woolley gave the adjutant a single glance and then looked away. 'Get dressed,' he ordered. 'We're moving back to the Front. Fricourt. Take-off at dawn.'

'But they can't,' Woodruffe said automatically. 'They're—' He turned and looked behind him. Killion and Richards, half-undressed and filthy, were carrying Church; his feet dragging in the mud. Behind came Kimberley, holding his head, and Finlayson, barefoot and wrapped in a blanket. Lambert, limping badly, wore a French police helmet, and Dangerfield was wiping mud from his eyes: he had just fallen down. Only Gabriel and Dickinson were fully dressed and erect. As he watched, Lambert tripped over his own stumbling feet.

The adjutant turned away in shame and disgust. But Woolley was no longer there. His chair was there, and beside it his empty bottle, but Woolley had gone. The pilots dragged themselves over and blinked painfully at the tableau, harshly delineated by the pressure lamps. They shuffled into a semi-circle and squinted at Woodruffe.

'We're off to Fricourt,' he said miserably. 'Take-off at dawn.'

Out of the darkness came a squat metal canister. It bounced and rolled between them and lay in the shadow of the chair. Some of them leaned forward and tried to see what it was. The thunderflash exploded with a stunning ferocity that shattered their jagged nerves and twisted their sagging faces with terror. They were home again.

Force 7: Moderate Gale

Whole trees in motion

Goshawk Squadron landed at Fricourt in light drizzle with blinding hangovers, and got away with only two accidents, thanks to the grace of God and an unusually long field. Dangerfield eased his SE5a into a three-point landing while he was still twenty feet above ground and smashed his undercarriage. Lambert touched down shakily, got lost and drove into some bog where his wheels stuck fast, the nose buried itself, and the tail reared high like a flag on a steeple. When they came out with ladders to rescue him he was asleep.

The squadron spent the rest of the day settling in. Three replacements arrived: Callaghan, Peacock and Blunt, straight from Flying Training Schools in England. The adjutant, holding his head with one hand, took them to Woolley. 'Replacements, sir,' he said. 'Their names—'

'I don't want to know,' Woolley said flatly. He looked at their fresh, serious, eager-to-impress faces and turned away. He was eating a cold sausage; his tongue located a piece of gristle and spat it out. 'I am a genial, jovial and well-liked commanding officer,' he told them. 'My warmth and charm are exceeded only by my old-fashioned courtesy and my fucking sympathy.' He stared at Lambert's stranded plane. 'As long as you are in this shoddy squadron, there are certain words you will not use. Here they are. *Fair, sporting, honourable, decent, gentlemanly.*' Woolley felt in his pocket, took out a flimsy telegram, read it, blew his nose on it, and threw it away. 'Those are bad words,' he said. 'Bad, murdering words. Don't even think them.'

The replacements saluted and withdrew, feeling bewildered. The adjutant billeted them separately, each sharing a hut with an experienced pilot. Callaghan got Finlayson. He found him sitting on a bunk, holding a bottle of milk in one hand and cup of gin in the other. 'Hullo!' said Callaghan. Finlayson winced. 'I say, are you all right?' Callaghan asked. He noticed the dirt and congealed blood on Finlayson's head. Finlayson thought for a good long time, while he stared at Callaghan's bright new buttons. Then Finlayson put down his bottle and cup, rolled over, and was sick into a fire bucket. Callaghan felt his pent-up excitement go flat. This was not the way he had expected it to be, at all.

Next morning, Woolley briefed the squadron on its first combat patrol. 'Just sweeping-up,' he said. 'We've got ten miles of Front to look after. We'll fly in two sections. Rogers leads the other. Each section flies a zig-zag from here to the Front and back. Nobody crosses the Front.'

'What if we're chasing a damaged Hun, sir?'

'You're an idiot, Rogers.'

'Yes, sir.'

Woolley called the replacements to one side and asked them if they had flown an SE before. None had. He looked at them like an auctioneer trying to improve a poor lot in a cattle market. 'I won't depress you with the truth,' he said. 'Just remember this. If the engine fails on take-off, keep going straight ahead and crash-land. Never try to turn back. Never. If you manage to take off, follow me and do *exactly* as I do. Can you make your head move?' he asked Blunt.

'Yes, sir.'

'Show me.'

Blunt turned his head. 'Move it right round,' Woolley ordered. 'Now up and down. Turn it all the way.' The others watched Blunt rotate his head. 'Do that all the time,' Woolley said. 'Search for the man who is searching for you.' He sucked in his ill-shaven cheeks and stroked his thin lips, and stared at them. 'Finders keepers,' he said.

The replacements got their planes off the ground and Woolley marshalled them into a broad arrowhead, with Dickinson and Church out on the flanks. The cloud ceiling was at two thousand feet. The countryside lay dead and cold, waiting for spring. The roads shone like strips of lead; every footpath was waterlogged. Nearer the Front the land began to erupt in craters, set and changeless: boiling porridge caught in a photograph. Then the Line itself – supply trenches angling cautiously up to an elaborate hem-stitch of Allied positions, with the wire lying beyond, scruffy and irregular, a tidemark in no-man's-land. They turned and flew back. There was no enemy air activity at all. For an hour they flew a repetitive zig-zag from their base to the Front and back, until Callaghan's neck was stiff and his eyes ached; but when he suddenly spotted an aircraft he wanted to shout the news.

After a few moments he realized they were flying on an interception course. Then he remembered that Woolley had changed the course before he, Callaghan, saw the plane. Reluctantly he conceded that Woolley saw it first.

It turned out to be French: a Nieuport. Woolley led them down in a mock attack, the arrowhead formation swooping in a long, curling dive that went under the Frenchman's tail and zoomed up and levelled out, back on patrol. The excitement of that plunge affected Callaghan. If only they could catch a German! But the war was asleep today.

After two hours Woolley turned for home. Blunt gratefully recognized that they were losing height, and rested his neck; then felt guilty and started searching again. They were within sight of the airfield when Woolley inexplicably wheeled left and they climbed towards the mattress of cloud. Blunt couldn't see the reason for that. He was four or five lengths away from the next plane when one by one they angled into the quilted greyness.

Cloud frightened Blunt. It seduced his imagination: woolly wisps streaming past told him nothing; he could be flying into a mountainside . . . or diving . . . or two seconds away from a collision . . . What if the cloud went up to five thousand feet? Or six? Or ten?

Blunt felt the sweat break out in his armpits and trickle down his ribs. He shut his eyes tight and locked his fists around the joystick. Part of his mind queried the value or purpose of sweating. What possible good could wet armpits do? Deep purple shapes bloomed and turned orange on his eyelids, then everything went bright grey. He opened his eyes. They were in weak, hazy, winter sunlight.

Woolley flattened out, turned right and prowled over the surface for about a quarter of a mile. Then he led them down into the bloody cloud again.

Blunt closed his eyes and loathed Woolley. He locked his fingers around the joystick again and gripped it tightly in the angle of the dive, hearing the engine-note climb and the wing bracings develop a piercing whistle that merged into a slow shriek. Fear slowed his thoughts, and grudgingly granted him one consolation: at this speed they must come out at the bottom a damn sight faster than they went through at the top.

He opened his eyes and searched for a break in the streaming fog. There was nothing, and suddenly there was everything: solid, sodden fields slightly canted over, and three, four German aircraft flying across them at fifteen hundred feet. Three Pfalz scouts and a lumbering two-seater observation plane. A reconnaissance patrol.

The formation swam up as Woolley held the flight in its dive. At ten lengths the furthest Pfalz turned to meet the attack, far too late. The six SE5as went through the German formation like an Act of God, spraying fire in a red-hot probe. Woolley, Callaghan and Peacock scored bursts on the two-seater. Dickinson and Church engaged the scouts. Blunt saw nothing ahead but he shot off a dozen rounds on impulse as he plunged through a great hole. He remembered only details: the shiny, slate-blue skins of the German wings; the old-fashioned, pinch-waisted crosses; the swept-back tail-fins. Then he was hauling back on the control column and edging in on Woolley as the flight hurtled up in a long recovery from its dive. Centrifugal force clamped his back-side and spine against the seat. He screwed his neck around to try and find the enemy. Ragged black smoke led to the two-seater; the Pfalz scouts had gone, vanished.

Woolley levelled off two hundred feet from the burning aircraft and flew parallel. The pilot had collapsed inside his cockpit. The observer lay sprawled across his gun, his blond hair streaming romantically in the wind. Something erupted with a soft boom, like a distant starting-gun, and the aircraft crumpled. Its tail stood up and it fell, spinning slowly as if it were gently unwinding itself.

It crashed on one side of a thick hedge. A herd of cows had been standing on the other side, and Blunt watched them stampede away, fanning out like clumsy messengers with news for all parts.

'I can't get over your not being related to C. G. W. Peacock,' Rogers said. He shook his head and frowned at his drink. 'It really is the most remarkable coincidence.'

Peacock clasped and unclasped and reclasped his hands in an embarrassment of humility and candour. 'Never even met him, I'm sorry to say,' he said. He put his hands in his pockets. Nobody else had their hands in their pockets. He took his out.

'Hampshire,' Rogers said. 'Opening bat. Useful bowler, too.'
'We . . . live in Norfolk.'
'Norfolk?' Rogers looked at him doubtfully. 'D'you know, I don't think I've ever met a cricketer from Norfolk.'
'No, we . . . don't seem to go in for . . . cricket. Much.'
'Oh. Isn't there rather a lot of water up there?'
'The Broads, yes. Jolly good for sailing.'
'Ah.' Rogers drank his drink with the air of a man who had found out why Norfolk people play so little cricket.

There was an odd silence. The squadron had gathered in

the ante-room to the dining-room for a drink before lunch. Everyone felt relieved to have left Pont St Martin, with its freezing tents, and to be here in Fricourt, where the airfield had hutted accommodation and a village down the road. Everyone was pleased about the German two-seater, whose remains lay outside in the back of a lorry; but nobody was going to say so while Woolley was in the room.

Rogers turned to Blunt. 'There was a Jonah Blunt who turned out for Somerset occasionally,' he said.

'Sorry.' Blunt flushed with shyness. 'Different Blunt.'

'I used to play cricket,' Church stated. 'I played for England, Scotland, Ireland and Wales.'

'Pay no attention,' Dickinson told the replacements, 'he's only showing off in front of the visitors.'

'In that order,' Church said firmly. 'England, Ireland, Scotland and Wales. I was *very* good.' He smiled craftily at Blunt and got himself another drink.

There was another pause. Peacock glanced warily around him. He noticed tiny signs of strain: finger-tapping, abrupt yawning, twitching of the eyes. Some pilots stood serenely, studying their cigarette smoke; but then Peacock saw their white knuckles.

The only exception was the CO. He leaned his backside against a table, arms folded. He didn't look pleased with himself, or with anyone else, either. He looked like one of those Irish rebels whose photographs one saw in the papers: swarthy, intense, indifferent to any opinion but their own. Smudged by cheap newsprint. Hanged.

Peacock wondered if all fighter squadrons were like this. People at home said they were a gay, defiant, rather reckless band of cavaliers of the sky. Peacock turned away and saw Finlayson picking his nose.

An airman came in: lunch was ready. They finished their drinks. 'This is a lot better than Pont St Martin,' Dickinson said. 'That mess tent was horribly draughty.'

'My billet has cockroaches,' Lambert complained. 'Big ones.'

'Clever wee beasts,' Finlayson said. 'They won't live where they can't get food and comfort. Consider yourself lucky.'

'I suppose *we* should consider ourselves *jolly* lucky,' Peacock said. 'I mean, to have a German plane shot down the first time we went up.'

Lambert shrugged.

'I never expected the first scrap to be so *easy*,' Callaghan said. 'I must say it gives a chap confidence, that sort of thing.'

Woolley stopped in the doorway and turned around. Everyone else stopped. 'You found it easy?' he asked Callaghan.

'Well, sir . . .' Callaghan was confused at finding himself the centre of attention. 'I mean . . . they didn't really stand much of a chance, did they, sir?'

'Isn't that as it should be?' Woolley hadn't moved, but the other pilots were shifting and looking away.

'Yes sir, I suppose . . . all I meant was, it's nice to start off with a gift from God, so to speak.'

Killion groaned and beat his fist against his forehead. Callaghan glanced unhappily from him to Woolley.

'Understand this,' Woolley said. 'While you are in this squadron, which I think will be a short time, you will never use the word "luck". Luck never killed anyone except the fool who believed in it.'

'Yes, sir,' Callaghan whispered. Woolley turned and went in. Callaghan squeezed his hands to control the trembling. Dickinson nudged him. 'In a sense you were right,' he said. 'That two-seater *was* a gift from God. But God around here is the old man, and believe me, he organized it.'

The conversation during lunch was a little more relaxed. Killion took pity on Callaghan and tried to discuss Freud, which only confused Callaghan the more. Eventually Richards told Killion to shut up and then found himself obliged to say something else in his place.

'I knew a Dermot Cavanagh in Dublin,' he said. 'I don't suppose . . .'

'We're not really Irish at all. Must have been once, but . . .

Funny thing, we had another sort of Anglo-Irishman at our flying school, only he passed out before I did. I heard he was posted here. Rather hoped to see him, actually.'

'Well, you know how it is. People come and go.'

'Yes. Still, I'd like to keep in touch. O'Shea, his name was.'

'I shouldn't bother if I were you.'

'But couldn't I get hold of his address, somehow? He and I—'

'Believe me, it's not worth it.'

Callaghan opened his mouth to beg to differ, saw Richards' expression, and shut it.

The adjutant came in. 'I do think it's rotten the way none of you chaps speaks French,' he said angrily. 'You get into all kinds of trouble, and they come to me and complain. Save me some lunch,' he told a steward.

'Are they causing a stink over what we did at St Denis the other night?' Lambert asked.

'No, no. But don't worry, that'll come before long.'

'We should have paid the bill, you know,' Dangerfield said. 'Dinner for ten, plus wine.'

'I'll send them a cheque,' Rogers said. 'Remind me to send them a cheque, Woody.'

'I think I'll get you to make out several cheques. In fact you might as well sign the lot and give them to me.'

'Thinking back on that occasion,' Kimberley said, 'isn't it odd that we haven't heard a squeak from the frogs about it?'

'Frogs croak,' Church said.

'It's not odd at all,' Woodruffe said. 'For a start, we got posted the very next day. That put them off the scent. For another thing, I told a friend of mine at Corps to shuffle his documents if the frogs started looking for us. He's put us down as posted to Belgium *en route* for Italy.'

'Masterly staff work,' Lambert said. 'What a blessing it is to have fundamentally dishonest officers.'

A black-shawled Frenchwoman appeared at the window and rapped on it. 'Oh my God. Her again,' Woodruffe said.

111

'Don't let her in or I'll never get any lunch. I can't understand a word she says.'

'I speak a little French,' Blunt offered.

'Go ahead,' Woodruffe said. 'Tell her there's nothing we can do.'

Blunt let her in. An old man shuffled after her and hooked a horticultural implement of a hand around her arm. The woman sniffed back her tears, and drew the shawl around her body, which was heavy and useful like a sack of potatoes. Only the eyes lived in her face.

She faced Blunt and spoke bitterly in rapid French. He tried to slow her down with gestures which she interpreted as signs of denial, and so she poured it on. He looked helplessly at the adjutant, who was eating; then at Woolley, who was cleaning his ears with a matchstick; and turned back. '*Pas bon, pas bon*,' he told her, smiling miserably. '*Je ne comprends pas.*' It sounded feeble.

She stared, and said something that might have been a question or a rejection.

'*Parlez plus lentement, s'il vous plaît, madame*,' he said. '*Très, très lentement.*'

'He is asking her how much her daughter charges,' Lambert said in a stage whisper.

She took Blunt's arm and spoke urgently. She pointed to the window. She spoke again, led him to the window and pointed. The old man went with her and stayed there, peering through the dirty panes, scrabbling absently for something to hold on to.

'*Un moment, s'il vous plaît*,' Blunt said. '*C'est très difficile.*'

'Now he is asking how much *she* costs,' Lambert said. Several pilots laughed. Blunt went towards the adjutant. 'I'm not at all sure, sir,' he said. 'It sounds as if something has died.'

'It can't be the old man,' Kimberley said. 'I just saw him move.'

Woolley said something to a steward. The man went out. Woolley continued his ear-cleaning.

'Send them to the police, for God's sake,' Dickinson said. 'What do they expect us to do?'

'It does seem odd,' Blunt said. He went back. '*Je ne comprends pas, madame. Expliquez-vous encore, s'il vous plaît.*'

She looked from Blunt to Dickinson, who was peeling an apple. She began to cry. Through her tears she repeated her previous words, only with more anguish and entreaty.

'She's cutting her prices,' Lambert said. 'I knew she would.'

'*Mais nous ne sommes pas la police,*' Blunt told her awkwardly. '*C'est dommage, mais . . .*' He paused. 'Damn and blast. What's French for "Why don't you?".' Nobody had any suggestions. '*Peut-être les gendarmes . . .*' he began.

Then the woman surprised them all. She pointed downwards with both hands, shook them violently, and made the sound of a machine gun.

'Good God,' said Rogers. He was quite startled.

Woodruffe stared at her trembling hands and face. He swallowed uncomfortably. 'Don't just stand there,' he said, 'find out what the hell she means, say something.' He put down his knife and fork.

'*Uh . . . madame . . .*' Blunt thought desperately. '*Je regrette . . .*' She snorted. '*. . . que . . . que tout ce que vous . . . er . . . disez n'est pas clair.*'

She glared. She stamped to the window and thrust the old man aside. '*Vos avions!*' she shouted. '*Vos mitraillettes!*' She stamped back and seized Blunt's arm, rapping on his wristwatch. '*Aujourd'hui!*' she screamed. '*Aujourd'hui vous avez tué ma petite!*' And then she really began weeping.

'Jesus Christ,' the adjutant said. 'I hope I didn't get that right.' He looked at the stiff, unhappy faces of the pilots. 'Come on,' he called out over her sobs. 'You were up there, you should know.'

The mess steward came in with Woolley's piano-accordion and gently laid it on the table.

'All I got was "aeroplanes" and "today",' Finlayson said. 'What the devil is the old bitch up to?'

113

'She says we shot her daughter,' Blunt said.

Finlayson held his breath, and then let it out in a rush. 'Bloody nonsense,' he snapped. 'How the hell could we? She must be mad.'

Woolley eased the broad straps around his shoulders and opened the bellows with a wheeze.

'As far as I can make out,' Blunt said, 'the girl was in the fields under our dog-fight, and somebody's bullets hit her.'

'That wasn't a dog-fight,' Kimberley said contemptuously.

'Shut up.' Woodruffe turned to Dickinson, while Woolley played a few experimental chords. 'Dicky, you were there. Could you – could we have done that?'

'I suppose so.' Dickinson made a helpless gesture. 'Anything's possible, isn't it? We were low enough. Anyway, high or low, the damn bullets have to end up somewhere, haven't they?'

'It's a wonder more people aren't killed,' Church said darkly.

Woolley edged his way into a shanty: *The Death of Tom Bowling.*

'I still don't see what we can do, anyway,' the adjutant said.

'*Ah . . . madame . . .*' Blunt hesitated, waiting for a pause, and finally tapped her on the arm. '*Je vous en prie . . . uh . . . Que voulez-vous?*'

This brought on such a bout of weeping and incoherence that the old man shuffled forward to lend his support. Blunt retired in despair. 'What can anyone do?' he asked. 'If she's dead, she's dead.'

Woolley swung into a second chorus, and gave it greater volume. There was now a touch of jauntiness about his phrasing.

'Wait a minute, wait a minute!' Richards cried. 'What exactly did she say? She said *ma petite*, didn't she? How do we know it was her little *girl*? It could have been her little anything.'

'Little cow,' Dickinson suggested. '*Vache* is feminine.'

'Ask her how old it was,' Woodruffe told Blunt.

'Ask what?' Blunt called across the vibrant sea-shanty.

'How old it was,' Woodruffe shouted. He looked impatiently at Woolley, but Woolley was putting his heart and soul into the music.

'Uh . . . *madame* . . .' Blunt said. '*Votre petite* . . . uh . . . *quel age?*'

She turned away and sank to her knees. With her arms crossed over her breast, she rocked to and fro, while long, shuddering sobs twisted her face. The old man looked accusingly at Blunt.

'I don't think it can be a cow,' Blunt called to the adjutant. Woolley released three loud chords, and started on a ponderous version of the Sailors' Hornpipe.

For a few moments the pilots sat there, appalled by the racket, upset by the tragedy, unwilling to leave. Woolley picked up the tempo. His fingering was dreadful and his chords were wild approximations, but he pressed on, bashing out his hornpipe in direct competition with the Frenchwoman's lament.

Rogers stood up and said: 'This is no good.'

Woodruffe shouted: 'What?'

Rogers walked out. Lambert got up, and with him Killion and Church. Soon the rest of the squadron was trailing cautiously and apologetically past the French couple, until only Woodruffe and Blunt were left. Woolley began the hornpipe again. Blunt looked confusedly at the adjutant, but Woodruffe had his head in his hands.

Blunt went to the door. Woolley followed, playing him out. He hooked the door shut with his foot, and walked away, spilling wrong notes behind him like a gardener sowing weeds.

Fifteen minutes later Woolley had the squadron in the air. They repeated the morning's patrol, landed, refuelled and took off again. No German aircraft were seen.

Once, Woolley took his flight a little farther over the Front than usual, just to provoke the gunners. For the new pilots it was a disturbing experience. Dirty blots of smoke appeared, leaking quickly into the sky like bad ink on cheap paper. Then came the wicked *crack-boom!* and the tossing, jarring turbulence. Next the murdering puffs of explosive charge and ragged steel fragments dissolved into weak smoke and the plane was butting through the piece of sky which, seconds before, had been laced with violence; and meanwhile, other shell bursts erupted just as unpredictably ahead, and behind, and below.

Woolley browsed this area, changing course and height every fifteen or twenty seconds to confuse the gunners. Finally he had exhausted the new pilots' capacity for fear. They loathed the German guns and they looked with longing and detestation at Woolley, but in each of them fear had given way to a curiously objective fatalism. Some shells were distant. Some were close. The next might kill you. So what?

They survived and flew home, and Peacock found himself savouring the memory. Even mortal danger was not entirely unpleasant.

Kimberley's engine failed and he crash-landed in a field, without harm; the others touched down safely. The adjutant watched them stroll back to their billets, unbuttoning their flying coats, stamping and kicking to work the stiffness away. They shouted obscene greetings to him, treating him like a commissionaire, or a barman. Nobody asked about the French couple.

Woolley trudged towards the adjutant. He recognized the pastel forms in his hands: indents and returns and vouchers and reports, all the papers that had to be signed to authorize the war to continue. Then he saw bolder colours: huge red crosses against a white panel on a muddy truck. He started to run, turning away from the adjutant. He was carrying his handbell by its clapper, and he shifted his grip to the handle and began clanging. Startled pilots stood aside. Church was too slow and Woolley's shoulder barged him out of the way. The bell clashed all the way to Woolley's billet until he kicked open the door. Then it was still. Margery was sitting on the bed holding a bottle of Guinness that foamed all down her hand and wrist.

'I heard you coming,' she said. 'I never could open these damn things.'

'How did you know this was my hut? Did they tell you?'

'Certainly not. To have asked would have been indiscreet. I went around and smelled them. This one smelled like yours.'

Woolley took the bottle and licked the Guinness off her wrist.

'I don't smell so bad,' he said.

'All men smell lovely,' Margery said. 'But you smell magnificent.'

Peacock, Callaghan and Blunt walked to the village after dinner. It was night; a brisk breeze drove chubby clouds to the east, effacing and revealing the stars as if polishing them for display. When the wind dropped an occasional rumble in the distance reminded them of their first taste of war's excitements. The sharp night air made them step out. Stepping out made them feel bold and confident and strong.

Peacock said: 'I've been thinking about our commanding officer. You know, he can't be more than twenty-three at the most.'

'He's twenty-three,' Callaghan said. 'Rogers told me.'

'How old is Rogers?'

'Twenty-one and a good bit.'

'The old man looks twice his age.'

'He's got that sort of face,' Blunt said. 'You know, degenerate.'

'He's not my idea of a leader, I must say,' Peacock said. 'Not the sort of chap you'd want to be captain of a team.'

'That uniform!' Callaghan said. 'He'd get shot if he turned up like that in England.'

'You really trod on his pet corn before lunch, didn't you?' Blunt said.

'All I said was we were lucky to get a two-seater on a plate

117

on our first flight,' Callaghan protested. 'No cause for him to be so stuffy, no cause at all.'

They walked in silence for a while, passing the first, blacked-out cottages.

'Actually, Dickinson told me that it almost certainly *wasn't* a matter of luck,' Peacock said. 'He seems pretty sure that the old man saw them coming.'

'Yes, but how did he know they would stay on that course?' Blunt asked. '*That* must have been luck.'

'Dickinson thinks not,' Peacock said. 'He said it was ten to one the Huns would fly over our field, since the two-seater was on reconnaissance and they'd want to take a picture or something.'

'Oh,' said Callaghan. 'Of course.'

'You seem to have been pretty thick with Dickinson,' Blunt said. 'Did he give you any other advice?' Blunt still felt hurt about the old Frenchwoman.

'As a matter of fact, he did. He said if you fire long bursts, you risk jamming your gun, so you should get in close and fire short bursts. Apparently the old man has been hammering this into them for weeks.'

'Apparently the old man is a bit of a Prussian,' Blunt said.

'One tries to be open-minded,' Callaghan said, 'but that sort of approach does put one off, rather. Frankly, I'd respond more if a chap came up to me and said, "Look here, we've been doing this for rather a long time now and we find that this way seems to bring the best results."'

'Exactly,' Blunt said.

'Oh, well.' Peacock pointed to an inn. 'I suppose we should be glad the fire-eater is on our side, and not the Germans'.'

'From all I've heard,' Callaghan said, 'some of the German pilots are jolly decent chaps.'

'Of course they are. It's absolute nonsense to say that chivalrous men can't fight a chivalrous war,' Blunt said. 'That's why I put in for the RFC. We're literally the only sportsmen left.'

*   *   *

Killion saw the three men come in, and turned his back on them. He was sitting at a corner table with an English girl called Rose Franklin. She was a nurse at a hospital on the other side of the village, and Killion had met her the previous evening by simply walking into the hospital and asking the first girl he saw if she would come out with him. Because Killion was young and trembling with desperation, Rose Franklin had agreed. She had laughed very loudly, but she had agreed. Rose was a strikingly handsome girl, big-breasted, high-coloured, dancing-eyed. It was Killion's bad luck that she was boisterous, unromantic, insensitive and recently married. Nevertheless, her presence was potent, and he persevered.

'F-funny,' he said, his sexual hunger overcoming his stutter, 'I knew as soon as I saw you.'

'Did you, now,' Rose said brightly. 'And what did you know, may I ask?'

Killion frowned with terrible sincerity. 'Well, you know,' he said, clenching his fists on the table. 'Y-you and me.'

'I certainly *don't* know. Are they friends of yours, over there? They seemed to recognize you.'

'I bet you're j-jolly good at s-s-swimming. Anyone can t-tell just by looking. Are you k-keen on swimming?'

She laughed, more for the exercise than anything else. 'Well, if you go to the seaside you have to bathe, don't you?'

'Not half!' Killion spread his hands on the table, in the hope that she would rest an arm within stroking range. 'D'you like that? I think bathing is jolly good f-fun. Especially when you don't have to w-wear anything.'

She laughed again, but reproachfully. 'I really couldn't say about *that*.'

'They have s-swimming pools where you can swim in the b-b-b-buff. It f-feels awfully g-good. You ought to t-try it.'

Rose re-arranged her gloves and purse. 'How stuffy it gets in here!' she said. 'It quite affects my head.'

'Have some m-more wine,' Killion urged. He tried to add to her full glass.

'Golly! The very idea. If anyone from the hospital sees me I'll never hear the last of it.' She stared unblinkingly over his shoulder.

'No, honestly, I m-mean it,' Killion tried to smile, but felt foolish, so he went back to looking sincere. 'You really are the m-most m-marvellous girl.'

'There's something written on the wall over there.' She tilted her head and frowned. 'Do you read French?'

'No,' said Killion. 'Not a bloody word.' That made her jump.

'Yes, it's definitely him,' Callaghan said.

'If you ask me, it's a grave mistake for a chap in our position to get too involved with women,' Blunt said. He sipped his wine. 'Not too dry for you, is it? I can always make them change it . . .' Blunt had ordered the wine. The others told him it was just right.

'Actually, I prefer my wine on the dry side,' Peacock said. 'I've never been one for a sweet wine. Never.'

'I think you'll like this one,' Blunt said. He picked up the bottle and studied the label. 'You've got to be awfully careful with some of them.'

'Can it be his wife?' Callaghan asked. 'She's wearing a wedding ring.'

'No, no. He's not married,' Blunt said. 'None of them is married, and a good thing too. Far too many young marriages these days.'

'Take my elder brother,' said Peacock. 'He got married during his last leave. Barely twenty-one at the time.'

'Utterly ridiculous,' Blunt said.

'If I don't see another girl until I'm twenty, that'll be all right by me,' Callaghan said. 'Female company is vastly overrated.'

'Passed nem con.,' Blunt said.

'Freud,' Killion said. 'S-Sigmund Freud. You ought to read about him, honestly.'

'Oh, foreigners!' Rose laughed, exercising her healthy chest. Killion watched, fascinated. They *moved*. What ecstasy it would be to see them really move . . .

'F-Freud says everything goes back to s-s-s-s—'

'Golly! Is that the time?'

'—ex. He s-says it's the most important th-thing between p-people.' Killion sat with his legs tensed and looked earnestly, beseechingly at her.

'I say! What long words we use, for such a little boy. If you were in my ward, the first thing you'd get would be a jolly good haircut. When did you last go to the barber's, may I ask?'

'Oh, Rose . . .' Killion groaned. 'Can't you be n-nice to me? Can't we l-l-like each other, just a b-bit?' He looked down to hide his misery. 'Damn it Rose, I might be killed tomorrow.'

'Pooh! What about my Edward? *He's* fighting in the *trenches*.' She made it sound as if her husband were in the employ of a superior company. 'He could be killed at any time. He might be dying *now*.'

'Then take m-me,' Killion urged. 'Do, Rose, do.'

Rose gathered her gloves and purse. 'You can take *me* home,' she said. 'The very idea!'

'Can't say I'm too awfully keen on this idea of going for the enemy *pilot*,' Blunt said. 'I mean, *deliberately* going for him.'

'Is that what they teach here?' Callaghan said.

'Oh yes, it's the old man's creed. They say he expects people to shoot the other chap *in the back*, if they possibly can.'

'Sticks in the craw, a bit, that,' Peacock said.

'One can't help sort of including the other chap in the general area of fire,' Blunt said, 'but I don't see the need to go out of one's way to commit murder. Do you?'

'No, no.'

'Of course not.'

'The way I look at it,' Blunt said, 'the chap can't stay up if his plane won't fly. And it seems to me that everyone overlooks a very vulnerable spot. Next time we meet a Hun, I know what I shall have a pot at.'

'What's that?' Callaghan asked.

'The propeller. One bullet in the right place, and down he goes.'

'Yes,' said Peacock. 'Of course. Odd that nobody's thought of it before.'

Rose Franklin stopped Killion at the gates of the hospital. They hadn't spoken since they left the inn. 'Thank you for a lovely evening,' she said.

'Oh well,' Killion mumbled. 'You know.'

'I've been thinking about what you said. You must get terribly lonely. And I've got Edward, you see.'

'Oh well.' Killion twisted about and beat his gloved hands together, anxious to get away.

'There's a girl who works in the hospital who I think might ... I mean I think you would ... Well, I can't promise anything, but I know she's awfully keen on ... men.'

Killion stopped hopping about and gazed at her. Sex blazed in the night like a beacon guiding a traveller to a city of delight.

'Well, d'you want me to or not?' she asked impatiently.

'Oh, y-yes, yes!' Killion cried. 'Yes, p-please!'

'Come around tomorrow night. I can't make any promises, mind.'

Killion ran all the way back to camp. At last!

'Suppose we had a child,' Margery said. 'What should we call it?'

Woolley stopped shaving and looked at her in the mirror. She was sitting on his bed with a blanket around her shoulders, trying on his flying-helmet. After a while she noticed his reflected look and looked back, chewing on the leather chinstrap. The drying lather got up his nose, and he sneezed. More dry lather flew off and drifted away. 'I'm sick of that question,' he said. He brushed on fresh lather.

122

'I never asked it before. Did I?'

'No.'

'Well, we might. In fact if we go on like this we're almost bound to. I mean, I don't especially *want* to, but . . .'

'Oh, bollocks. Of course you want to. All women want to. Nobody yet in the whole history of mankind has had the strength to resist doing what lies in their power to do, just to prove that they can. Given a choice between doing something and not doing something people always do something, even if it's the wrong thing.'

'Good gracious. Philosophy,' she said, surprised. 'I never heard any of that before.'

'Well.' He twisted his face to shave the side of his mouth. 'It's true. It explains this war, doesn't it?'

'Oh God, not that again. I came here to get away from that.' She hunched up. 'I am so sick of dead men . . . They all seem to get hit in the head nowadays. Ours do, anyway. It's such a waste. We use up miles of bandages and gauze and lint and dressings, and then they die anyway . . . Can't they tell them to keep their stupid heads down? I feel like . . .'

Woolley finished shaving and towelled off the soap. 'Goodness gracious,' he said. 'Philosophy.' He sat down and shared her blanket.

'Your feet are cold.' She dragged off another blanket and pushed it around his legs. 'Anyway, I don't see why God had to put men's heads on top of their stupid bodies if it means they just get blown open with shells, that's all.'

'God has a very curious sense of humour. Hence fornication.'

She thought about it. 'Why hence?'

He drew her to him. 'All right then, don't count fornication,' he said. He put his lips to her hair and blew softly.

'But I want to count it. Tell me.'

'No. You'll just be insulted.'

'I promise.'

'Well, don't blame me.'

'Tell me, tell me!'

Woolley considered. 'All right. It's obvious, once you look at it objectively and dispassionately. The whole business is grotesque. It's like two bicycles fighting.'

'Fighting what?'

'Fighting each other, fathead.'

'I don't see that at all.'

Woolley sighed gloomily. 'I said you'd go all huffy.'

'I'm not huffy. I just don't agree. For a start, bicycles only go when they're upright.'

'So do human beings.'

'That has nothing to do with it.' She wriggled away from him and stared him in the face. 'Does it? Go on, admit it has absolutely nothing to do with it.'

'Look, why don't you let me demonstrate—'

'No. Not until you admit you were wrong.'

Woolley sniffed and looked around for something to blow his nose on. 'All right. I admit I was wrong.'

'You're just saying that to shut me up. You can be so rotten damn patronizing.'

'Have you got a handkerchief?'

'No. And if I had I wouldn't lend it to anyone as rotten damn patronizing, stupid and heartless as you.'

Woolley was startled. 'My dear Margery,' he said. 'What—' He stood and blinked at her with his finger under his nose to stop the drips. 'I apologize. I really do.'

'How can you? You don't know what for.' Her voice was thick with suppressed tears. Woolley said nothing. 'If you knew how ridiculous you look, standing there with nothing on and your finger up your nose.' She threw a handkerchief against his chest, and he caught it.

'I think we'd better have a drink,' Woolley said. He fished out a bottle of whisky from a kit-bag, and cleaned two glasses on his towel.

'Anyway, suppose we do have a child,' Margery said damply.

'Out of the question.' Woolley half-filled both glasses. 'My family has been sterile for generations.'

124

'Oh, shut up. You don't care because you won't be the one to have it. I shall be left here looking ten times as fat as I do already and the poor little bastard won't even have a real name.'

'Here's to generations yet unborn.' Woolley clinked her glass. 'Long may they stay that way.'

Margery drank and took off the flying-helmet and lay face-down on the bed. Woolley sat beside her and wrote in whisky with his finger all along her back, starting from the neck.

'What's that?' she asked. She sounded empty, drained by her anger at the end of a day of travelling and love-making.

'I'm christening the bloody baby,' he said. 'Lie still.' He reached her bottom and let a couple of drops fall down the cleft. 'There! Just drowned a flea. Little bugger made a run for it, but I swamped him.'

'Liar . . . What did you christen it?'

Woolley checked off the names all the way down her spine. 'Hardy; Lyons, Weston; Barber, Harrop, Leach; Wallace, Halse, Hampton, Stephenson, Bache.'

She tried to make sense of it, while he parted her hair neatly on either side of her neck. 'Who are they?'

'Aston Villa's team in 1913, when they won the Cup.'

'Oh.' She took a sudden, deep breath, and wriggled deeper into the bed. 'I thought it might be the people in your squadron.'

'Oh, God . . . them. The Children's Crusade. I got three new ones yesterday. Dribbling infants. Not a day over twelve, any of them.'

'It's not their fault they're young. You were young once.' She turned on her side and pulled the blanket around her neck. 'I bet they're all nice boys. Nicer than you, anyhow.' She was falling asleep. 'Nicer than me, probably . . .'

Woolley watched her eyes close and the lids stop flickering. He finished his drink and started on hers. She looked very tired: there were puffy smudges around her eyes, and brack-eting her mouth were tiny lines like the first cracks in plaster. He wondered if he could do her dreadful job; or rather, how long he could stand it if he ever tried it. He turned down the lamp and wondered how he was going to get in without wakening her; when suddenly she started up, crying out with despair, fighting to be free of the blankets. Then she saw him. 'Oh my God!' she said. 'Oh my God. Nightmares. Already.'

'You're all right,' Woolley said. 'Move over, now. I'll be with you now.'

Someone knocked on the door. 'Shit,' Woolley said, one foot in the bed. 'Who the hell is that?' he called.

'It's me, sir,' came the adjutant's voice. 'I saw your light was on and I thought you ought to know. Dispatch rider from Corps, sir.'

'Whatever it is, don't read it. Give him a mug of cocoa and a big kiss and send him on a month's leave. Now bugger off.'

'Too late, sir, I'm afraid. Squadron's ordered to transfer to the field at Achiet with all speed at first light.'

Woolley took his foot out of bed. 'Achiet?'

'Yes, sir. He needs your signature.'

'Oh.' Woolley opened the door and took the dispatch and Woodruffe's fountain pen. 'Miss Brooke, Captain Woodruffe.'

The adjutant saluted. Margery smiled weakly.

'We have met, actually,' Woodruffe said. 'You introduced us before, sir.'

'Balls. I've never seen this woman before in my life. Your pen leaks.' He gave the dispatch back and wiped his fingers on his thighs. 'Make reveille an hour earlier. Now piss off.'

'Goodnight, miss,' Woodruffe said. He saluted.

Woolley closed the door. 'Achiet,' he said. 'Fancy. I lost half a crown there, two years ago. And my virginity.'

'In that order?' Margery asked sleepily.

'Be fair. It *was* her living.' He climbed in and hugged her.

'You owe me about five hundred pounds,' she whispered.

The next day was bright and cold, with a stiff breeze blowing straight down the field. Woolley briefed the pilots on course and height, and they dispersed. The planes were already

126

warming up; it was a short flight, only thirty miles; with luck they would be on patrol again that afternoon. It depended on supplies of fuel and ammunition at the other end.

Woolley went off to give final orders to the chief mechanics, and to Woodruffe, who was driving Rogers' limousine over. As they talked, planes began to taxi out and rev up. One by one they jounced over the ruts, and formed up in pairs. The long, square noses aimed up-wind, and bored forward until the wings developed lift and carried them, rocking and bucking, high over the hedge.

Rogers and Lambert took off together; then Killion and Church, then Richards and Gabriel. Callaghan and Peacock went next, with Blunt and Dangerfield taxi-ing out behind them. The first two left the ground at almost the same instant and climbed easily with the help of the headwind. At a hundred feet Peacock's engine failed. It just stopped dead. He panicked. The breeze that had been lifting him, now began dragging him back, making everything heavy and sluggish. The nose dropped alarmingly. There were tiny fields ahead, but Peacock could see nothing but hedges and trees. If he fell down there he'd crash, like the two-seater. As his dive steepened he felt the speed pick up again; there was still life in the controls somewhere. Peacock shoved everything into a turn, straining to get a view of the airfield he had just left. The SE5a was too heavy. There was too much weight hanging from the wings to let it glide through an awkward bank like that, all the time losing the upthrust from the breeze; losing it twice, because now it followed the turning plane.

Halfway through the bank Peacock lost it altogether. His plane fell sideways, helplessly, like a book toppling from a shelf. Blunt, coming up behind him and hauling back on the control column to get his plane over the hedge, saw Peacock sliding out of the sky and tried to turn inside him. But his plane too was heavy, and it responded reluctantly. Blunt changed course just enough to collide with Peacock head-on. The impact ruptured both fuel tanks. For a moment the embracing machines hung in the air, waiting, it seemed, for some act of coronation. Then the flames bloomed, and the wreckage fell, magnificently orange and red. It made the other planes droning around the dull sky look puny.

Force 8: Fresh Gale

Breaks twigs off trees; generally impedes progress

In mid-March the sky over France was all exuberance. Ragged flotillas of cloud sailed before a brisk west wind. Sunlight sought out the gaps and flickered over the new-green fields far below. The sky was a place of awakening, of vigour, as full of life as the million seeds in the earth. Woolley hacked a long, scarlet gash in it with a burst of machine-gun fire and pulled up hard into a tight, half-rolling turn so that he could look back and down.

Still the bastard would not burn.

It was a Fokker Triplane. It flew steadily homewards, nose fractionally down but wings beautifully level, trailing streamers of torn fabric like favours. In the fuselage, holes as big as fanlights showed bright sky on the other side. The upper wing was as bare of fabric as a garden gate. No pilot could be seen.

Woolley and Dickinson and Callaghan had ambushed a patrol of six Triplanes. Dickinson had burned one and gone down with it to confirm the kill. Callaghan had damaged another and been damaged himself. After less than thirty seconds of action everyone had vanished except Woolley and his own sedate victim, whose pilot was already dead. Woolley dived from alternate sides and blasted the aircraft with the close attention of a man beating a carpet. In five attacks he emptied every bullet in the drum, battering away at the vitals: the engine, cockpit, fuel tank. The Triplane absorbed them all and droned on.

He levelled out on a parallel course. He stood up, holding the controls between his knees, and dragged the Lewis gun down its sliding mounting. Cold air like rushing water battered at his face, beating in his cheeks and making it hard to breathe. The hot stink of the engine tickled his nostrils. He unclipped the empty drum and slammed on a full one, thrust the gun forward and sat down with a thud that shook the cockpit.

The Triplane flew its useless pilot home, unhurriedly, with dignity. Woolley side-slipped and fell behind it, then climbed and injected a long burst into its belly, searching forwards until he saw the bullets slashing up between the wingroots. The Triplane shuddered but would not break and would not burn. He curled away so close that his wash disturbed it.

Woolley swore, cursing the enemy into flames. This was his fourth patrol of the day and only his first kill of the week. The Germans would not fight without a clear advantage. Always they had the wind behind them. Pursuit meant slogging home. Woolley approved and resented. Even now, when he had succeeded in attacking, this Triplane refused to be destroyed.

He double-checked the sky, climbed, dived, and blazed away again. Nothing. It was like firing into a sand-pile.

He flew alongside and swore again: at God, at the rubber bullets, at the serene stability of the enemy. Then he saw that its nose had sunk a couple of degrees, and it was gradually pulling away. A lick of colour pulsed out of the engine, dissolved, came again and grew strong. Orange flame drew out and broadened. The nose dipped further, and the flame suddenly raced along the wings and around the cockpit. In an instant the whole aircraft was outlined in fire like a set-piece at a fireworks display. The explosion detached the separate wings as if they had been plucked feathers. Woolley felt the blast wash over his SE, pushing it aside, and he turned with the motion and set course for home, dissatisfied at the inefficiency of it all.

Dickinson landed at Achiet and went to the adjutant's office to report his kill and his availability. He found Woodruffe with a tall, one-armed man in a raincoat and a bowler hat. Like many tall men, he had a perpetually upright, weary look, as if he usually slept leaning in a corner. He was examining the dust on top of a cupboard.

'Ah, Dicky,' Woodruffe said. 'Did you have a good flight? This is Inspector Philippe of the French civil police. He's looking for Goshawk Squadron. Any idea where they might have gone?'

'The last I saw they were all flying away.'

'Yes. That would be three days ago, now.'

'My goodness. Is it as long as that?'

Woodruffe turned to the inspector. 'I'm almost sure they said Brittany, although some of them might have gone to Bordeaux. You could try both.'

'Yes,' the inspector said.

'We didn't see much of them,' Woodruffe went on. 'They flew out as we flew in. No time to chat.'

'No,' the inspector said.

'Are you sure they were here?' Dickinson said.

'Quite sure.' The inspector levelled his surviving index finger at the Squadron blackboard, which listed the patrols. Across the top it read 'Goshawk Squadron'.

Woodruffe clapped his hand to his brow. 'Good Lord! You must think us very ill-organized, inspector.' He rubbed it out and chalked in '73 Squadron'. 'There!'

The inspector looked at it, looked at Woodruffe, and said nothing.

'Any message, in case they drop in?' Dickinson asked.

Philippe picked up his dispatch-case. 'Please tell them,' he said, 'a warrant has been issued against them for manslaughter.' He nodded at Woodruffe and went out.

They watched him get into his car. 'Manslaughter?' asked Dickinson.

'The restaurant owner. Chap we stuck up on the chair. He fell off when the police charged in. Hit his head and died, apparently.'

'Oh. Seen Callaghan?'

'He staggered in ten minutes ago with a broken tail. I think he went to have some tea.'

'*Tea?*'

'That's what he said. Oh, I forgot. We're out of booze.'

'But my dear fellow, how *awful*.' Dickinson sat down and looked at the adjutant, appalled. 'There *has* to be booze, there simply must be. The whole thing is quite impossible without booze. It . . . it can't be done.'

Woodruffe blinked, feeling uncomfortable. Woolley came in, and the adjutant quickly got up.

'Woody says there's no booze, sir,' Dickinson said.

'Did you confirm your Hun?'

'Oh, yes. He went off with a lovely bang.'

'Why is there no drink for the squadron?' Woolley asked the adjutant.

Woodruffe shuffled a little stack of telephone messages. 'It seems that Colonel Hawthorn refuses to approve the indent,' he said.

'Who's he?'

'Apparently our new Corps Liaison Officer for Admin. and Supplies. He's been appointed to, as it were, look after this section. Been given a bomber squadron and one or two fighter squadrons and us. He . . . straightens things out.'

'Get him on the phone.'

'Actually, sir, you can meet him now, if you want to. He went over to inspect the ground staff. Mechanics and armourers and so on.'

'What for? Pox?'

'Something a great deal worse, I'm afraid. Clean webbing.'

Woolley looked sick. 'D'you mean that our mechanics have stopped work while some fat arse-hole from bloody Corps inspects their scrofulous webbing?' he shouted.

The adjutant looked out of a window. 'Brasses, too,' he

said. 'Colonel Hawthorn told me he puts a lot of stock in men's brasses.'

Woolley lurched towards the door. Dickinson saw his face, heavy-eyed and working like a drunk's. 'Also the silk scarves,' Woodruffe added quickly. 'He cancelled the indent for silk scarves.' The door slammed, and his telephone messages fluttered to the floor.

Gabriel, Lambert and Church met the F2B at the rendezvous point and headed for the Front. The two-seater looked old and battered and slow. They could see the patchwork of new fabric over old, where the repairs hadn't been painted yet. There were moth-holes in the wing-tips, and the fuselage seemed warped. It flew very slowly.

They crossed the Line at 3,500 feet. As soon as the anti-aircraft fire began to thin out the F2B dived to begin photographing below cloud level. The three fighters stayed above and searched for defenders.

For twenty minutes nothing happened. Lambert distrusted it. Usually, on reconnaissance escort, the Germans drove the camera plane home within ten minutes, and often they got it before it recrossed the Line. This was Lambert's fourth patrol of the day. He kept thinking how nice it would be to lie in a hot bath and soak out the cold and the dirt. The F2B creaked through a 180-degree turn and began photographing another strip. Naked Balinese dancing girls held tankards of ale to his lips. Flak burst, black and bad-tempered, far below. More hot water . . . Church waggled his wing-tips: time to turn again. What luxury it would be to get out and stretch.

For five more minutes they ploughed the sky. Lambert forced his treacherous mind to keep alert, and made his tired eyes keep searching the wastes. Again the camera plane turned, and they swung to follow it; and between them and the Line three trim shapes plunged in and out of cloud in a dive pointed at the F2B. Albatros D IIIs: little blue-grey, lethal toys.

Gabriel was looking the wrong way at the crucial second.

By the time he had moved his head, Lambert and Church had gone, falling away in a howling power-dive. He raced after them. The camera plane was grinding up in a labouring climb, turning to present the smallest target. The German planes reached it seconds before the SEs. Gabriel saw bullets sparkle and flash all around the F2B; and then a longer streak from the British observer's rear-firing gun.

Lambert and Church bowled past the two-seater and eased into a long right-hand turn to follow the German planes, Lambert firing short bursts to attract their attention. Gabriel had cut inside the turn and was racing to meet them on their other flank. In the end all six planes came together more or less head-on.

Lambert and Gabriel managed to grab an enemy, but Church had to swerve to avoid Gabriel and he lost sight of the third German. By the time he had got clear of the dog-fight the Albatros was a couple of hundred yards away, closing on the two-seater as it chugged westwards against the implacable wind.

Church speculated with a long-range squirt, clicking his tongue in self-reproach as he did. The Albatros ignored him. He fired again, and this time it twisted violently. He had hit it, or the pilot was jumpy, for the Albatros banked steeply to the left, flattened out, looked at Church, and dived for home. Church went after him.

Lambert had his German in a tight circle and was chasing his tail; not far away. Gabriel had trapped the other plane in the same way. Alternatively, the Germans had trapped Lambert and Gabriel. What mattered was that the two-seater was getting away. Meanwhile each pilot strained to force an advantage. It was like driving the machines around an invisible Wall of Death. Lambert found that he could look across the circle and see right inside the German pilot's cockpit. The man had a black moustache. Villainous.

Gabriel's man wanted blood and he blazed away at Gabriel's perpetually vanishing tail. Gabriel encouraged this with tiny bursts. After two noisy minutes the German fell silent.

Gabriel waited for him to break away and in that instant got in a good burst, peppering the cockpit. The Albatros dived, and Gabriel turned away to check the state of Lambert's health. He was drifting into a cloud, still chasing the other plane's tail. A few seconds later they emerged, a hundred yards apart. The German saw Gabriel waiting, and dived for home.

Church had followed his Albatros right down to ground level. He flattened out and chased the German up a wooded valley. The other pilot was either new or nervous; probably both; he zig-zagged desperately to avoid Church's sniping. The valley narrowed and hampered escape, and now Church began to score. Bits of the Albatros were blowing past him. He was crying with delight, as he often did in anticipation, when his engine started to cough, and he sailed slap into a rocky cascade. Burning petrol floated down the stream like a Wagnerian funeral, terrifying the trout.

Woolley turned a corner and saw Colonel Hawthorn instructing Corporal Hemsley in the about-turn. Hemsley got it wrong. Hawthorn stopped him, and walked to where he could be seen by the rest of the squad of mechanics and fitters and armourers. He transferred his swagger-stick to his left arm, thrust his hands alongside the piping on his breeches, and aimed his jaw at the horizon.

'Skuh-wod, ay bout,' he sang, '*tun*!' He rotated on his right heel and left toe and brought the left boot alongside the right with a delicate crash which trembled his pink jowls. He paused to let the demonstration sink in. Woolley reached up and pulled the switch on the air-raid warning.

Like a tortured donkey, the klaxon brayed its amplified signal. The noise ruptured the afternoon, shattered the parade, sent men pounding across the tarmac, colliding, cursing, racing for the trenches on the edge of the airfield. Nobody hesitated. A low-flying German plane could hop over a hangar and massacre a squad with one sudden burst. It had happened.

Hawthorn blinked and flinched as men sprinted past him. He held his swagger-stick in his left hand and massaged it with his right. As the parade vanished, his confidence went with it, leaving a flatfooted, overweight colonel with poor eyesight and a build that suggested two sets of underwear.

The last man dashed around a corner. Hawthorn turned and saw Woolley. For a moment they stared at each other, while the klaxon remorselessly threw out a yard and a half of raucousness every two seconds. Hawthorn signalled to him. Woolley stood where he was.

Hawthorn's dispatch-case lay where it had been knocked over. He picked it up and walked across. 'Colonel Hawthorn,' he announced. 'From Corps.' He looked pointedly at the solitary and tarnished crown on Woolley's shoulder. Woolley did not move. 'I'm Corps Liaison Officer for Admin. and Supplies. I take it you're Major Woolley, the CO here.'

Woolley took out an old, soiled handkerchief and blew his nose. He looked into Hawthorn's restless, enthusiastic eyes and found no intelligence.

'Air-raid warning?' Hawthorn inquired. Woolley turned it off. Echoes from the last blast bounced off hangar walls and escaped into the vastness of the airfield.

'You blocked this squadron's booze order,' Woolley said.

Hawthorn looked away. 'I'd advise you to give your chaps half an hour's rifle drill every day. I wouldn't care to be in your shoes if the general took it into his head to inspect you now. *Very* rusty.'

'I want that booze delivered today,' Woolley said.

'No doubt you do, Major.' Hawthorn chuckled grimly. He could afford to. 'You're going the wrong way about it, though. Don't you usually salute a superior officer?'

'Yes.'

Hawthorn flushed. 'You'll get your beverage allocation when I'm satisfied with it, and not a damn day before. I know all about irregular units like you Flying Corps wallahs. There's been a sight too much laxity permitted with stores and equipment. If you ask me, some of you odds-and-sods have been playing the old soldier. Well, Corps happens to think so too.' He held up his dispatch-case and tapped it with his swagger-stick. 'From now on, all your indents and pro-formas and requisitions go through *here*.'

Woolley took out his revolver and blew a hole through Hawthorn's dispatch-case.

The man staggered. For a moment the flesh hung slackly on his face as he gaped at the damage, and then he sucked up his lips and took a deep breath. 'My God, Woolley, you'll pay for that!' he said in an astonished, passionate whisper. 'You'll pay a thousand times over. Put yourself under close arrest, Major. At once.'

'Bollocks. I want that booze.'

'Somehow I don't think you're going to need it!'

Woolley raised the revolver and pressed the muzzle against the glittering badge on Hawthorn's peaked cap. 'My men need it,' he said. Hawthorn's brow furrowed with the effort of evading the weapon. His hands squeezed tightly on his case and stick. 'These pilots can't fly without it.' Woolley pulled the trigger, and Hawthorn's cap spun to earth ten feet behind him.

The explosion made the man's mouth gape and his eyes water. 'I warn you, Major,' he croaked, and had to clear his throat. 'I warn you, Major, you may think you are acting in the interests of your men, but all you are doing is ruining your own career.'

'If you don't get that booze here soon,' Woolley said, 'I'll kill you.'

A couple of airmen had come out of the trenches to see what the shooting was about. They watched from a distance.

'You're a little mad, Woolley,' Hawthorn said. He breathed deeply, playing for time. 'But not completely insane. Not completely. Not so foolish as to put your head in a noose. Even in wartime, murder is still murder.'

'I'll kill you now,' Woolley said flatly, 'and stick your fat body in my plane, and in ten minutes I'll throw you out behind the German lines, unless you get me my booze and my scarves.'

'Cut your losses, Woolley.' Hawthorn indicated the airmen. 'Too many witnesses now.'

Woolley reached down and shot the spur off Hawthorn's left boot. The impact knocked his feet from under him. He got up very slowly. The airmen did not move.

'This is the most arrant, selfish, unpatriotic swindle I ever heard of,' he said thickly. 'Don't talk to me about your bloody pilots. They don't need a bottle of Scotch a day and new silk scarves every week.'

'I don't know why I bother to tell you,' Woolley said. 'They need booze because the stink from the engine gives them the runs. They also need booze to stop them from thinking about what they do all day. And you, you po-faced runt, you've no idea what they do.'

'On the contrary.' Hawthorn had trouble with that word. 'Artillery observation. Take photographs. Spot for us.'

'Shit. They go up and try to fry the enemy alive, two miles high. You never even set fire to a man on the ground, so you don't know what it's like to burn one.'

Hawthorn lifted his dispatch-case and looked at the hole, and said nothing.

'The silk scarves go around the neck.' Woolley rested the hot barrel against Hawthorn's neck. 'The neck must turn. The enemy is trying to creep up behind and fry you. The head rotates. The silk lubricates. The machine goes on working. Remove the lubricant and it seizes up. Overheats. Catches fire.'

'All right,' Hawthorn muttered. 'But you can't tell me your hardworking pilots wear out a silk scarf every other week, so you don't need new ones all the time.'

'The scarves wear out when the pilots do,' Woolley said. 'Unless you want us to use non-inflammable silk?'

Hawthorn took out a handkerchief and mopped his face. Woolley touched it with the muzzle of his gun. 'Silk,' he said.

On the way to the adjutant's office, Hawthorn said bitterly: 'You'll never get away with this. How am I going to explain the holes in my hat and case? And a broken spur . . .'

'Tell them you got shot up by enemy aircraft,' Woolley said. 'You'll probably get a medal.' He pushed open the door. 'Woody, this officer will telephone Corps HQ and have everything delivered today.'

'How splendid,' the adjutant said. 'May I sound the "All Clear" now, sir?'

'Yes.' Woolley went away.

'I wonder if you could ask them to send us some decent toilet paper?' the adjutant asked. 'I can't believe the general staff use the same quality they send us here. Could you?'

Hawthorn nodded dumbly.

After forty minutes at his ceiling of fifteen thousand feet, Killion felt drowsy and slow, like his aeroplane. The air up there was too thin to support either of them properly.

He tugged at the flask of whisky inside his tunic and eventually worked it out. It took a long time to open it and when he drank, it tasted warm against his mouth, as if it had been in the sun; only there was no sun, not even at fifteen thousand. Cirrus at more than twenty thousand screened it out. Killion felt the encouraging, rewarding liquid charge slowly down his throat. He drank another toast to himself. It was his twentieth birthday. He was going to get a Hun.

Killion should not have been flying; he was supposed to be on reserve. But it was his birthday, so he invented a hiccup in the engine to let him take it up for height testing. It was his birthday; he had letters from his mother and his grandmother, who sent a five-pound note and a newspaper photograph of the royal family. And tonight he was going to meet a magnificent girl called Jane Ashton who worked in the YMCA canteen in the village of Chavigny. It was a happy day for Killion, too happy to be spent on the ground.

Down through the drifting cloud he could sometimes see the hazy plan-view of a German airfield. Sooner or later, something had to land there. Meanwhile Killion let the SE bumble along, barely dragging enough air under her wings to maintain height. Occasional planes crossed the landscape, far beneath, but nobody toiled up to challenge him. The enemy was oddly restrained these days. Killion was too exhausted by the feeble air, and the cold, and the need to watch the airfield, to try and think of a reason. He held the control column between his legs and sprawled across the cockpit, his frozen nose over the edge, and allowed Jane Ashton to drift around inside his head like smoke.

He dozed momentarily: his legs relaxed and the plane wobbled him awake; and there was a whole squadron of tiny Huns wheeling towards the tiny airfield. Killion immediately put the nose down. The engine stopped its fretful clacking and began to bellow with satisfaction as the air became stronger. He steered through the middle of every cloud in his path. With all that activity below it was unlikely that any German pilot would look upwards. The ground staff must have seen him, but what could they do? He streaked out of a thin patch and saw the aircraft bigger now and shinier, curling around in a wide arc to start landing. They were too big to be fighters, even two-seaters. They were bombers. Twin-engined German bombers. Probably Gothas. Another birthday present.

Red flares began coming up from the airfield, but the first bombers were committed: they had nowhere to go but down. Killion steepened his dive and began picking his targets. He still had five thousand feet to go. One bomber was just touching down; three others were strung out in approach; the rest were reforming. He decided to attack right down the landing path, diving from behind them, and he nudged his throbbing aircraft slightly to one side. He could feel the warmer, stronger air rushing past, making the whole machine vibrate. Anti-aircraft guns opened up, hopelessly off-target, nervous of hitting their own planes. Three thousand feet. Killion reached up in a panic; he'd forgotten to cock his gun. Two thousand feet. Tracer laid stitches across the sky: the bombers still in formation were firing long shots at him. Now machine guns on the ground showed flame, and as he curled around to line up with his targets he saw smaller aircraft – Rumplers or maybe Aviatiks – taxi-ing across the field. One thousand feet. The rearmost bomber was shooting at him, but its pilot was dodging to spoil Killion's aim, and the bullets sprayed wildly. Killion cackled with pleasure at the trouble he was causing. He plunged on the bomber and raked it from tail to nose; then let his dive carry him under it and pulled up in time to plant a burst in its belly before climbing into a half-roll which brought the next plane almost within range.

This time the enemy pilot could not even dodge: he was almost on the ground. Killion raced down at almost three times the German's speed, and saw his shots plucking and smashing at the lumbering fuselage. Bullets from somewhere rapped his own aircraft, and then he was hurdling the bomber and flattening out above the battered grass of the field. He flew through a wild cross-fire of small-arms and caught up with the third bomber just as it was taxi-ing towards a hangar. That had to be slaughter. Killion opened fire at a hundred yards and emptied this drum in a series of probing bursts that brought a bloom of flames to the aircraft just as he skimmed over it.

Now Killion was defenceless. A Rumpler, straining to make height, saw him coming, turned panicking away and hit a tree. Killion jumped over a barracks through a cross-hatching of furious ground fire, and fled to the west. A huge explosion drowned the enemy fire and Killion caught a glimpse of a burning bomber slowly sliding along on its nose. Then he was over a railway line, over a wood; out of sight and reach of the guns. He hedge-hopped all the way home.

Men were shovelling dirt into steaming bomb-craters when he landed. He was told that Woolley wanted to see him right away. Killion found the pilots in the armourer's stores, silent and resentful, checking the rounds in Lewis drums.

'Where the shit have you been?' Woolley demanded.

'Height-testing, sir,' Killion said. He felt apprehensive yet jubilant.

'You're a cunt, Killion. You were supposed to be here, on reserve. While you were farting about, we got bombed.'

'Yes, sir.' Killion saw that he was very angry.

'Three mechanics dead, Killion. Three.'

Killion stared at the rounds in Woolley's dirty hands and said nothing. He felt that Woolley had no right to be so contemptuous, so damaging; Killion alone could not have stopped a bombing raid; besides, hadn't he just destroyed two, maybe three of the enemy? You couldn't talk to Woolley, you couldn't live with him. Killion felt hatred flare inside his whisky-bound guts. He refused to speak, or move, or do anything.

'Too many guns jam,' Woolley said. 'From now on you'll check every bullet before it goes into your drum.' He looked at Killion as if urging him to argue so that Woolley could knock him down. Killion shuffled over to a box of ammunition. 'Look out for over-size or deformed rounds,' Woolley said, and managed to make the advice sound like a curse.

Killion got to work. For a while there was nothing but the click of ammunition, the scrape of boots, and the stink of Woolley's rancour. Then Callaghan came in.

'I was told you wished to see me, sir,' Callaghan said stiffly. 'My batman was just running a bath.'

'Start looking for over-size rounds,' Woolley said. 'Your batman can scrub his own arse for once.'

Lambert tittered, then laughed aloud. Callaghan frowned. 'Could it possibly wait for half an hour, sir? I'd rather like—'

Woolley dropped a box of ammunition. Rounds spilled and ran across the floor. Everyone stopped work. 'Get outside,' Woolley ordered.

'Really, sir, I—'

'*Get out!*' Woolley drew his revolver and drove Callaghan through the doorway. 'You'll get a bath, you stinking schoolboy, like they get in the goddam trenches. *Run!*' Callaghan stood, hanging on to the rags of his self-respect. Woolley lashed out with his boots. Callaghan ran.

Woolley chased him to the nearest bomb-crater. A

shattered drain half-filled the hole with lumpy, scummy water. Woolley ordered him into it. When he hesitated Woolley fired. The rest of the squadron watched and heard Woolley cursing, kicking clods down on Callaghan, shooting into the water. They heard Callaghan splashing and collapsing in the quagmire of his own making.

'This is how those poor sods live!' Woolley bellowed. 'This is what they get from arsehole to breakfast. Get your head *down*!' He aimed across the water. The air split, smoke and flame grew, the bullet slammed into the crater wall and sprayed Callaghan with mud. Callaghan was now utterly terrified. He hurled himself away and tried to climb out. He gibbered and choked over an appeal for mercy. 'Get your head *down*!' Woolley shouted. Again the revolver exploded, again Callaghan staggered away from the spurt of dirt. He retreated to the deepest part and stood up to the chest in filth, weeping.

'I want to hear you swear,' Woolley demanded. 'Swear!'

'Bugger,' said Callaghan pitifully. 'Bugger, bugger.'

Woolley fired into the muck, sewage spattered over Callaghan's face. 'You piece of shit,' Woolley said. 'You couldn't fight a retired German whore. Swear, swear!'

'Shit,' croaked Callaghan. 'Shit, piss, oh my God, oh Christ, bugger, bugger, oh please, fuck, sod, fuck, oh please sir, fuck.'

'This is where you live now,' Woolley said. 'You stay in there or I'll shoot you.' He walked away.

After ten minutes, Callaghan peered wretchedly over the rim of the crater. Woolley, sitting on a box thirty yards away, took a snap shot at him. The bullet went high. Killion heard it as he hurried down the road to see Jane Ashton. It was his birthday, and he had had enough of war for today.

Force 9: Strong Gale

*Slight structural damage occurs;
chimney pots and slates removed*

K illion had arranged to meet Jane Ashton outside the
Chavigny canteen. It was a big place and he waited for
twenty minutes while girls came and went. After the dozenth
girl Killion began to be afraid that he would not recognize
her; but when she came out, even with a single dimmed-out
light bulb behind her head, she was so much more than his
memories of her.

Jane Ashton was a slim girl, with short, soft hair curling
around a face so pleasant that people automatically smiled
when they met her. Yet her eyes were serious, even spec-
ulative. You might wish to help her but you wouldn't think of
advising her; and usually she needed no help, either. There
was a delicacy about her which dominated Killion, and a
womanliness which sent the blood pumping to his head. She
made him nervous and reckless at the same time. So had
every other beautiful girl, of course; but Jane Ashton was
now not only the first beautiful girl Killion had kissed good
night, she was the first to kiss him in return, and kiss him as if
she had a great deal to give as well as take. Even now the
shock trembled him, and when she put her arm in his he was
afraid to speak.

'That was an awful day,' she said. 'How are you?'

'I'm twenty.'

'I'm twenty, too.'

'There must be a joke about that, but I've forgotten it.' She laughed, and he felt proud because he hadn't stuttered. 'I should have brought you a present,' she said.

'You have.' Killion was amazed at his own sophistication: it worked, it worked. They walked towards the village while he struggled to contain and enjoy his feelings. 'Would you like to eat at the same place?' he asked, taking no risks.

'Yes. Did you have a good birthday?'

'Good and bad. Tell me something.'

'What?'

'Can I see you tomorrow?' That sounded jerky, unsure, not at all sophisticated.

'We should wait until tomorrow,' she said; but it was a suggestion, not a statement. Their feet stumbled on the cobbles, and she gripped his arm. 'It's simply asking for trouble,' she said. 'We'd only be storing up grief for ourselves.'

'I know. But can I?'

'I may have to work.'

'The next day, then?'

'God . . . I was going to lead a quiet life. I gave up men after the last time.'

'Give up giving up.'

'We mustn't start . . . we mustn't get . . .'

'No. But can I see you tomorrow?'

'Oh, why? It's pointless. Anything could happen at any time. It's silly.' He said nothing. 'Besides, I have to wash my hair.'

He wanted to speak, to say anything so as not to seem sullen or graceless, but there was nothing; and they went into the restaurant stiffly, not looking at each other. When they were holding menus she looked away. 'You should have asked me later. It's been a rotten day, you see.'

'I just had to know.'

'What if you got posted?'

Killion looked in the menu for an answer and was saved by

145

the arrival of the waiter. He ordered a lot of food and a lot of wine.

'I see you're trying to guarantee results,' she said, but lightly.

During the meal they talked about England, mainly London where they had both lived. They exchanged experiences and enthusiasms. She drank a lot of wine for a small girl, and enjoyed it. They were at the brandy stage when she said; 'You know, you got all that sex psychology wrong, before.'

'Nonsense. You're repressed, that's all.'

'Not half as repressed as you are. You see sex behind everything, and so you imagine that everything has sex behind it.'

The French couple at the next table heard the scurrilous word and stared reproachfully at this affront to their palates.

'It's a good rule-of-thumb,' Killion said loftily.

'Only because it's *your* thumb,' she replied. He blinked with surprise. She took his hand and squeezed the thumb. 'Look, if I were hungry, I mean *really* hungry, starving. I would look for food everywhere, wouldn't I? So everything I saw would be in terms of food. If I saw this candle it would remind me of a carrot. Well, that's what you're like. You're hungry, and you see everything in terms of food. Well, there is a lot of food about, but once you start trying to live in a world of nothing but food, you're going wrong.'

'It's a nice mistake, though,' Killion said wittily.

'No, it's *not*.' She surprised him by her intensity. 'You can't see it now, because you can't. But when you see it like that you don't just distort the world, you distort your*self*. Don't you understand? You're trying to see more than exists, and so you're *squinting*.'

He refused to look at her. 'Nice speech.'

'Oh, don't sulk. I can't like you when you're so childish and . . . heavy.' He blinked at the words *like you*.

'How do you know so much about it anyway?' he mumbled.

146

She took her hand away. 'I'm tired of men who look at me as if I were a fillet steak, that's all.'

He took her home to the cottage near the canteen. He was intensely miserable and, hidden by the darkness, tried to apologize. His stutter resisted him. 'I'm s-sorry.' He held both her hands in his and looked down at the pale blur of her face. He felt tears, stupid, pointless, treacherous tears. 'I can't help b-b-b-being the w-w-way I am.' He gave up in disgust. Her fingers tightened around his own, harder and harder, pulling him down. Briefly he refused, not wishing her to know about the tears, and then they kissed. Her mouth was searching for him, and giving to him. Killion's head surged: girls weren't like this; she had seemed not to want to . . . She had said . . . He gave up. Her arms slipped inside his tunic and encircled his thin body. Relax and enjoy your problem, he told himself.

After a while she let go of him and buttoned his tunic. 'You can't come in,' she said.

'Why not?' He was all courage again.

'Because it would be a waste of time, for medical reasons.' She straightened his invisible tie. 'Or didn't you get that far in your anatomy lessons?'

'Oh,' he said. 'That.' Killion was both elated and deflated.

'Come tomorrow, if you still want to.'

'Yes. Good.'

'It will all end in tears,' she said, and went inside.

'Church must have had very small feet,' Lambert said. 'His socks don't seem to keep me warm at all.'

'He wore eights,' Kimberley said. 'I hope you had them washed first. You know what Church was like.'

'It's the worst thing about flying,' Lambert said. 'Cold feet. I'd sooner be too warm than too cold.'

Dickinson said: 'I knew a pilot who had cold feet one minute and was extremely hot indeed the next.'

'Who was that?' Callaghan asked, interested.

'Pay no heed to him,' Lambert told Callaghan. 'Dicky's remarks are in the worst possible taste.'

147

They were all in a room near the adjutant's office, waiting for Woolley to get off the phone to Corps HQ and tell them where the day's flying would be. It was only 7.30 AM, and still dark.

'I wonder *why* people get cold feet,' Killion remarked. 'From a medical point of view, that is. At a time of crisis, you'd think the body would try even harder.'

'In a crisis, the body just panics,' said Rogers. Like everyone except Callaghan and Gabriel, he was sipping whisky with his coffee. 'The bowels, in particular, behave with childish irresponsibility.'

'Please,' protested Dickinson.

'Well, so they do. And it's such a nuisance. Especially when everything freezes.'

Callaghan tittered. He was still trying to establish himself after the siege in the flooded crater. 'I can't think of anything *worse*,' he murmured.

Lambert pulled hard on his socks, failing to stretch them. 'I can,' he said.

Woolley opened the door and stamped in. His teeth were clenched against the cold, and his sleeves were pulled down over his knuckles. He stood for a moment, frowning, his head nodding, not looking at anyone. 'Shit,' he grunted. He went out.

There was a pause; then Finlayson said: 'That could mean almost anything, couldn't it?'

Dangerfield leaned across and whispered, with the grotesque drama of an elderly gossip: 'I think he wants to be *friends*, you know. *Deep* down. He just can't bring himself to *say* it.'

Woolley came back with a wooden model of a biplane. He put it on a table where they could see it. 'Somebody has started using his brains,' he said. The model looked like a stretched-out SE5a, only smoother and cleaner. 'The engine generates 160 horse-power, so the speed, ceiling and rate-of-climb are all good. Top speed is about 120, ceiling is over 22,000, and I don't know the other, but you can guess.'

Woolley pointed at the wings. 'Thick wings. The controls still answer at high altitudes. Very strong construction. You could dive it hard and the wings won't come off. Sensitive. Easy to turn. Might be too easy if the pilot wasn't careful. Plenty of wallop; two machine guns mounted on the engine and firing through the prop. Big prop, too.'

Rogers leaned forward and licked his lips. 'What a darling creature,' he said softly.

Finlayson made a scornful show of lighting a cigarette, so that everyone looked. 'It's a nice *model*,' he said, 'if you like *models*. Personally I'd sooner fly what we've got, even if they are slow, tired and sick of the palsy.' His hand was shaking.

'Well, bully for you,' said Woolley flatly.

'I do like that tapered wing,' Rogers said. 'Do you think we might get these, sir? What are they?'

Woolley took a bacon sandwich out of his tunic pocket. 'The enemy calls them Fokker D VIIs,' he said. 'If you try hard you might get one this morning.'

'Oh my Christ,' said Lambert. 'Now they've got something better than Triplanes.' He looked sick.

'I don't fancy arguing with one of those,' Kimberley said. 'That's a wicked-looking bastard, that is.'

'Isn't there any chance of our getting better planes, sir?' Rogers asked. 'Couldn't we get Camels, or Bristols?'

'I expect so.' Woolley champed on his sandwich. 'I haven't asked for any, and they haven't sent them.' He discovered a piece of bone in his bacon and spat it out. The pilots were looking at him with a mixture of dread and shock.

'But sir—'

'The SE5a is the best gun-platform made. It's rock-steady. It won't dip, or wobble, or swing, or scratch its ass when you tell it to keep still. I want two things from an aeroplane: I want it to fly me up to the enemy, and then lie still while I shoot the enemy down.'

'It's too slow, sir,' Richards said quietly. 'It's too slow, and it won't fly as high as we need to go. The enemy can get on top of us. In a Camel—'

'Get there first,' Woolley said, 'and catch them coming up. I'm not changing planes.'

For a moment, that silenced them. Finlayson threw his cigarette at the model. 'The Kaiser's wife could fly rings round us in one of those,' he said.

'Nobody ever killed the enemy by flying rings around him. You kill him with guns, not the aeroplane. I have always maintained,' Woolley said with ponderous irony, 'that the way to avoid a long argument is to shoot the other man before he starts. All you have to do is get up close, keep your temper, and shoot straight. Camels wobble. Spads wobble. Bristols wobble. SE5as do not,' he brought up a long, curling belch, 'wobble.' Nobody smiled.

'Now for the second piece of good news.' Woolley went over to the wall map. 'The General Staff has at last discovered what fighters are for. They are for fighting. From now on we shall not hang around our side of the Front, waiting for the foe and getting shot down by the French artillery. We shall fly over the German lines, looking for trouble. We shall *fight*. Right? As soon as it's light, my old school chums Finlayson, Richards and Callaghan will come with me and patrol the area Roeux-Riencourt. Rogers will take Dickinson, Gabriel and Dangerfield and patrol Riencourt-Flesquières. Lambert is the lucky one. He goes balloon-busting, with Kimberley and Killion to help.'

'Excuse me,' Lambert muttered. He hurried out, knocking over chairs, and ran to the latrines.

When Lambert found Kimberley and Killion they were out on the field, looking at a map laid on the bottom wing of a plane. The grey light from the east did nothing to improve Lambert's face. 'Where are these bloody balloons?' he said.

'Queant,' said Kimberley. 'That's just between—'

'I know, I know.' Lambert leaned against the fuselage and shuddered. 'I've seen those sods before, they always keep a few Fokkers lurking at about five thousand. How many are there?'

'Three, yesterday,' Killion said.

'Oh God.' He walked down to the tail and pressed his hands on the rudder, wet with morning mist. 'Bloody sausages,' he said. 'Bloody lousy murdering sausages. I shall never eat another sausage as long as I live.'

'Come on,' Kimberley said. 'We might as well go.' Planes were taking off. Lambert came back, wiping his wet hands on his face.

'You ever been balloon-busting?' he asked. They had not. 'Dear mum, it's a bastard,' he said. 'They've got a ring of anti-aircraft guns all round them. Then they've got the ground crews with dozens of machine guns and hundreds of damn rifles, all blazing away. If you get through that you've got to give the balloon a good hard squirt to make it burn, and if you do make it burn it goes up with a hell of a whoomph and you've still got to get away.'

'Past the big guns, the medium-sized guns and the little guns,' said Kimberley.

'Did I mention the Jerry fighters?'

'Yes.' Killion offered him his flask, but Lambert just closed his eyes. 'They let these sausages up pretty high, though, don't they? About a thousand feet, it says here. The ground fire shouldn't be too accurate there—'

Lambert waved a limp hand. 'They pull 'em down,' he said, his eyes still closed. 'They pull 'em down as soon as they see you coming.'

'They won't see us if we fly low.'

'The observers in the balloons will.'

'Oh,' Killion said. 'Um.'

'I'm getting cold,' Kimberley complained. 'What d'you want to do?'

'Oh, bollocks, I don't know.' Lambert opened his eyes and looked bleakly at the map. 'If we go in high the Jerry planes will get us. We've got to go in low. I'll bust the balloons, you two split-ass about and distract their attention.'

'What if they pull the balloons down first?' Killion asked.

'Oh, shut up,' Lambert said. He trudged away.

*   *   *

151

Hugging the ground, dodging clumps of splintered trees, hopping over hedges and walls and old fortified lines, Lambert led Kimberley and Killion so low that they had little opportunity to take their eyes off the terrain and look for balloons. But his reckoning was good: they skimmed the British trench system and raced across the ruptured wastes of no-man's-land exactly opposite the given map reference.

As it happened, the Germans had moved the balloons one thousand yards to the left.

Lambert kept on going and made height as fast as possible, to clear the angry patter of small-arms fire and the explosive stutter of machine guns. At five hundred feet he banked hard and headed for the balloons. Inevitably they were being hauled down, fast. Both of them.

Kimberley and Killion swung out to broaden the attack and confuse the ground fire. Flak blotted the sky ahead, making remote grunting sounds. Lambert's mind registered the presence of aircraft high above, but they were irrelevant. He was studying the nearer balloon, calculating where it would be when he got there. Dimples like heavy rain spotted his wings as stray bullets went through, and then he reached the belt of anti-aircraft fire. The grimy blots grew closer and bigger, sudden thunderclaps made visible, and hurled the little planes from side to side. As Lambert laboured to get back on course another blast flung him lopsided. The next pitched him violently upwards, or kicked him forward. The controls felt sloppy and disjointed. The explosions made his head hurt. Through the smoke he saw the balloon dropping, its basket swinging wildly. Now he could see the heads of the observers.

Abruptly the flak ceased and he flew into clear air: too near the balloon for the German gunners. The bag was down to five hundred feet. Lambert felt mildly surprised that he had arrived. He lined up the dead centre of the target and scored with a long, spiralling burst. The way his bullets plucked at the fat bag was slightly obscene. He kept on firing until he could see each individual rope on the net, then hauled the

152

nose up and vaulted the balloon, realizing as he did so that if it caught fire now he would be fried.

No flames came. He looked behind: the balloon was still dropping. Kimberley and Killion were prancing about the sky, failing to distract the defences, and Lambert strayed into a hail of machine-gun fire, splashed with flak. He forced the unhappy plane into an Immelmann turn and dived back on the balloon. From a hundred feet he raked it from side to side and back again. This time he curled away before he could overshoot, and as he kicked the rudder bar across he saw a glowing redness develop. Before he had completed his turn the whole sphere was blazing, and two parachutes were unfolding below it. For a moment Lambert went rigid with horror as it looked as if the fire would fall on top of them; but they drifted clear.

The second balloon was a quarter of a mile off, and by now very close to the ground. Kimberley and Killion made mock-attacks while Lambert dived through the intense machine-gun fire and a screen of flak so dense that he lost sight of his target. Something clouted his left shoulder with a blow that numbed the arm and knocked him across the cockpit. The plane staggered and refused to fly straight; it lurched crab-wise out of one shell-blast and into another. Lambert's eyes went hazy; he felt unconsciousness rising in him like a tide; it drained reluctantly away, and he was through the barrage again.

But now the balloon was in the wrong place . . . it should be in front . . . the plane wandered away from it, sluggish and disobedient. Lambert strained to force it back but the controls insisted on turning for home, and so he had to slip past the balloon, all plump and shining grey, soon to be on the ground.

Feeling sick and disgusted, Lambert let the plane lumber over the Front. The bruising flak searched for him again, but he ignored it and eventually it went away. He looked for the other two aircraft.

They were still over German territory, quite high, about

half a mile apart, and heading for home. There was a lot of flak but the Fokkers had gone. As Lambert watched, one SE5a took a hit from a shell and fell sideways. Rich black smoke, like costly velvet, unfurled from its engine. The plane began a slow, spiralling descent which developed into a steep side-slip. Lambert watched it as long as he could, but his own plane was losing height, and he limped over the British lines at fifty feet. High above, the third plane flew home, apparently unconcerned by war, destruction or anything.

Lambert nursed his coughing, shaking aircraft back to the field and thankfully touched down on the first available yard of turf. He cut the engine and felt the tail skid sink, bounce, settle and finally run. There was something odd about the way the plane was rolling; one wheel was broken. Lambert slumped and watched the grass go by and listened to the strut tearing itself apart. The plane juddered to a halt and the undercarriage noisily collapsed. The right wing buckled. Lambert got out and left it all.

Woodruffe came over from his hut and met him. 'Are you all right?' the adjutant asked. Lambert showed him his left shoulder. 'Something hit me,' he said. He wanted a drink, now it was all over.

'Nothing there, old chap,' the adjutant said. 'Not even a hole. What did it feel like?'

'Let's have a drink.' Lambert sat down on the grass and put his head between his knees. 'They moved the damn sausages,' he said. 'I hate sausages . . . I feel rotten, Woody. I think . . .' He lay down and blinked, while the blood roared behind his ears. The adjutant sent a man for whisky.

After a while, Lambert's head stopped roaring and he could see clearly. He saw an SE5a high above, circling and circling. 'Why doesn't the silly bugger land?' he asked weakly. Woodruffe helped him drink some Scotch and put him in Rogers' limousine, which a mechanic had brought over. Together they sat and watched the plane circle. After about ten minutes it came down and flew a cautious lap, and then landed. 'Killion,' Woodruffe said. Black fumes were coming off the engine.

They drove over and picked him up. 'Where's Kimberley?' Killion asked. He had oil all over his face and hands.

'You should know,' Lambert said. He was lying in the back seat, drinking. 'He was right next to you when he got hit.'

Killion climbed into the car. 'I couldn't see a damn thing,' he said. 'This oil kept blowing back and messing up my goggles, it was all I could do to get home. I must have got a splinter in the engine, somewhere.' He spat out of the window. 'Filthy-tasting stuff.'

'Well, we got one balloon,' Lambert said. 'I hope they're bloody grateful.'

Woolley landed with Finlayson and Richards an hour later; then Rogers came in with Dickinson and Gabriel. Danger-field was already there, having struggled home with a broken rudder line, probably clipped by shrapnel. Calla-ghan had made a forced landing in a field, but they had seen him get out. Woolley sent Finlayson off with a truck to lead the driver to Callaghan. Meanwhile, the ground crews refuelled, re-armed, and slapped patches on the worst holes. Everyone was fairly pleased: each flight had killed one German and damaged others, and no German planes had crossed the Front on that sector. Woolley went over to the adjutant's office.

Two Frenchmen were sitting, drinking coffee. 'And here *is* the Commanding Officer, now, gentlemen,' Woodruffe told them. Everyone stood up. 'Did you have a good flight, sir?'

'Where's Lambert?' Woolley demanded.

'I believe he's . . . resting. In his billet.'

'Get him.'

Woodruffe went into the next room. The Frenchmen sat down. Woolley took off his helmet and vigorously massaged his scalp. He picked a match out of an ashtray and cleaned his finger-nails. Something sprang to the floor and he mashed it with a large flying-boot. One of the Frenchmen glanced to see what it was. 'French,' he told them. They looked at each other blankly.

The adjutant came back. 'Yes, he *was* resting. These gentlemen, by the way, are from the French police.'

'Did you get the booze? And the scarves?'

'Yes, sir. And two replacements arrive tomorrow.'

'New machines?'

'Well, Corps says six good aircraft should be flown here today.'

'*Should?* The first goddam pilot I see sitting on his ass, I'll send him to Corps to shoot a general.'

'Yes sir.' There was a pause while Woolley kicked monotonously against a filing cabinet. Woodruffe indicated the visitors. 'They would like to arrest about half the squadron,' he said.

Woolley looked at him. 'Don't be fucking stupid,' he said.

'We have warrants,' one of the Frenchmen told him. He unfolded some documents. 'Against Captain Dudley Arthur Rogers for manslaughter and conspiracy to defraud. Against Lieutenant George Yates Finlayson for manslaughter, assault and conspiracy to defraud. Against Lieutenant Frank Alan Michael Church for manslaughter, arson, assault, rape and conspiracy to defraud.' His English was good. He riffled the other warrants and put them away.

'Rape?' said Woodruffe. 'Not rape, surely. That must be a mistake.'

The man gave a very faint smile. 'You might say that the whole affair was a mistake,' he said.

'Get rid of these farts,' Woolley said.

'You should know, sir, that I understand you,' the Frenchman said.

'If I might explain,' Woodruffe said hurriedly, '"Fart" is a term of familiar respect in the British Army. Rather like "bastard".'

'Kick these bastards off my airfield,' Woolley said.

'You should also know that we consulted with your Corps commander this morning,' the Frenchman said, 'and he ordered that we should be given every possible assistance.'

'He is a fart *and* a bastard,' Woolley said.

An airman opened a door. 'Captain Lambert, sir,' he said. Lambert came in, looking scruffy and pale.

'You did a piss-poor job on those balloons,' Woolley told him. 'I came over there fifteen minutes ago and they had two of the buggers up again, and the Boche artillery was pounding shit out of our lines.'

'Oh, Christ,' Lambert said. He sat down and fumbled for a cigarette.

The Frenchman sorted his warrants. 'Captain Gerald Frazer Neil Lambert?' he said.

'I did get *one*,' Lambert protested miserably. 'They moved their rotten sausages during the night, they saw us coming, they pulled them down. You couldn't . . .' Woodruffe struck a light, but Lambert's eyes didn't see it, and the flame burned itself out. 'We lost old Kimberley, as it was,' he said.

'What did they lose?'

'I got one—'

'Did you get the observers?'

Lambert took in a long, shuddering breath. 'They damn near went up with the balloon,' he said. 'They jumped, and I thought their parachutes were going to catch fire.' He discovered the cigarette in his hand and examined it as if it were a mistake.

'You didn't kill them?' Woolley stared bleakly, like a butcher with an incompetent errand-boy.

'No, I got the balloon, I didn't . . .' Lambert shrugged. 'I didn't . . . I got the balloon, that was . . . I got the goddam balloon, didn't I?' he demanded angrily.

'*I got the goddam balloon!*' Woolley parodied in a shrill voice. 'Go back and get the goddam observers! *You shoot down the gas-bag*, dummy, to make them *jump out* so you can *machine-gun* them while they go down! By Christ! You think you pop balloons for sport?'

'You should have told me,' Lambert muttered.

'Told you? Should have told you we go up to kill men and

157

not pop balloons? I should have told you the Huns have balloons the way you have the runs, but they are short of skilled observers? I should have told you that snot comes out of your nose?'

The Frenchman stepped forward, and his colleague moved with him. 'We will start with this officer,' he said. 'Captain Gerald Frazer—'

'You're not taking any of my pilots,' Woolley said harshly. 'You can stuff those warrants right up the Corps commander's bum.'

'Then we shall return in force and compel the arrest.'

'No you won't.' Woolley glowered at him. 'No you won't, you French turd, because Captain bloody Lambert is under military arrest already.'

'Indeed. What charge?'

'Cowardice in the face of the enemy.'

The adjutant covered his face with his hands. Lambert looked at Woolley with dull loathing. The French policemen raised their eyebrows fractionally, and picked up their hats. Woolley scratched his stomach.

'After all we have heard,' the Frenchman said, 'I am surprised that you still find the services of Captain Lambert so necessary.'

'Is that a fact,' Woolley said. 'Well, he's got that job still to do, hasn't he? He's got to get after them balloons again, today, as soon as possible. And I want those observers dead this time.' He gave Lambert a grubby smirk. 'Gerald,' he said.

Lambert stumbled as he came out of the adjutant's office, and collided with two airmen. 'Where's Lieutenant Killion?' he demanded.

'Dunno, sir,' replied one. 'We're on cookhouse fatigues, sir.'

Lambert stared at him, licking his lips. He suddenly felt cold; shudderingly cold. 'Cookhouse?' he said. 'So what?' The words came out slurred. He heard the slurring and wondered what caused it.

'You might try Mr Kimberley's room, sir,' the other airman suggested.

'Don't want Kimberley. Want Killion,' Lambert shivered and put his hands in his pockets. 'Can't have Kimberley,' he muttered.

'I think I saw him go in Mr Kimberley's room, sir.'

Lambert walked heavily away. There was a deep puddle in the path and he walked through it.

'Charming,' said the first airman.

'He's not to blame,' the other said. 'Poor bastard's tiddly. Smell the whisky on him?'

Killion was sitting on Kimberley's bed, reading one of Kimberley's books, when Lambert came in. 'Here's a funny thing,' he said. 'I bet you didn't know the Scotch thistle doesn't really grow all that much in Scotland at all.'

'Great news,' Lambert said.

'It grows mainly in England. But bog myrtle grows mainly in Scotland. So does bog asphodel. Scotland and Wales.'

'Great news,' Lambert sat down and rested his head in his hands.

'There's an awfully pretty flower here somewhere, called golden something . . . They say it likes chalky uplands . . .' Killion leafed through the book. 'It looks a bit like a cowslip,' he said. 'I didn't know old Kimberley was interested in botany, did you?'

'Great news.'

Killion glanced at him, and turned back to the Scotch thistle. 'What is?'

'We're going back.'

'Back where?'

'Back to the same place.'

'Oh.' Killion put the book in his pocket and went to the chest of drawers. He found half a dozen handkerchiefs and a green silk scarf. 'Just the thing for my girl!' he exclaimed. He put it around his neck and showed Lambert, but Lambert wasn't looking. 'Have they got the balloons up again? I suppose they must have. When are we going?'

159

'As soon as they've patched up my plane. Four o'clock, five o'clock, I don't know. We'll have to get someone to take Kimberley's place.'

Killion rummaged through the bedside locker. 'Chocolate . . . want some chocolate? I say, a wristwatch! What on earth did he want with two watches? Not very accurate: five minutes slow. I suppose you saw the old man about it.'

'He wants me to machine-gun the observers this time.'

Killion was brushing his hair with a pair of silver-backed brushes from the top of the chest of drawers. He stared at Lambert through the mirror. 'What, in the basket? You can't *see* them in the basket.'

'Not in the bleeding basket,' Lambert said angrily. 'After they've jumped out, while they're going down.'

Killion didn't like the idea at all. He sat on the wooden chair in the corner and looked at Lambert as if he were a self-confessed criminal. 'You can't do that, though, can you? I mean, they're completely helpless. It's like—'

'If you so much as mention sitting ducks or fish in a barrel,' Lambert said acidly, 'I'll kick your teeth in.'

'But what good will it do? Did he tell you that?'

'He says Jerry is short of skilled observers. He says there's no point in busting a balloon if the observers can go up in another. They can replace the balloons but not the observers.'

'He can't *make* you do it, you know.' Killion ate some chocolate while he thought about it. 'You're within your rights to refuse, you know. He wouldn't dare court-martial you.'

'Oh, shut up.' Lambert got up, opened the window, closed it, leaned against the wall. 'I didn't join this rotten squadron to become his hired assassin,' he muttered.

'No,' Killion agreed. 'Of course, that's where the old man would probably differ.'

'I've just realized.' Lambert looked at him with such energy that for a moment Killion thought he had discovered a way out of it. 'Woolley never knew the observers weren't killed *until I told him*. How could he? He tricked me into telling

160

him. What if I'd said we killed them all? He couldn't prove otherwise.'

'How did he trick you?'

'He asked me what happened to them. Whether they were dead.'

'Oh.' Killion sniffed. 'Diabolical cunning.'

'If I'd only thought . . . Still, that's the answer, isn't it? Bust the balloons, bugger off home, tell him we shot everything that moved.'

'He might get a different report from our gunners. Frankly I think you should just tell him to go to hell. He wouldn't dare court-martial. It's sheer, cold-blooded murder, and in full view of everyone.'

Kimberley came in. 'Hullo,' he said. 'You two hiding from someone?' He had a dirty bandage above one eye, and mud all over his breeches.

'What happened to you?' Lambert asked.

'Just about bloody everything. I got bitten by a rat. Look.' He showed them the mark on his hand. 'Our trenches are full of them, horrible great brutes. God, I'm tired.' He lay down on the bed. 'I was just coming home when I got hit in the engine. Fortunately it didn't go off, but it made a hell of mess, and I came down in a shell-hole just outside our wire.'

'In no-man's-land?' Killion said. 'You were lucky you didn't get shot.'

'Yes . . . Excuse me, but is that my scarf? Thanks. Just put it back in the drawer . . . Well, they got me out, and into our trenches, and patched me up, and I was just leaving when the Huns started shelling. Have you ever been shelled? It's horrible. It's nothing but screaming and colossal explosions and everything shaking and you keep thinking the next one is going to hit you, and you pray for it to stop, and it goes on, and on, and on. You want to scream out and make them stop it, and you want to cringe up your body and hide it some-where, and there's nowhere to hide, and the shells keep screaming down and blowing everything up all around you. That was when I got bitten by the rat.'

161

Killion and Lambert watched him curiously. This was stocky, stolid Kimberley, the Derbyshire ploughboy.

'How long did it last?' Killion asked.

'An hour, I think. I've no idea, I lost count of time. It took me ten minutes just to stop shaking so I could walk. They took me out with the wounded. Just think. Those men have to stand that over and over again. I never knew it was like that. We lost a lot of men. Direct hits on the trenches.'

'Was it really accurate?' Lambert asked, stupidly.

'They couldn't miss, they just couldn't miss. They had that sausage up again, the one we didn't get. The Jerry observers were looking right down on us. It was murder. Like shooting fish in a barrel.'

'Well, if it's any consolation we're going back this afternoon to have another go.'

'So we should. Those balloons are just murdering our poor bloody infantry. It's a crime to let them do it, a bloody crime.'

'Woolley wants us to kill the observers,' Killion said. 'Fire the balloon, make them jump, then shoot them as they parachute down.'

'Couldn't agree more. Shoot the buggers dead. Then their guns won't be able to see what they're hitting.'

'It doesn't strike you as . . .' Killion hesitated, 'a bit cold-blooded?'

Kimberley looked at him sideways. 'Listen,' he said. 'If someone threw a bomb at you and ran away, would you shoot him in the back, or would you let him get some more bombs and try again?'

'It's not as easy as that,' Lambert mumbled.

'It's as easy as that,' Kimberley said. He closed his eyes. 'Now piss off and leave me alone.' He sounded angry.

Lambert's plane was ready at 3.45 PM. He tried to telephone the British artillery unit nearest the balloons, but the operator couldn't get through. The line had probably been cut by shell-fire.

It was a fine, clear afternoon, dry and bright in an

unexpected spell of sunshine. Lambert waited until 4.15. He wanted to go in with the sun behind him. He took off first and circled the field, testing the controls. The rudder felt as if it were covered with barnacles, and the engine sounded old and tired, but there was no reason for grounding the plane. He performed a laborious loop, the signal for Kimberley and Killion to join him.

Again they skimmed the ground all the way to the Front, but this time the Germans had no chance to hear the warning buzz of engines, for they were shelling again. Lambert was climbing hard over the German wire before the first balloon began to move.

The ground fire was much worse than it had been that morning. Lambert glimpsed a flickering of muzzle-flames from a hundred machine guns, and heard the deft tug of bullets speckling his machine, with sometimes a *spang!* as a round struck metal. He realized, without interest, that the enemy firepower had been tremendously increased during the day. Kimberley and Killion were still with him, he observed, but fanning out to distract the gunners. Killion waved to him. Lambert stared, and looked back at the balloon.

Suddenly the flak awoke and got in fifteen seconds' vicious pounding before giving up. It was like being ambushed with filthy snowballs; they materialized without warning, crashed painfully against the eardrums, and buffeted the aircraft. The balloon loomed up, gross and jerking, and the storm fell away. Lambert climbed hard at his descending target. For a moment there was nothing to do but let the shabby old SE haul him up the last stretch, so Lambert actually relaxed and momentarily enjoyed his peace. He sprawled sideways and took in the twitching frightened balloon with its crosshatched plumpness rounded out by the golden sun on one side, curving into purple dusk on the other, and the heavy, ugly, functional basket. At two hundred feet he began firing. He could not miss. The balloon was a target indecently big. His bullets streamed into its chubby underside, slitting and probing.

The flames came almost immediately. Lambert kept on firing, criss-crossing the balloon, underscoring the obvious, until at last he had to turn away.

When he looked back the gas-bag was roaring, a spherical furnace illuminating the early dusk. The basket was still there. Then it became detached. Lambert dived, but nobody came out of the basket. It dropped fast, keeping its upright stance at first, then turning as if emptying itself, and the men fell out. No parachutes opened. Lambert watched the tumbling bodies until they were little spinning, waving irrelevances; and turned away.

The kill infuriated the gunners. They sent up a thick screen of flak between the Goshawk planes and the second balloon, damning anyone who tried to break through. The usual haphazard spray of machine-gun fire sprinkled the air, inaccurate and half-spent at that height, but it only needed one bullet in the head to destroy a whole aircraft. Lambert was now very afraid. Something smashed into his instrument panel and thin oil streaked his goggles. He circled, looking for the other two, and then found he couldn't level out: the outer half of the left wing was shredded, as if by hailstones.

Lopsided and vulnerable, he tried to climb the barrage and get to the second balloon. The barrage climbed to meet him. He saw Kimberley and Killion curling in from either side, and wondered that they were both intact.

Weaving and dodging, the three planes shuffled across the blotched and shuddering sky. Continuous eruptions created a wilderness of blast and air pockets; they barely recovered from one sickening jolt before something hurled them in the opposite direction, or the plane stumbled into a vacuum and hit bottom fifty feet down. Often Lambert lost sight of the other two. He slumped inside the cockpit as far as he could, out of sight of the pounding high-explosive, protected by old canvas against jagged shell-fragments; and dimly recognized the familiar sensation of hot urine soaking down his right leg.

Like flies in a thunderstorm, their very lightness carried the British planes through. Anything short of a very near miss merely blew them away. Three strong men could lift an SE5a, fully loaded; so blast blew the planes about, aged them, weakened them, but it did not destroy them. Lambert raised his shaking head to see the sky ahead clear of flak, with the balloon in the centre. There were also three circling Fokker Triplanes.

This balloon had not descended. Lambert realized that far below the barrage was still pounding away; that the observers' reports were still going down the telephone wire, correcting ranges and bearings, selecting new targets from the shop window of the British Front. This attack was important to the Germans.

Hence the Triplanes. They came out of their circuit one by one and bore down on the SE5as, each of which was now heading for the balloon from a different quarter. Lambert saw his German change from profile to head-on-view: a black, kite-like pattern, edged with gold, dropping out of the pure purple of the dusk. He turned slightly to meet the attack. The German fired a couple of rounds to clear his guns. Lambert blinked to rid his eyes of a sudden haziness, and then the German was on him, with a curiously muffled stutter that swelled and was lost in the bellow of their engines as they passed in a blaze of flashing muzzles and white-hot exhausts and shining propeller blades.

Lambert heard something crack and thrash itself to death in the slipstream, but the plane still flew and although there was a stink coming from the engine it was not on fire. While the Triplane recovered and returned he closed in on the balloon. Killion and Kimberley were keeping the other Germans honest. The balloon rotated gently in the evening breeze, presenting its serial number to him. With the Triplane boring in from behind he fired a long burst at the dead centre of the bag, and saw the fabric split and flare.

Lambert dropped his right wing and dummied to go around the right of the balloon, and just as the Triplane started firing he banked steeply to the left and got away. He missed the burning bag by ten feet, standing his plane on its tattered wing-tip, and held the turn until the whole scene came in sight again. The observers were straddling the side of the basket. Then they jumped.

Lambert hesitated, finding excuses in wanting to oversee the complete destruction of the flaming balloon, or wondering where the Triplane was, or perhaps they had a third balloon somewhere . . . The parachutes opened like conjuring tricks, and still he circled. A hundred yards away a smoke-ball appeared: the flak was back. The parachutes drifted away, controlled now by their own laws, out of the war. Still Lambert circled, uselessly, neither doing nor not doing.

A sheet of flame created itself away to his left, like a scrap of brilliant paper, and a Triplane was on its back, trailing smoke. Kimberley came pounding across the sky to the parachutes. Lambert saw his own Triplane diving to protect them and he plunged after it, far too late.

Kimberley let fly at the dangling men from a hopeless range. He duelled briefly with the Triplane, lost it, and came round in a wide, searching turn. He flew into an anti-aircraft shell with the precise catastrophe of a drunken driver speeding into a wall. The petrol tank exploded in a bloom of yellow and red, and then there was only a lot of smoke, with bits falling: bits of wing, bits of wheel, bits of pilot.

Lambert held his dive. The Triplane came after him and made a long, angled pass, but he was unaware of it. He reached the parachutes and killed the observers in two attacks from close range. Then he dropped to roof-top height and fled for home through the deepening dusk. Killion landed right behind him.

'I'd like to introduce myself,' said the replacement. 'My name is Shufflebotham. I just came today.'

'Oh.' Rogers looked at him. The man was neat and clean and nervously ingratiating. 'I'm Rogers. Have you got somewhere to sleep?'

'Oh, yes. The adjutant—'

'That's all right, then.' Rogers went back to oiling his cricket bat. He seemed anxious about its condition.

'Can I buy you a drink?'

'Got one.' Rogers indicated the half-full bottle of Scotch on the floor between his legs.

Shufflebotham watched him work for a few moments. 'Sorry about my name,' he said, unconvincingly. 'Damn silly name, really. I ought to do something about it.'

'Oh?' Rogers said. He waited. 'Oh,' he said.

Shufflebotham wandered away. Lambert was putting records on the gramophone. He was drunk, and he dropped one. Shufflebotham picked it up for him. Lambert played a record.

'Jolly little tune,' Shufflebotham said.

'What?'

'I don't think we've met. My name is Shufflebotham. Awfully sorry . . .'

'Nonsense.' Lambert blinked at the blur of the spinning label. 'That's a waltz. Know it anywhere.'

'No, no. My name is Shufflebotham.'

'Never heard of him. Not in this squadron.' He picked up his bottle and tramped away, treading on Dickinson's feet.

'Who's that?' Dickinson said, waking up.

'Shufflebotham,' Lambert said angrily. 'Not in this squadron, never. Fellow's got the wrong squadron. Never, never, *never*.' His narrow, bloodshot eyes glared at the replacement.

'Wait a minute,' Finlayson said. 'You're a bloody liar, Lambert. Wait a minute. I *know* you're a bloody liar.'

'Where?' Lambert demanded. 'What?'

'There *was* a Shuttlecock in this squadron,' Finlayson said. 'I'm almost bloody certain of it.' He sniffed morosely. 'You always were a bloody liar, Lambert. Hey,' he turned on Dangerfield. 'You remember the bastard, don't you?'

'Who's that?'

Finlayson looked back at Lambert. 'Come on, then, who was it?'

'Nobody,' said Lambert. 'There never was one. Never.'

'I'm afraid it's all a bit of a misunderstanding,' Shufflebo-tham said with a light chuckle.

'Who is this screaming hysteric?' Finlayson said.

'You mean *Shackleton*,' Dangerfield announced. 'You remember old Shack, Dudley? Came down in a tree and broke both his legs. You remember, he used to do those tricks with matches.'

Rogers thought. 'No,' he decided.

'Oh, come on,' Dangerfield protested. 'How can you forget old Shack?'

'I never knew him,' Rogers said. 'Before my time probably.'

'I win, then,' Lambert said loudly. 'You're all bloody liars.'

'*Listen*,' Finlayson said. He went up to Lambert and hiccuped rum fumes into his face. 'Listen, I can remember this fellow whatsisname as clear as you.' He waved at Shufflebotham. 'Clearer.'

'All right, then,' Lambert challenged. 'All right, ask old Woody.'

'*You* ask old Woody.' Finlayson closed his eyes to help him think. 'The burden of the evidence rests on the other side to *dis*prove whatever it is, and not on the *other* side to disprove the other side's evidence. That's English justice.'

Lambert turned to Dickinson. 'Is that right, Dicky?' he asked, confused.

'Better ask old Woody,' Dickinson said.

'That's what *I* said,' Finlayson confirmed. 'You ask old Woody.'

The adjutant came in, followed by a one-armed major. 'Aha!' said Dangerfield. 'Now for a duel between giants. Lambert wants to ask you something, Woody.'

'Fire ahead.'

'I forget,' Lambert said. There was a chorus of booing and laughter. 'There never was one, that's why!' he shouted.

'Are these the officers named in the arraignments?' the major asked Woodruffe.

'Yes. Manslaughter and fraud all round, more or less, and

rape, arson and assault sort of sprinkled through. This is Major Gibbs,' he told them

'Have a drink,' Dangerfield offered.

'It's damn ticklish, really,' the major said. He accepted some whisky. 'Thanks. I've been sent down to arrange your indictments before a French civil court on all these charges. Cheers.'

'But it's all balls,' Richards said, emerging from behind a newspaper. 'Tell them to go to hell.'

'It is their country,' Woodruffe pointed out.

'They don't deserve it. We're fighting much harder than they are. Besides, look at the rations they sell us. Look at the eggs we get, they're tiny. It's scandalous.' Richards was trembling with indignation.

'Well, never mind about that,' the major said. 'We can't get you before a French court anyway, as long as you're all awaiting court-martial.'

'I'm not awaiting court-martial,' Gabriel declared. He put down his pocket Bible and looked around with a certain grim satisfaction. 'Nor am I charged with any crime under French civil law.'

'Good,' said the major. 'Then maybe you can give me a hand. We've got to get one set of charges or the other in motion, and I'm your defence counsel.'

'We plead guilty but insane,' Lambert said.

'I shall have nothing to do with unrighteousness,' Gabriel stated firmly. 'The soul that sinneth, it shall die.' He looked calmly from Gibbs to Lambert. 'But if a man be just, and do that which is lawful and right, he shall surely live, saith the Lord God.'

'I don't think you understand,' said Gibbs. 'I just need someone to help with the paperwork.'

'Oh no. That's quite impossible. If ye shall despise my statutes, or if your soul abhor my judgements, I will even appoint over you terror, consumption, and the burning ague. And I will break the pride of your power.' He tapped his Bible with his finger. 'You see, it's out of my hands.'

169

'Jesus Christ,' Finlayson growled in disgust.

'Who else?' asked Gabriel.

'What about the other girl who lives here?' Killion asked.

'She's hiding behind the curtains,' Jane Ashton said. 'Why are you shivering? Perhaps you'd better put some clothes back on.'

'Who's shivering?' He swished the wine around in his glass to disguise the tremble. 'Anyway, I've had a hard day.'

She stepped out of her skirt and undid her hair. Killion watched from the corners of his eyes. 'Let's bring the mattress through here, in front of the fire,' she suggested. She cocked her head. 'If you can wait that long, that is.'

Killion turned away, pretending to look for somewhere to put his glass. 'All right,' he said. 'Are you sure it will go through the door?' He picked a china ornament off the mantelpiece and looked at its base. 'Neat, but not gaudy,' he said. 'Is it yours?'

She came up and put her arms around him. 'Oh *Jack*,' she said. Killion felt the warm and cool curves and points pressing against him. He put the ornament down very carefully. It fell over. 'It's all very well for you,' he said meaninglessly. 'You live here.'

'Oh, come *on*. Stop muttering away to yourself.' She reached down and began tickling towards his groin, and he broke away.

'Where is it?' he demanded.

They dragged the mattress through, and stood panting with exertion on either side of it. Killion said: 'You really do look absolutely wonderful.' There were tears in his eyes, and he did not look away.

'Thank you.'

They lay down, and started to begin the endless discovery of the pleasure of each other, and the endless pleasure of each discovery; while outside there was a faint, remote rumble which could have been shell-fire, or heavy traffic, or even a loose window vibrating in the wind.

*　　*　　*

170

'If we had a house,' Margery said, 'what would we call it?' She was frying eggs and bacon and mushrooms on a camp stove in Woolley's billet.

'Cléry-le-Grand.' Woolley was looking at a large-scale map, and drinking Guinness.

'What? Seriously.'

'Seriously, I can't think of anything more serious than Cléry-le-Grand. Right now it's just about the most serious little piss-pot of a frog pox-factory in the whole world.'

She glanced at the map, and went back to spooning hot fat over the eggs. 'It depends what sort of house it is, I suppose, but what if it was a, you know, biggish place, in the country somewhere. Like Hampshire. What about that? What would we call it?'

'Dunromin. Taj Mahal. Justanook.' He rubbed a grimy thumb in his palm, collecting dirt off both surfaces. 'Bide-a-wee. Cosycot. Cedar Lodge. The Moated Grange. The Station Hotel. The Bottom of the Barrel. The End of the Road. The Skin of our Teeth. The Broken Reed. Bottomsup.' He went back to the map. 'Cléry-le-Grand.'

'We used to live in a house called The Nest.' She forked out the bacon, letting it drain before she arranged it around the plate. 'We didn't give it that name, but all the same it made a difference. I mean, it wouldn't have been the same if it had been called something else.'

'We lived in hundred and ten Canal Row,' he said. 'If it had been called hundred and twelve we'd have had our own lavatory.'

She slid the eggs, one by one, on to slices of toast in the middle of the plate. 'It *does* matter,' she said. 'You give names to the things that matter to you, and where you live matters.'

'As long as the postman puts the begging letters through the right door,' he said. He felt a throbbing strain at the outer corners of his eyes, and pressed them with his finger-tips. Margery's face was hidden by her hair as she bent over the stove.

'I'd like to live somewhere nice, that was called something

nice,' she said. The mushrooms were being dotted around the eggs, bright and buttony. 'What I want more than anything is to have somewhere I can look forward to.' She put the plate in front of him, and he began eating.

'I once had a week in a boarding-house called St Monica's,' he said. 'What I look forward to is never seeing it again.'

'Why don't you want to live somewhere nice, for God's sake?' she asked. 'Haven't you ever wanted a home of your own?'

Woolley grimaced. 'This bacon,' he said. 'Bloody salty.'

She reached forward and overturned the plate so that it landed on his lap. Mushrooms bounced about the plank floor. He stared at her.

'You're an absolute bastard,' she said. The tears came, and rapidly dissolved her angry expression to one of utter despair. Woolley sat, knife and fork in hand, and tried to think what to do.

'Why have you got two watches on?' Jane asked. She held his wrist and smoothed the soft hairs on his arm.

'Extra precaution,' Killion said, 'in case one goes wrong. Hey! That reminds me.' He jumped up and went to his tunic. 'I brought something for you.'

He handed her his green silk scarf. 'How beautiful!' she said. 'You *are* kind.' She kissed him.

'Try it on,' he said. She put it around her neck and let the points fall between her breasts. 'What a perfect day,' she whispered.

Force 10: Whole Gale

Trees uprooted; considerable structural damage

T he following night Killion was awakened by the drum-
ming of a loose pane of glass. He found his watch: 5 AM.
The window frame vibrated steadily, producing a buzz like a
trapped fly. Killion got out of bed and went over and rested
his brow on the cold glass. He heard a dull thunder that was
not the blood in his ears. He opened the door and listened.
From the east came the roar of ten thousand blast furnaces.
Killion stood and let the cold air chill him, as a kind of left-
handed penance for not being at the Front where all that
pounding and pulverizing of flesh and bone and blood with
steel and explosive was taking place.

Somebody walked past, and said: 'Damn noisy, isn't it?' It
was Dickinson.

Killion asked: 'Is this it, d'you think?'

'No, no. They're just loosening up. The real barrage comes
later.'

Killion got dressed and went to the mess. He saw some
figures on the roof and climbed a ladder to them. 'This is
definitely worse than Passchendaele,' Rogers was saying. 'I
mean, just look at it.' The entire eastern horizon was red. 'It's
like the Great Fire of London, 1666.'

'I suppose it *is* the Hun, and not us,' said Finlayson
gloomily.

'We haven't got the guns to do a quarter of that damage,'

Dickinson said, 'and in this weather it would take a week to bring them up. Good God Almighty!' A huge explosion bloomed and reverberated on the skyline. 'Somebody holed out in an ammunition dump.'

As if this were a signal, the entire barrage magnified and intensified itself. Now the horizon was brighter, with little curling lights flaring into the glow. The battering clamour seemed to shake the air. 'It's not possible,' Rogers muttered. 'No one can live through that.'

'We kept it up for ten days before Passchendaele,' Finlayson said. 'I wonder how long they'll do it for?'

'They haven't got ten days to waste,' Dickinson told him. 'I'll give you fifty to one the Jerry infantry is drinking its *Schnapps* in the front row of the stalls right now.'

Rogers produced a flask that had belonged to Church, and they circulated this while the appalling display went on.

'How far are we from there?' Killion asked.

'About twenty miles. Far enough,' Dickinson said. 'Nobody's advanced twenty miles in this war since the soldiers settled down to do their gardening.'

A figure climbed on to the roof and came towards them. It was Gabriel. 'What d'you think of *that* for hellfire?' Finlayson asked him sourly.

'The Lord shall smite thee with an extreme burning, and with the sword, and with blasting, and with mildew; and they shall pursue thee until thou perish,' Gabriel said firmly. 'Thy carcass shall be meat unto all the fowls of the air, and unto the beasts of the earth.'

'It beats me why you want to fly with us at all, Gabriel,' Rogers said. 'If that's the way you feel.'

'To me belongeth vengeance and recompense,' Gabriel told him. 'Their foot shall slide in due time: for the day of their calamity is at hand, and the things that shall come upon them make haste.'

'Ah,' Rogers said. 'Well, I suppose that's different, then.'

'The Lord will smite thee with the botch of Egypt, and with

174

the emerods, and with the scab, and with the itch, whereof thou canst not be healed.'

'How disgusting,' Dickinson declared. 'I shall go and make them cook me some breakfast.' He climbed down the ladder. 'The botch of Egypt, indeed! And the emerods . . .' His words were lost in the violent pounding from the east.

Rogers and Lambert took off at first light to see what was happening. More than three hours after it began, the German barrage was still going full blast. They heard it through the clatter of their engines, but they could not see its results. Dense fog covered the Line. Whatever war was being fought below them was taking place either at the long range of bombardment or the short range of a brawl. It was curious. Rogers had flown over the Front many times, and he thought of it as two huge armies entrenched against each other, launching and repelling attacks massively and obviously; but now, he supposed, the fog must have dissolved the armies into isolated soldiers, each fighting his own tiny battle, with no way of knowing whether his side was winning or losing.

Well, Rogers thought, it's the same for both sides. Our chaps can't see their chaps, but their chaps can't see ours. And our chaps will be ready for them.

Lambert, nervously watching a couple of single-seaters at height, thought: please God get me home, I don't want to land down there . . . His face was twitching; he tried to stop it, and failed; looked for Rogers and couldn't see him; lost track of position and direction and why he was up there at all. His brain moved with a mocking ponderousness, deliberately not helping. He panicked because he wasn't keeping a look-out. Found his flask, gulped from it. Nobody fired at him. Rogers was alongside. Slowly his panic faded.

The fog was still thick when they crossed the German Line, but it thinned out on higher ground. Rogers took advantage of the absence of flak to fly low. Everywhere that he saw ground, he saw troops moving up. The grey lines patterned the green-brown earth like odd bits of carpet. He turned north and searched for more openings and found more troops. They hurried forward, ignoring the planes. Other patches revealed supply columns, horsedrawn wagons, ambulance units, strings of gun carriages. Then more troops, more troops. More. Hurrying forward with the absorbed attention of worker ants moving their colony. Hurrying towards the square miles of deafening battering that had been provided to smash open the British Line for their benefit.

After a while Lambert stopped looking. He had seen too many troops already. There was no point in measuring how much was too much.

The sun was shining at two thousand feet, but it did no more than lacquer the fog. Rogers gestured towards home. As they recrossed the submerged inferno, they saw other aircraft, Germans, further down the Line. Presumably the attack was not considered a secret any more, for nobody made any move to intercept. In any case, there was nothing anyone could do about the men in the trenches until the fog lifted. And precious little after that.

'Like all bad ideas,' Woolley said, 'this one is brilliantly simple.'

He sat on the big table in the mess, one bare foot tucked up, and cut his yellow toe-nails with heavy scissors. The pilots stood out of range of the parings.

'You will load your aeroplanes with TNT,' he said, 'fly in line-astern to Corps HQ, and crash on to the roof of the Corps commander's château, in alphabetical order.'

Nobody laughed. Dickinson lit a cigarette, and they watched the match burn out.

'When you have done that,' Woolley said, 'you will fly to Berlin, where you will stand to attention in your cockpits and piss on the Kaiser, thus ending the war.' He sheared laboriously through a horny overhang.

Lambert looked at his watch, and yawned.

'And after *that*,' Woolley said, 'you will come back here

and stop the German air force from examining the hole which their artillery has just blown in the British Line, a hole about the size of Lancashire, and that will be the biggest waste of time of all, because the German Army found that hole an hour ago, and is now galloping through it as fast as its little legs will carry it, heading in the direction of . . .' he snipped the final toe-nail and straightened his leg to study the result '. . . *us*.'

Rogers had been looking out of a window. He started, and turned, pretending a well-bred confusion. '*Aw*fully sorry, sir,' he said. 'Miles away, I'm afraid. *What* is it you want done, again?'

Woolley pulled on a sock. 'Just get up there and fend them off,' he said. 'Stay over the Jerry lines, and keep them busy, that's all.' He stamped his foot into his flying-boot. 'Keep them away from the fighting until the poor bloody infantry gets a chance to stop running.'

'How long do you think that will be, sir?' Callaghan asked.

'About a week.'

They looked at him, but Woolley was serious.

'Well, that seems simple and straightforward enough,' Rogers said.

'You're simple,' Woolley told him. 'The plan is utterly bloody impossible, but if you can't see that, you're probably better off.'

'I hope you told the Corps commander it was impossible,' Finlayson said sourly.

Woolley laughed through his nose. 'On the contrary, you sickly convalescent, *he* told *me*. He doesn't expect us to succeed, but on the other hand he doesn't expect the German attack to succeed, either. He's got to do something with us, we're on his ration strength. If you want his exact words, he said "Get up there and make bloody nuisances of yourselves until I tell you to come down".'

'What a way to win a war,' Lambert said in disgust.

'Don't talk daft. You're not here to win the stupid war, you're here to help make sure nobody loses it. You're not

Henry the Fifth on a flying bloody charger, you know. You're a semi-skilled mechanic, just like the municipal ratcatcher, on piece-work. Keep your mind on your job, or some big grey bastard will bite you in the thumb.' A fitter rapped on the window. 'They're ready. We'll fly in pairs. Shufflebotham, you come with me.'

Goshawk Squadron flew all that day, and came back from the patrols badly mauled. German aircraft crossed the Line in a constant stream: two-seater observation planes, single-seater scouts, twin-engined bombers, heavily escorted photographic planes. By noon all the squadron's reserve aircraft were in use, and the mechanics were sucking blood from cut fingers and grazed knuckles as they worked too fast on battered planes which had just creaked home with streaming canvas and smashed spars, or labouring engines, or cracked fuel lines, or crippled controls, or lopsided undercarriages. Half a mile away smoke still rose from Dangerfield's machine, where he had crash-landed on fire after stopping a burst of tracer in the wing. The fire had spread to the fuselage and reached the cockpit by the time he got the wheels on the ground and jumped out. He flew again within the hour, fat blisters coming up on his right hand and not much left of his eyebrows.

In the late afternoon Dangerfield and Killion were flying together on their fifth patrol when they saw a formation of five Pfalz fighters climbing towards them. Dangerfield had started the day tired; now, after repeated bouts of combat and the shock of his crash-landing, he was weary beyond anything he had ever known. He watched the Pfalz D VIIs coming up out of the east, with all the loathing and resignation of a slum-dweller who sees yet another street-brawl lurching his way.

Two against five. The advantage of height, the disadvantage of numbers, and of fatigue. Dangerfield felt a deep desire to rest his head and just let the enemy go by. He had done enough, it was unfair to ask for more . . . He slumped and

178

waited for God to save him. Suddenly, definitely, he decided to quit, turn back, go home, leave everything until tomorrow. He straightened up and waved at Killion, pointing hard to westward.

Killion waved back and dived into the attack. Horrified and enraged, Dangerfield watched him go. Killion looked back. Dangerfield swore and thrust into a dive. His disgust mixed with despair as the Germans drove towards him, and the emotions drugged his tired brain. When the enemy formation scattered he took a second too long to pick out an opponent, and one of the Germans slid under his tail. The first burst from his machine gun hammered through Dangerfield's weary back and smashed his instrument panel.

Killion saw the SE5a topple and fall over, but he was too busy fighting off the circling scouts to see if Dangerfield crashed. A formation of six Camels came to his rescue and the battle broke up, drifting away to other parts of the sky, leaving Killion to cruise home, alone.

The adjutant found Woolley with the armourer, checking ammunition before he allowed his machine-gun drums to be filled. Woolley looked as if he had been fighting a forest fire: his eyes were red, his face was filthy, and one ear had bled down his neck. He sucked at a bottle of Guinness, and went on fingering the rounds.

'Corps wouldn't tell me the latest position on the phone, sir,' Woodruffe said. 'I had to go over and get it in person. They say too many of our telephones have been captured, you never know who you might be talking to at the other end.'

'What have we lost?'

'Well, it's not as bad as it might have been.' The adjutant settled down and looked through his notes. 'They attacked along about sixty miles, from Lens down to La Fère, more or less. They just about levelled our Front Line with that bombardment.'

'I know. I saw it.'

'Yes, of course. Well, they broke through on about a forty-mile stretch. Where they really gained ground is up towards Arras, they made about five miles there, and down around St Quentin. It looks as if we might have to pull back behind the Crozat Canal and hold St Simon. That would mean they've taken something like ten miles at that point. Of course we're digging in now—'

'Five miles. Ten miles. How long is it since anyone advanced five miles in one day?'

Woodruffe shifted uncomfortably. 'Not since 1914, unless you count—'

'How did they do it?'

'Well . . . that's the extraordinary thing, nobody quite knows. The bombardment destroyed our first system, of course, and there seem to have been a lot of gas shells landing amongst our gunners – those that weren't killed – and they say the Hun did a lot of damage with his trench mortars and those awful minenwerfers. But it was the mist that really let him in. The Jerry troops just sort of walked right through in a lot of places, and the next thing anyone knew we were retreating. It took Corps rather a long time to adjust, I believe. They're not accustomed to moving five miles in one day. Especially backwards.'

Woolley held up a bullet and showed it to the armourer. 'Piece of shit?' he said.

'Piece of shit, Mr Woolley.'

He threw it into a bucket. 'Presumably the cruel, implacable, scheming Teuton hordes will do the same tomorrow,' he said.

'Ah, well, now that's an open question,' the adjutant said. 'Corps rather thinks not. Corps feels that with all the losses they must have taken, the Germans will almost certainly be consolidating tomorrow. Evacuating wounded and bringing up supplies and generally tidying up.'

'Corps is an arse-hole full of farts.'

Woodruffe smiled uncertainly. 'Also, sir, you must remember that we've brought up all possible reserves to plug the gap.'

'You amaze me,' Woolley said. 'You truly do. What happened today? They attacked our Line. It wasn't a very brilliant Line, but at least it was a Line, with trenches and wire and stuff. They bashed hell out of it so much that it burst wide open, and we had to use all our reserves to hold them. By which time they were miles inside our Front.'

'Yes, but we shall do better tomorrow,' Woodruffe insisted. 'I mean, we won't be taken by surprise tomorrow, shall we?'

'And tomorrow they won't be attacking strong positions, they'll be hitting us out in the open. Good Christ, if they can make five miles a day when they have to fight through four systems of trenches and get right inside our Battle Zone, how bloody far d'you think they'll go when we've got nothing to hide behind except cow turds and haystacks?'

'The reserves are fresh,' Woodruffe said. 'The reserves will hold them.'

'The Hun has reserves, too. What happens when he makes another hole? What do we plug that with?'

'It's never happened before,' Woodruffe said stiffly. 'I suppose we should have to ask the French for help. Or the Americans. Frankly, sir, I doubt if the occasion will arise.'

'You mean you hope it won't. It looks to me as if we've forgotten how to retreat. I don't suppose the Germans have forgotten how to advance, and if they do it again tomorrow we shall have to learn something new, won't we?'

Major Gibbs came in. 'Ah, Woolley. Sorry to bother you, but this squadron has assumed unusual significance in the present difficult situation. The French have been accusing us of lack of cooperation lately – military cooperation, that is. Naturally they are plotting to get us to take over the dangerous bits of the Front, and launch all the expensive attacks, and so on. Typical dago trickery. Anyway, they've seized on this legal brouhaha as an example of Albion's perfidy, so to speak. How can they help us if we don't help them? That sort of thing. I needn't tell you what a nuisance they can be.'

'Then don't. The French can go and fuck themselves, for me.'

181

'Me too. Unfortunately we need their help too much at the moment. Unless we get some French reinforcements soon, we're going to have nothing left to fight with. Assuming that the Hun keeps attacking, of course. Anyway, Corps commander has promised them immediate action, which being translated means: a couple of your pilots will have to face the music, I'm afraid.'

Woolley finished his Guinness. 'Next week,' he said.

Gibbs shook his head. 'Now.'

'Tell Corps we're flying from dawn to dusk. Tell them about the war against the Germans.'

'That's exactly it, though. The generals are falling over themselves to get French divisions sent up as reserves. We can't risk any friction. It's all thoroughly political, but you must see the military sense behind it.'

'But surely we can't need reinforcements as desperately as all *that*,' Woodruffe said.

'Oh yes we do. We do indeed.'

'All right, you can court-martial someone,' Woolley said. 'Invite the French police along.'

'On what charge?'

'Desertion in the face of the enemy.'

'Good Lord, that's a bit stiff. The penalty's death.'

'Serve the bastard right. I never did like him.'

'Who is it?' the adjutant asked.

'Any of 'em.' Woolley looked at them with stony satisfaction.

It was three miles to Jane Ashton's place. Killion trudged it with a kind of dogged stupidity, too tired to think after the all-day violence. He passed bivouacking troops on their way up, and had to stand in gateways while supply columns clattered by, or lines of ambulances rumbled back. He got lost, he forgot where he was going; he gave up and sat down; he set off again. When at last he got there and knocked on the door with a sticky bottle of claret, a stranger let him in.

'I'm Mary,' she said, as if there were nothing more to be

said about that. 'You must be Jack. Jane's in the bath, I'm cooking dinner.' That accounted for everyone.

'I see,' said Killion. 'You're the other girl.' He blinked at the bright lamplight. Jane should have been here, not . . . whoever this was. Mary? Mary.

'What's that you've got?'

'This? Bottle. Wine,' Killion explained.

Mary took it. 'I could have used some half an hour ago, in the sauce. We'll just have to drink it. Sit down. You look like something the cat brought in.'

Killion sat down and fell asleep. Jane woke him. 'Dinner's ready, Jack,' she said.

'Don't want any,' he mumbled. 'Too . . . tired . . .'

'Rubbish,' Mary told him. 'If I've cooked it you'll eat it. You can wash your hands in the bathroom. They look as if they need it.' She began dragging chairs up to the table. Jane smiled and helped him up. He washed his face in cold water and came back red-eyed but awake. The table was laid, and a roast chicken lay waiting for him to carve.

Mary organized the plates and kept an eye on his carving. Killion felt her watching, and sawed clumsily at the bird. Hot grease spotted the fresh tablecloth. Eventually he managed to hack off a wing, in two parts. The knife slipped and cut his finger. He sucked it, sniffing, and then started on a leg. Drops of blood fell on to the chicken. 'Here, give me that,' Mary said impatiently. 'Suck your finger.'

Killion sucked and sipped while Mary sliced the chicken rapidly and efficiently. Jane watched him. 'I feel like a walking wounded,' he said.

'I thought you said he was a medical student,' Mary muttered.

'So I was, once,' Killion protested.

She discarded the shattered wing. 'You'll never take my appendix out, I can tell you that.'

'Poor Jack.' Jane kissed him behind the ear. 'Have you had an awful day? I hear it's been bad at the Front.'

'Flying all day. Flying, flying, flying. Never stopped.'

'I don't know what you men make such a fuss about,' Mary said. 'As far as I can see you don't *do* anything, you just *sit* up there. Take some more potatoes.'

'Honestly, I've got enough.'

'Rubbish.' She gave him more. 'You need to keep your strength up. The war's going to last a long time yet.'

'Anyway, what do *you* do?'

'Me? Same as Jane. I work in the forces' canteen. We seem to spend most of the day rejecting indecent propositions.'

'Here's to indecency,' Jane said. 'The only thing that never dies.'

Mary sniffed, but she drank the toast.

The meal was solid, orthodox and delicious. Killion tucked in. After twenty minutes he was quite awake, and he suddenly noticed Mary's face. 'Good heavens,' he said. 'How good-looking you are, Mary. I only just noticed.'

She half-smiled. 'What was I before, then?'

'I don't know. Maternal, maybe.'

'But you didn't say so.'

'No. Still, we know each other much better now, don't we?' She began collecting their plates, and Killion saw a wedding ring on her finger. He swung around on Jane. 'You're not saying much, funny face.'

'Perhaps I'm waiting for you to ask me how I am.'

'Ahah. How are you?'

She looked away, played with a spoon, looked back. 'Only wonderful,' she said. They laughed, unexpectedly, even Mary. They had spoken their unknown passwords; now they recognized each other. For half an hour their talk was easy and pointless, and then Killion began to wonder whether Mary was going to stay in all night and he became uncomfortable, chatting pleasantly to someone he wanted to get rid of.

When Jane went into the kitchen, Mary cleared her throat and looked at him seriously.

'Jane has told me a lot about you,' she said. 'Of course, I'm two or three years older than she is . . . I have no possible

184

right to interfere, of course; however, I *would* just like to ask you one thing. Do you plan to marry Jane?'

Killion had never even thought about it. 'Of course,' he said.

Mary seemed satisfied. She leaned back.

'Of course I do,' Killion said. The idea attracted him.

'I shall be going on duty in ten minutes, you see,' Mary said.

'Why, of course,' Killion said again. 'I mean, why not?'

Jane came in. They both looked at her with satisfaction; Mary sober, Killion a little drunk. She raised an eyebrow. 'Have I done something clever?' she asked.

Simultaneously, Mary said 'No', and Killion said 'Yes'.

When Mary had left for the canteen, Jane asked: 'What was all that yes-no about?'

'Nothing. Everything.'

'Well, tell me then.'

Killion stood up. 'Mary wanted to know if I planned to marry you. Of course I said I did.' He sat down.

Jane perched on the arm. 'Well, *I* certainly don't intend to marry *you*,' she said.

Killion was shocked. Jane smiled cheerfully, so that he thought she was being charitable, or even contemptuous, and he looked down at his hands. Then he looked back. 'But don't you love me?'

'Yes, I do. Does that mean we have to get married?'

'Uh . . .'

'I think it's a good reason for *not* getting married.'

'Really? But we could fix it up now, if we wanted. I mean . . . Well, this week, anyway.'

'What good would that do?'

'I've no idea. Mary seemed to think—'

'Mary's different. She can't help hating me because I'm single and she's a widow.'

'She doesn't hate you.'

'She hates the fact that I've lost nothing and she's lost everything.'

'Oh. Well. Yes. I see. Well, I suppose we needn't get married, need we?'

Jane slid on to his lap and kissed him on the mouth. 'My lovely Jack . . . We would make a perfectly rotten married couple.'

'But lovely lovers.'

'Lovely.'

She groped underneath and found something angular in his tunic pocket. 'Are you carrying a gun, just like the cowboys?'

'It's for you.' He dragged out a beautiful, silver-backed hairbrush. 'Sorry about the monogram. I won it off a chap at poker.'

'What was his name?' She fingered the lettering J.T.D.

'Dangerfield.'

'It's beautiful. Won't he need it?'

'No. He got posted.'

'Poor Dangerfield.'

'Poor me. *I* nearly got court-martialled tonight.'

'Why? Because you were gambling?'

'No, no. It's all to do with the CO. He wanted to court-martial me, only I heard them trying to find me so I hid in the latrines and I don't know what happened in the end. I think they gave up on me and started looking for Finlayson instead. Maybe the old man decided to court-martial old Finlayson instead . . .'

Jane was not listening; she was unbuttoning his tunic, and then his shirt. 'Shall I undress you?' she whispered; and Killion nodded. Away in the east the barrage had begun again, but as they lay in front of the fire it was remote and harmless. Nothing could touch them now.

Next day the German attack repeated itself with meticulous Prussian efficiency. The bombardment chewed the British defences as savagely; the dawn advance was cloaked in the same white mist of invisibility; within hours the storm troopers had overrun the new Front and the retreat was on again.

Woolley had the squadron in the air very early. They crossed the booming fog-bank, shapeless and lethal like some fungoid growth, and patrolled behind the German lines in flights of two or three.

For an hour and a half no German aircraft came near. The flak was heavy, relentless as hounds chasing a cornered stag up and down high ground. Rogers was flying with Lambert. They droned about, surrounded by the black, dissolving snorts of high explosive. As they climbed so the flak followed them; as they dived so it came down to harry them. They dodged and doubled back between ten and twelve thousand feet, where the gunners were not accurate; but the chance of flying into a burst was always there.

The changes of height and course became automatic after a while. Rogers was thinking about a cricket match in which he had made a good score, reliving the running between the wickets, as he bucketed about between the shell-bursts. He braced himself to clout the ball, and watched it race away, like a round of tracer . . .

He started, sweating guiltily: he hadn't been checking the sky. The flak cracked on, bad-temperedly, puffs of charcoal, sharp-edged in the cold sunlight. Two miles below, the mist was thinning, revealing God knew what disasters. Rogers waggled his wings and they turned for home.

Within minutes they met another flight: Richards and Gabriel. The flak tailed off, mercifully, and Dickinson and Finlayson angled across from the north to join them. In this formation half the squadron, with guns unfired, intercepted a solitary German two-seater heading eastwards. Almost certainly it had been on camera-reconnaissance, photographing the British reserves being rushed up. Where was its escort? Perhaps the Germans thought it would be less conspicuous on its own. Perhaps they hoped that it would be able to hide in the fog. But now the fog was collapsing, evaporating, dying.

Rogers and Lambert dived ahead of the two-seater and turned it. The machine seemed to manoeuvre heavily, as if

187

pregnant. The other four Goshawk aircraft came down in an angled line which allowed each gun to rake the target from nose to tail in a continuous devastation of bullets. The teamwork was superfluous, because the pilot was dead before the second burst hit him, his plane was on fire before the third burst cut it apart, and the fourth simply knocked sideways a wreck which had only to fall to the ground.

Finlayson found Major Gibbs and the adjutant waiting for him.

'I know you've got a lot on,' Woodruffe said, 'but Major Gibbs says it's absolutely essential that you be charged properly, according to King's Regulations.'

'Oh Christ,' said Finlayson. He sat down on an oil drum. 'Is the old man still playing that game? I thought that was last night's bad joke.'

'We must have something to show the French,' Gibbs said. 'A formality, and some documents. Something they can see and feel, and be impressed by, and tell all their pals in the Ministry of Justice about.'

'Let them squeeze the old man's balls, then. They're about the biggest thing in this squadron.'

'Quite. But at the moment, I suggest we adjourn to the adjutant's office. The French lawyers are waiting there now, and I'd like them to hear the CO actually make the charge.'

'So would I,' said Finlayson bitterly. 'I'd like to know exactly where and when I deserted in the face of the enemy.'

'Oh, I forgot to tell you,' Gibbs said. 'That's all been changed. He's decided to make it cowardice now.'

'Cowardice?' Woodruffe frowned. 'Are you sure? He told me he was going to make it incompetence.'

'Good God, I hope not. I can't change everything at this stage. It'll *have* to be cowardice.'

The two French civil servants shook hands with everybody. They seemed competent and satisfied. Woolley was making a long telephone call. The line was bad and he kept shouting. Gabriel sat by a window, reading his Bible.

Woodruffe saw Finlayson looking at him. 'Gabriel has agreed to defend you after all,' the adjutant said.

'I don't want the silly bastard!' Finlayson exclaimed. Gabriel turned a page.

'I'm afraid you must,' Gibbs said. 'Everyone else is liable to court-martial too, and you must be represented.'

Woolley shouted: 'Bollocks!' and hung up. 'Get on with it,' he told Gibbs. 'We're off again in ten minutes.'

Finlayson and Gabriel stood up. The Frenchmen watched carefully. Woolley picked his teeth with a matchstick. Gibbs read out the charge: there was a great deal of florid preambling, all about the defence of the realm, and the jurisdiction of the provost-marshal, and the patriotic obligations of the King's subjects to defend the royal allies against the common enemy, most of which Gibbs and Woodruffe had cooked up to impress the French. The charge itself was brief. Lieutenant George Yates Finlayson had displayed cowardice in the face of the enemy all the previous week. Signed, Stanley Woolley, Major.

Despite the transparent nonsense of it all, Finlayson felt his guts tighten at the word *cowardice*. His head was half-bent; he looked up at Woolley, stiff with disgust and hate; and saw Woolley watching him coolly, almost curiously.

'Jolly good,' Woodruffe said. 'Now, what I propose is, I propose a week's adjournment before we fix the date of the hearing, if that suits the defending officer.'

Gabriel took his Bible from under his arm as if it were loaded, and opened it. 'And if ye will not for all this hearken unto me, but walk contrary unto me,' he read out, 'then will I walk contrary unto you also in fury; and I, even I, will chastise you seven times for your sins. And ye shall eat the flesh of your sons, and the flesh of your daughters shall ye eat.' He closed the book and nodded to Finlayson and Woodruffe.

'Time to fly,' Woolley said. To Finlayson's surprise, he took him by the elbow and steered him, quite gently, to the door. When they were outside and walking towards the aircraft, Woolley said: 'The French make such a fuss, you see. And we need their reinforcements, or something.'

'Yes. Woody explained.'

'I could have made it something piddling, like embezzling the mess funds, but I thought it might as well be, you know, melodramatic.'

'I see.'

'The frogs like melodrama. Besides, Goshawk Squadron has never been known for doing things half-heartedly, has it?'

'No.'

'I knew you'd understand. I didn't want it to get you down. After all, it's not going to make any difference, is it?'

Finlayson watched Woolley's face for a trace of sarcasm and found none. 'Why should it?' he said.

'You're right,' Woolley said warmly. 'Nothing's going to make any difference.' They parted.

Finlayson met Rogers. 'I think the old man's cracking up,' he said. 'I think he's finally out to lunch. I've never seen him like this before. He's just been *nice* to me.'

'I thought he was going to charge you—'

'Yes, yes, he did all that. But *nicely*, as if it didn't matter.'

'Oh.'

They looked uneasily towards Woolley. He was leaning against his machine, arms resting on the upper wing, head resting on his arms, eyes closed.

'Odd,' said Rogers.

Force 11: Storm

Small houses and sheds moved

It was the third day of the German assault.

Dickinson was in hospital with bullet wounds in the leg. Three replacement pilots had arrived the night before, straight from England, none having flown more than twenty hours. Woolley refused to see them; he had retired to his hut and practised the accordion.

In the morning he put one replacement and two experienced men in each flight. Their mission was less ambitious than the day before: just to clear the air over the battlefield. Attack any and every German plane, stay over the fighting, use up left-over ammunition on German troops. The replacements listened carefully and tried not to show their excitement. 'A special instruction for our newcomers,' Woolley said heavily. 'Don't get shot down, but if you do get shot down, try and ram a Hun on the way.' That made them blink.

Rogers, Lambert and an eighteen-year-old called King took off together. The front was nearer now, and Rogers climbed to five thousand feet over the airfield before he turned east. King was clumsy with the aircraft, never having flown an SE before, and Lambert watched nervously. It was a gusty morning.

The sky over the Front was dotted with wheeling, plunging, dodging aircraft. From a distance they looked like birds; there were no formations, and the movements seemed random and pointless. Then one of the specks flared with a sudden, intense brightness that lasted as long as a struck match, before it dropped. A smear of smoke was all that was left, and it rapidly grew ragged and thin. The other machines went on circling and dodging as before. As the Goshawk flight got closer they could see the flickering criss-cross of tracer.

Rogers held off until they had climbed to twelve thousand, then prowled about, searching for an easy target. Everything was tangled and confused and fast-changing. Lambert fired a couple of rounds to attract his attention. Six Fokker D VIIs were diving from fifteen thousand feet. Rogers put his nose down and they escaped into the chaos below.

For the first thousand feet there was nothing; then a couple of private duels; then a sprawling mêlée of about twenty aircraft spread over half a mile of sky. Rogers hoped that King would go off and look for his own target, and not stick close to him. He saw a shaky-looking Halberstadt turn eastwards and went after it. Now he could smell the burnt-phosphorus of tracer in the air.

He glanced at Lambert and saw him blaze at a green-and-yellow plane, then bank hard away as tracer scorched past. Rogers' Halberstadt came looming up, its observer firing steadily: bright dashes which seemed to bend towards Rogers' machine. He jinked and tried a burst at long range, but the Halberstadt was diving hard now and pulling away. He zoomed to save height, heard the crackle of machine guns, skidded round in a savage, 180-degree turn, and instinctively ducked as a bright blue Pfalz hurtled over his head. By the time he had recovered it was gone.

Quite suddenly the whole battle had moved far away. Individual skirmishes flickered and stuttered in the distance. Rogers checked above and behind: no sign of Lambert, but King came wobbling by, grinning and waving. Rogers acknowledged. King pointed downwards and waved goodbye. He side-slipped neatly; he was getting the hang of the thing.

Rogers saw the left wing start to buckle in the centre. It fluttered for a moment and then folded right back against the fuselage, like a roosting bird. A strut had failed; collapsed, for no reason at all.

Rogers dipped a wing so that he could watch the aeroplane tumble away, lopsided, dwindling to a grey-brown fragment that flickered in the early sunlight. King did not jump, not that it would have made any difference if he had. Perhaps he couldn't get his straps undone. Perhaps he didn't want to. Perhaps he didn't know what the hell was happening to him. The SE hit the ground in a cluster of shell-holes.

Rogers felt relieved: at least it hadn't been a flamer. And now they wouldn't have to worry about collision on the way home. He went off to find Lambert.

Finlayson's flight consisted of Richards and a new boy called Tribe, a big, broad New Zealander. Finlayson spent fifteen minutes teaching Tribe the signals, and describing the blind spots of enemy aircraft. He emphasized the need to hold height; to keep searching around, above, below, behind; to get in close; to fire short bursts; to go for the pilot, not the plane. It was a waste of time. Tribe barely knew how to fly. On take-off he almost crashed into a hangar. In the air he never mastered the throttle setting, so that he either fell behind or pulled ahead. He seemed physically uncomfortable in the cockpit. Once Richards had to dive out of the way as Tribe, twisting and stretching in his straps, lurched across the formation. After that, Finlayson did his best to get Tribe to fly a hundred feet below them, but the man kept wandering up.

They reached the fighting at a height of eight thousand feet. Finlayson searched around for something simple to blood Tribe on. There was nothing simple, only tangled dog-fights. After five minutes the decision was made for them: they were jumped by six D-Vs which came dropping out of a stretch of dirty cloud.

Finlayson had no time to protect Tribe. Within seconds each man was twisting and skidding away from the attackers.

Richards zig-zagged violently as two D-Vs got behind him and took turns to fire. Each burst ripped the air like split canvas. He felt the SE kick, and tasted hot tracer fumes on his breath. In desperation he faked a dive and hauled the SE up on a tight loop. He glimpsed the enemy overshooting and banking steeply away, half-rolled and took a snap shot at a dappled D-V, then saw Finlayson behind it and yet another D-V behind him. Richards sprayed shots wildly and saw the second German swerve away. Where was Tribe?

He climbed and saw three Germans circling a lone SE and firing at it. The SE was doing nothing but loops. Loop after loop. Richards raced over and broke it up. The Germans turned on him, blocking his escape. Richards glimpsed Tribe, still laboriously and pointlessly looping. A D-V flashed across, firing and missing; Richards got off a burst and saw his bullets rip open the fuselage. He skidded hard in the opposite direction, anticipating attack, but none came. The enemy was diving away, for no reason, unless they were out of ammunition. Or low on petrol. He scanned the sky, suspicious of tricks and ambushes. There was nothing. They had decided to call it a day, that was all. Extraordinary.

Finlayson came toiling back up, and Tribe was at last levelling out. Richards flew alongside, waiting for Finlayson. Tribe stood up and hammered at his gun. He pointed at it and waved his hands in the wash-out signal. Richards pointed homewards, which was behind them, and turned to escort Tribe across the Lines.

Tribe paid no attention. Richards came back and signalled more clearly, but Tribe was busy with his gun again. Richards fired a few rounds. Tribe looked up, waved, and went back to work. Finlayson reached them and Tribe repeated the pantomime. They were flying steadily eastwards, deeper into enemy territory. Finlayson pointed backwards, towards home. Tribe looked back, studying his tail, trying to see what they saw wrong with it. It looked all right. He worked the rudder pedals to show them. Nothing wrong there. It was the *gun* that was jammed.

194

Finlayson gave him the wash-out signal several times, and turned westward. Tribe was puzzled, but he followed. When they were well inside the British Line Finlayson motioned Tribe to go on home, while he and Richards went back. Tribe mistook the signal for the 'enemy aircraft' warning, and searched the sky. He gave up looking and found that he was on his own. He wheeled around and chased after them.

Tribe caught them up as they were attacking a pair of two-seaters which were climbing away from the British Line, if there still was one, having just bombed an artillery position. Tribe knew better than to join the attack, unarmed and gunless. He circled above it, watching, in case there was anything he could do; until a passing Albatros fell on him and hammered a dozen bullets into his engine. Other aircraft joined in the fight, and before it could make a second attack the Albatros found itself under attack.

Tribe, not knowing how to fly when the propeller stopped turning, glided heavily eastwards and crash-landed in a field full of German infantry, who were having a meal before going up to join the attack. His machine struck several of the soldiers and actually killed one. Some German military police took Tribe prisoner and locked him in a barn, where they shot him fifteen minutes later.

Killion had Shufflebotham and a replacement called Beattie in his flight. He told Beattie to climb as high as he could and watch what happened, but not to join in the fighting. This Beattie did, and learned a lot.

When they landed, Finlayson came over to ask if they had seen anything of Tribe.

'Who's Tribe?' Killion asked.

'Tribe is, or was, a bad joke,' Finlayson said morosely. 'He nearly killed me, he nearly killed Richards, and then his gun jammed before he could do any real damage.'

'Never saw him.' They watched Woolley's flight land, and went indoors. Major Gibbs was waiting for Finlayson with some typed papers. 'Just sign these for me, there's a good chap,' he said.

'What are they?'

'Oh . . . depositions and arraignments and things. Legal junk to foozle the frogs. *You* know.'

'I want nothing to do with it. Sign it yourself.'

'Oh, come now, be reasonable. Nothing personal in this, you know. We're depending on you to cooperate, surely you see that?'

'I want nothing to do with it. If you don't like it, bloody well arrest me.'

'Me too,' Lambert said. 'I'm as guilty as he is. In fact I demand to be charged alongside him.'

'Hear, hear!' shouted Killion. 'Charge us all, charge us all, or don't charge anyone!' The others applauded.

'No, dammit, you can't *all* be scapegoats,' Gibbs said, 'that would be absurd . . . Finlayson, you really must do your bit, you know. I mean, one scapegoat is enough *as long as he does his bit*.'

'Bollocks.'

'Look here . . .' Gibbs sat down and thought. 'All right, I'll tell you what we'll do. *You* make a statement *denying* everything, professing innocence, know what I mean? I'll get it typed up. That'll do nicely. Also, we need a photograph.'

Finlayson laughed coarsely.

'But dammit,' said Gibbs, exasperated, 'we must have *something* to put in the French papers.' Woolley, Gabriel and Callaghan came in. 'Can't you do anything with him?' Gibbs appealed to Gabriel. 'I don't see how you can defend him unless he either denies everything or confesses something.'

Gabriel smiled winningly at Finlayson. 'Moreover Abishai the son of Zeruiah slew of the Edomites in the valley of salt eighteen thousand,' he said. 'Imagine that, *eighteen thousand*.'

'You seem bloody bright this morning,' Richards said.

196

'Ahah! I got two flamers.' Gabriel swung his arms.

'And what good did that do?' Lambert muttered.

'Oh, what good does any of it do?' Rogers interrupted. 'We kill them, and they kill us. The war still goes on downstairs, doesn't it? We're just a rotten little side-show up in the sky. Do you realize – all this was going on exactly the same *last* March? And the March before? *And* the March before? And d'you think that anyone will remember us next March? Or care?'

'That reminds me,' Lambert asked him. 'What became of our young friend?'

'I don't know. He folded his wings,' said Rogers. 'He sent in his resignation. Another triumph for gravity.'

Beattie turned white. 'You don't mean Tom King,' he said.

'I thought that was the capital of China,' Killion murmured.

'Was that his name?' Rogers shrugged.

'How did it happen? Was he shot down?' Beattie was agitated. 'Did you see it? Are you sure he crashed?'

'What does it matter?' Rogers was fed up with the subject. 'All I know is he spun in from five thousand on half a wing.'

'You mean he wasn't shot down? So he could have jumped, then.' Beattie turned on Woolley. 'Why don't they give us parachutes, for God's sake? You never knew him, you never knew what he was like . . .' Woolley looked at the twitching, furious face, and turned away. He scratched his armpits.

'I don't think I'll do any more flying today,' Finlayson said. 'I think I'll go to the pictures.' He stared across at Woolley, but Woolley stared back. 'I'm no good up there, anyhow,' Finlayson said complacently. 'I run away all the time. Don't I, Major?'

'I'd dearly bloody like to know what we're supposed to be achieving, that's all,' Lambert bitched. 'They're all over us in the air, and we can't stop them on the ground. We're just going through the motions.'

'Until the Yanks come,' Killion muttered.

'Then let 'em come,' Lambert said, 'and we'll keep the war

warm for 'em, but for God's sake don't tell me I'm helping to knacker the Kaiser by farting round in a clapped-out one-gun flying coffin, because I've seen too much of it.'

'The frogs have the right idea,' Finlayson said. ' "We won't attack. We'll defend, but we won't attack".'

'But surely . . . to win the war—' Shufflebotham's voice was drowned in laughter. Rogers and Lambert, Killion, Finlayson and Richards lay back and guffawed and waited for Woolley to do something about it. They watched him with sly greediness. For once they had him by the balls.

'You don't want to fly,' Woolley said.

'It's bloody mutiny, Major,' Finlayson said cheerfully. 'Don't you tolerate it. Have 'em all shot. That'll make 'em respect you.'

'If you don't want to fly . . . What do you want to do?'

'Speaking for myself,' Rogers said, 'I want to live.'

'I think I'll have the whole bloody lot of you transferred to the infantry,' Woolley said. There was an unreal atmosphere, like a courtroom where the jury has decided to impeach the judge.

'Oh, you can do that, certainly,' Lambert told him. 'You can throw your weight around. What you can't do is tell us what good we're doing up there, day after day. Can you?'

'There is no alternative,' Woolley said. 'It's not a question of good. *This fucking war has got to be fought.* So there.'

'The terrible part about that,' Richards said, 'is that it's perfectly true, and it's also the stupidest thing ever said.'

Woolley swung on him, eyes staring, brows raised, face stiff. The adjutant pushed open the door and cleared his throat. 'Corps on the phone, sir,' he said. 'We're off again. Squadron's transferred to Rosières. It seems that this field is in some danger of being overrun.'

As he spoke, the crack-thud of anti-aircraft fire sounded. Woolley shoved past him. A two-seater was cruising overhead at six thousand feet. The white balls of flak looked close, but Woolley knew better. Suddenly there was a heavier explosion, drowning the guns. A fountain of earth and smoke erupted in a nearby field. 'Cheeky bastard!' Woodruffe said. 'He's bombing us.'

'He's not,' Woolley said. 'He's spotting for their batteries. We're being shelled, old cock.' A second explosion blotted out a length of hedge. Woolley shouted into the hut: 'Get in the air! Quick as you can!' As Rogers came by he grabbed him, 'That's right, isn't it? You do want to live, don't you?'

Rogers twisted free and pounded across the grass. Woolley watched, and smirked. A shell scored a direct hit on a petrol tank, and he felt the wave of heat from fifty yards off. He made for his aircraft, walking fast.

Jane Ashton heard the shelling as she was packing to get out of her cottage. She opened a window and listened.

'They're bombing the aerodrome,' she said. 'I wonder—'

'Get a move on, before they start bombing us too,' Mary told her. 'If we don't get on that truck we'll be *walking* to Doullens.'

'It sounds very heavy.' She sat on the bed and chewed at a thumb-nail. 'I feel so damned helpless.'

'That's because you *are* helpless.' Mary was stuffing wet towels into a dirty pillowcase. 'What are we going to put the food in?'

'My God!' A violent explosion rattled the windows. 'Surely they can't make them fly through that, can they?' She stared at Mary, white-faced.

'I don't know what that question means, so I certainly can't give you an answer. Have we any more string?'

'I bet they move the squadron. It must be too dangerous up there now. They *must* move them. Mustn't they?'

Mary shrugged. 'Who knows? Perhaps they moved them already.'

Jane stared. She turned and dumped everything out of her suitcases.

'We'll never get a seat, my girl, unless you buck your ideas up,' Mary said sharply. 'You haven't time to fiddle-faddle about like that.'

'I'm not coming.' She was sorting out her clothes, packing some in the smaller case, throwing the rest aside. 'You go on as soon as you're ready, don't wait for me.'

'I can't possibly manage all the kitchen stuff on my own.'

'I don't care. Leave it behind. It doesn't matter, does it? What does it matter?'

Mary picked up a woollen scarf. 'Are you leaving *this*?'

'You have it, if you want it. Take anything.' Jane changed her shoes to a heavier pair. 'I'm not coming to Doullens. I've just realized, I can't come with you, Mary, I'm sorry. No, I'm not, I'm not sorry, I'm glad.'

'You're not making very much sense, I can tell you *that*.'

'I'll let you know where I am when I know it. Soon.'

'You're off after that stupid squadron. You're chasing that—'

'Goodbye, goodbye,' Jane said to shut her up. 'I've got to go, don't you see?' She grabbed the case. 'How can I go one way when he's going the other? How can I?'

'You don't even know *which* way he's going.'

'I do, I do!' She hurried out. Mary waited and watched her running down the road. 'Bitch,' she said aloud. 'Black bitch.' She found herself crying. 'Black bloody bitch.'

Rosières turned out to be a big old field, already occupied by a squadron of bombers and a squadron of Bristol Fighters. It was a converted racetrack, with the mess and administration in the grandstand. Goshawk Squadron drifted in by twos and threes. Some had chased the German two-seater all the way back to its own territory, furious at this interference by the military in their air war. Others had scrambled across the field, dodging shell-bursts, and had taken off only to forget where they were supposed to be going. Some flew to the wrong field and had to telephone around before they heard about Rosières and took off again. The adjutant drove Rogers' car and got there before anyone. Major Gibbs navigated.

It was a well-equipped field, probably the best on the

Western Front. It had a cemetery, a hospital, and an up-to-date War Room, with a direct line to Corps HQ and a vast relief map of the Front, beautifully cast in plaster of Paris and painted to show all the woods, canals, roads, railways, towns and villages along a fifty-mile stretch. The zig-zag stripes of trench-systems lay on either side like the skin shed by a massive snake. But when Woodruffe took Woolley to see it, nobody was looking at the trench-systems. A great arrow-head, outlined with coloured markers, had split the British Front wide open. Soldiers with bits of paper were moving the markers. Before long they would be off the map.

Here and there the advance had flowed around little bunches of markers, now isolated far behind the real Front. 'What are they?' Woolley asked an Intelligence officer. 'Targets?'

'Lord, no. Those are the last reported positions we got from various units. Let's see . . . that's the 21st/23rd Sherwood Foresters . . . these are the Manchester Regiment . . . over here you've got mixed units of the Black Watch and the Durham Light Infantry . . . All last reported positions, you see. Nothing fresh since then.' He picked up a marker. 'Two days ago, that lot.'

'Are they still there?'

'Oh, yes.' He thought about it. 'Well, they must be. One way or another.'

'Are we still falling back?'

'Well, we're holding them *here* and *here*.' He pointed to the extreme ends of the breakthrough. 'And we're consolidating along prepared positions, *here*.' He waved vaguely at the limits of the German advance. 'It's given us a chance to improve our overall strategic attitude by shortening our supply lines, you see.' A soldier moved some markers from one side of a canal to the other. 'The general situation is more or less fluid, in some respects,' the officer said.

'Woody, get Corps on the phone,' Woolley said. 'As far as I can see, Jerry should capture Arras the day after tomorrow, in which case the Americans can stay at home. The frogs won't fight if they lose Paris, will they?'

'*Paris* is quite safe, Major,' the Intelligence officer broke in. 'It's *Arras* we're concerned about.'

'You lose one and you've lost the other. They're shelling Paris already with those long-range cannons. From Arras they'll be able to flatten it. You see where you say we're holding them?' Woolley pointed to the extremes of the German breakthrough. 'Gateposts, mate. Pure gateposts. The gates themselves are wide open.'

Corps ordered trench-strafing. 'I flew over there two hours ago,' Woolley told the telephone. 'There isn't a trench to be seen. Our lot haven't got time to dig them, and their lot don't need to.'

'Well, strafe the blighters where they stand, then,' Corps said angrily. 'How the hell do I know? Just make sure you don't shoot the wrong men. They need all the help we can give. Fly low, damn you, and get the uniforms right.'

'Where are the French?'

'Mind your own bloody business.'

Killion and Gabriel took off together and crossed the fighting at about six thousand feet. From that height it was impossible to see any action; a great grey-brown mist of smoke covered the battleground, like an old forest fire burning itself out. To avoid attacking the wrong side, Woolley had told them to fly east until the German anti-aircraft fire opened up, and then go down and work their way westward.

Flights of Albatros patrolled at eight thousand, just below the real cloud, but they paid no attention to the SEs. As usual the flak opened up without warning, and it was horribly close. Killion saw a flash of red flames about fifty yards in front, as if someone had opened a furnace door; then a surge of black smoke drowning the brightness; and as it raced towards him he flinched at the deep-throated *woof*. Then came the harsh smell of cordite and the little chunks of shrapnel slashing at the canvas. The smoke was brown, not black. More barks were uttered all around them, and the planes bounced like boats in surf. They dived away from it.

At a thousand feet they flew into the battlesmoke drifting eastwards. They went right down to ground level and hunted around. Soon Killion lost Gabriel; presumably he went off to look at something interesting. A shattered village appeared ahead, and Killion raced over the roofless houses. The square was full of men and vehicles, with red crosses everywhere. He kept going, picked up the road to the west and followed it. A car appeared, coming towards him. He dropped a few feet until he was skimming the tarmac and gave it a brief burst. The car drove into a ditch and overturned.

War litter cluttered everything now: blown-up artillery, burned-out trucks and wagons, piles of bodies, dead horses. The fields were cratered like the moon; the trees flicked past like fence-posts, every last branch blasted away. Engineers pointed up at him from a broken bridge, and he circled and sprayed them with fire; they were still falling into the water as he left.

A mile away he came upon a German artillery position, just as it fired. The crash, and the flash of their muzzles right in front of him, made him rear up in a panicking turn; two seconds later and he'd have flown slap into that salvo . . . Machine guns rattled; the gunners were after him. He careered away into the drifting smoke, hoisted the SE over a hedge and saw white faces by the hundred underneath, filling all the field. Grey uniforms. He zig-zagged, flicking out sprays of fire to left and right. Bodies tumbled in neat rows of ten or a dozen; for a moment the automatic rhythm of the slaughter fascinated him and he waltzed the aeroplane across the crowded field with devastating precision, tumbling a dozen to the left, a dozen to the right, a dozen to the left . . . At last the drum emptied, and still the faces gaped.

Killion flew out of range, went up to five hundred feet and held the controls between his knees while he changed the drum. Then down again. He had lost the field, and was not sorry. For a while there was nothing, only broken ground and clusters of corpses at the usual places – behind houses, behind trees, behind other corpses. The smoke was thicker now, and the racket came from all sides. He followed a stream around a wood and banked past a bunch of men who were firing at a ruin. They looked neither grey nor khaki, but mud-coloured. Somebody was mortaring them. A fountain of dirt rose higher than the SE and rocked its wings. Killion sheered off, bullets pinging around him, he couldn't tell from where.

A farmhouse burned in the distance. He climbed to two hundred feet and flew over it. Shell-bursts smashed into a ridge of ground across which men were retreating, or perhaps advancing. He side-slipped down through the stink of high explosive and watched the activity. It was a retreat: they were firing behind them, and running on. He skimmed lower and saw the unmistakable flare of a kilt as a man staggered and fell.

Killion swung around and headed towards the advance. It was all smoke and the scream of shells; he saw no enemy, just the muzzle flames of machine guns and the isolated crack-flashes of rifles. A church loomed up and he flung the SE on to her wing-tips to miss it. He glimpsed the graveyard wall, studded with machine-gun posts, all battering away into the murk; straightened up and made three shallow dives parallel with the wall, stitching his bullets into the confusion of bodies grovelling and clambering for safety. By then heavy rifle fire was splitting the air around him from all sides, and he fled.

A mile to the east he came across a field battery being set up. The horses were only half-unhitched from the limbers and the gun crews had no small-arms ready. It was like stoning the lunatics in Bedlam. Killion rattled off his remaining half a drum and sailed home.

When Gabriel left Killion he went down to ten feet and hedge-hopped his way to the fighting without seeing anything that was worth a burst. He reached the area of shell-fire and

204

searched up and down, trying to establish some definite lines; but there was no Front any more. Scattered groups seemed to be firing in any direction, and the smoke and filth disguised all uniform. Once he saw a village being captured, but the fighting was too confused for him to interfere safely. Everybody on the ground had a go at him, however. Eventually he gave up and climbed to three hundred feet.

Immediately he saw, off to his left, the glint of a canal. A Halberstadt was flying just above it and shooting down at the tow-path. Gabriel dived, curling so as to catch the enemy plane from behind. The observer and the pilot were busy spraying fire at an endless line of troops lying in the dip behind the path. Gabriel hurried to catch up, closed to within ten feet of the tail, and held the SE steady for a hammerblow of a burst. It was so simple. One moment the Halberstadt was drifting along, raking death into the infantry, and the next it crashed hard on its nose into the tow-path and burst into flames. Gabriel climbed away and saw men running from the heat. Over his engine he just heard the hoarse roar of a cheer. Salvation, he thought.

He turned east, booming out the words of Psalm 47: O *clap your hands, all ye people; shout unto God with the voice of triumph. For the Lord most high is terrible; he is a great King over all the earth* . . . He found a sunken road and followed it, singing and listening to the clatter of his engine rebounding up at him. The road twisted, and when he turned with it a column of infantry six wide was marching towards him, rifles slung. Gabriel had to dive to bring his gun to bear on them, so he switchbacked along, hauling up to forty feet and then diving while he sprayed the packed mass. *He shall subdue the people under us, and the nations under our feet* . . . Gabriel rose and dipped, and hosed the column vigorously and efficiently, as if destroying wasps with boiling water. *God is gone up with a shout, the Lord with the sound of a trumpet* . . . Hoist up and ease down, and squeeze the trigger while the bullets pump into the stockaded soldiers, and release and pull out. What a long column. *Sing praises to*

God, sing praises; sing praises unto our King, sing praises. Down again, a touch of rudder to the right, how they scramble up those steep banks, squeeze . . . *For God is the King of all the earth*!

The drum ran out as the column ended, men fighting each other to get out of his way. Gabriel climbed and changed the drum. He decided not to go back to the column, since they would be expecting him now. He went looking for another sunken road, and found one, only this time it was full of horse-traffic: gun-limbers and ammunition wagons and water-tankers and a few old ambulances – a long column with men riding everywhere to save their legs.

He switchbacked again, leaving a devastation of plunging, rearing, bullet-holed horses, and cursing, fleeing men. The tail-end of the column saw him coming and sent up a hail of rifle fire, but Gabriel swept through. He climbed to a thousand feet and examined the damage below. Away in the distance he could see the first column; men were laying out bodies in the field, at least a hundred already. Gabriel went down in a power-dive and used up his last rounds on the working party. Then he headed for home. *Lift up your heads, O ye gates!* he boomed. *Even lift them up, ye everlasting doors; and the King of glory shall come in!*

Woolley, Finlayson and Beattie were the only Goshawk pilots who actually found the German advance that day and stopped it for a while. There was a report that a bridge had not been blown in time, that the Germans had grabbed it. The only way Corps could find out was by sending an aeroplane. Woolley made a patrol out of it.

The bridge was neither lost nor held. At one end men in khaki were throwing grenades; at the other end men in grey were trying to drag a field-gun into position. Once that field-gun began firing nothing would save the bridge. Woolley dived and shot it up and drove the German troops back. As he curled away they rushed forward. Finlayson skimmed over the bridge and drove them back. Beattie followed him up. By that time, Woolley had circled and was boring in for another attack.

The Germans tried three times. Each time, the gun crew was killed, and under cover of the last attack the British troops ran halfway across the bridge and rolled their grenades up to the abandoned field-gun. The Germans pulled back.

Woolley took his flight up to a thousand feet and circled, watching. After ten minutes he saw the Germans massing for a fresh attempt. As the first men ran forward, the SEs swooped and strafed the bridge. The attack died. The British were stronger now, and they had started mortaring the hidden German positions. Woolley went back up into the sky.

They prowled around for another fifteen minutes. Woolley knew that Corps was waiting for a report, but this was obviously more important. British reinforcements were creeping up all the time. Artillery from somewhere was trying to shell the bridge. It was too good to last: eventually six Albatros arrived to chase the SEs away.

Woolley and Beattie dived westwards. Finlayson turned to follow and at once his engine stopped. The comforting clatter up front simply ceased, and he heard instead the snarl of enemy planes above and the crash of explosives below and the stutter of a machine gun. He sat there drifting, naked, appallingly helpless. Obviously Woolley hadn't noticed it; he was probably shepherding Beattie. The machine started to stall, and Finlayson came out of his shock and thrust the joystick forward. The ground hurried upwards in a sort of pockmarked silence, dreamlike, and Finlayson nervously flattened the dive to look for a landing place. It was all stream-bank and shell-holes. With a vague fear of fire he went to switch off the engine, changed his mind for no reason and tried the reserve fuel tank. The engine fired at once and roared in perfect health. Finlayson scooted down the valley, soggy with relief until he heard the crackle of machine guns behind him and adrenalin rushed back into his bloodstream.

It was a single Albatros, and it chased him for a couple of miles until Finlayson got desperate and aimed the SE quite suicidally between two tall trees. The German wisely banked away. Finlayson squeaked through the gap and was free.

He knew that the reserve tank was small, and climbed for home, bearing 270 degrees. But the compass refused to settle and he found himself circling, with no idea which way was west. He climbed higher to search for landmarks and saw a vaguely familiar wood off to his right. It was shaped like a blunt diamond. He twisted his head, trying to remember how it lay and where it pointed. An old Fokker Triplane crept up behind him, easing in from the blind side. Finlayson saw a town he knew, and calculated that he was flying north. He banked left just as the Triplane opened fire, and took the bullets in his petrol tank instead of his body.

A long plume of white vapour sprang from the tank and trailed, flaring, in his slipstream. Finlayson switched off the engine. It was not inevitable that the vapour would catch fire. Not inevitable. He smelled the stench of petrol drowning the clean air. It was soaking into his boots, chilling his legs. He glided easily into the sun. He was at about five thousand feet. Where was the Triplane? Flying alongside, watching.

Finlayson fished out his Colt revolver and fired three shots at the Triplane. The bastard didn't even move. The drenching petrol crept towards the SE's red-hot exhausts and the whole aircraft went up with a rush. Finlayson shot himself in the head.

'Damn,' said Major Gibbs. 'The French won't like that.' He threw his brief-case on to the desk. 'I was afraid something like this might happen, you know,' he said. 'Just when we were doing so well, too. I've got a photographer coming over in an hour.'

'It can't be helped,' the adjutant said.

'I suppose there's no doubt? A forced landing, maybe . . .'

'Some chaps in 46 Squadron saw it happen. They even got his number right.'

'Ah.'

'I suppose you'd better see the old man. I take it you'll need a replacement.'

Gibbs nodded gloomily. 'The pressure's still on. The French won't be satisfied until we produce the goods.' He paused in the doorway. 'What about using Dickinson? I could stall them until he gets out of hospital. It's worth a try.'

'Didn't I tell you about Dickinson?'

'No. What? Not available?'

'Afraid not, Gangrene, or something. Last night.'

'Oh dear.'

'Sorry. I thought I told you. I *meant* to tell you, only all this rushing about . . .'

'Quite. Oh, well.'

They found Woolley in the bomber squadron's bar, which Goshawk pilots were allowed to use. All the survivors were there, standing in a wide circle, holding drinks. The atmosphere was uncomfortable; even the bomber pilots looked on warily. Woodruffe and Gibbs got themselves a drink and waited for Woolley to stop talking. He was saying something to Rogers about cricket: asking a question or checking an opinion. 'Of course,' Woodruffe murmured to Gibbs. 'Squadron party. Rogers' M.C. came through today. Celebration.'

'I remember!' said Woolley brightly. They looked at him apprehensively. 'G. W. Grace, that was it. He was pretty good, wasn't he?' He suddenly sounded forty years old.

'W. G. Grace, you mean,' Rogers mumbled.

'Ah!' Woolley said. 'Yes? He was good at cricket, was he? I mean . . . you know, as good as all that?'

Rogers stared at his drink and cleared his throat.

'I'd heard about him,' Woolley said. 'I thought I'd ask you.' He wiped his nose carefully, tucking the handkerchief up his sleeve. The gesture fascinated Lambert. 'I knew that cricket was a hobby of yours, of course.'

'Of course. Yes.'

209

Woolley smoothed his face and shaped his chin. He looked at the light fixtures, and tugged at the skin over his Adam's apple. Richards whistled a tune, but it sounded wrong, so he let it die.

'Um,' Woolley said. He looked sideways, his chin down. 'Are we all here? I don't see . . . Mr Killion. Is he coming, does anyone know?'

None of the pilots spoke. The adjutant said: 'I think he's gone down to the village, sir. He has a girl-friend down there, an English girl. He spends all his spare time down there, now.'

'Ah. Lucky chap, eh? I wish I . . .' Woolley hunched his shoulders and stared at nothing. Richards cleared his throat, a tiny sound. Woolley looked at him. 'He was going to be a doctor, wasn't he? Medicine . . . It's a grand thing, isn't it, medicine?'

'Is it, sir?' Richards said woodenly.

'Oh yes. Yes, I think so. I mean, where would we be without doctors?'

He looked at their faces in turn, and they all looked away, pretending to consider the question.

'How is Shufflebotham, sir?' asked Beattie.

'Funny thing, that.' Woolley seized on the subject. 'Nobody actually saw him. Big field like this, you'd expect someone to see, but no. Nobody actually . . . saw it. *Heard* it, yes. Funny thing, that, isn't it? Odd . . .' He had stretched the subject as far as it would go, and now he stood trying to stretch it further. Lambert put down his glass and knocked over an ash tray. Woolley looked at him worriedly. '*You* didn't see him, did you, Lambert?'

'No, no, no,' Lambert muttered. He went off to get another drink.

'So . . . how is he, sir?' Beattie repeated.

Woolley looked at Beattie for a long time. 'Not very well, I'm afraid,' he said softly. 'Broken . . . things. Arms. And head. You must be . . . Mackenzie.'

'Beattie, sir.'

'Really? Oh. We had a Beattie last year . . . I don't remember much about him, though. Would anyone like a drink?'

Nobody answered.

'It's on me, you know. CO's treat, this time.'

Nobody spoke.

'I saw a horse, in a field,' Woolley said. He looked around and found Richards and told him again. 'Saw this horse, in a field. Not far from here.' When Richards looked away, he said: 'You're keen on horses, aren't you? I seem to remember . . .'

'Sir.'

'We ought to get some. For off-duty.'

'Sir.'

'You could teach the others, perhaps. Chaps like me.'

'Sir.'

Gibbs touched the adjutant's arm and steered him away. 'What the devil's he up to?' he whispered.

'I should have thought it was obvious,' Woodruffe said softly. 'He's trying to make friends. God knows why.'

'Strikes me he's making a bloody fool of himself . . . Anyway, I need to get on with the other thing.'

'Go ahead, then.'

Gibbs walked over to Woolley. 'Awfully sorry to barge in on your celebration binge like this,' he said.

'Don't mensh,' Woolley said. 'You know everybody here, don't you?'

'It's about . . . Finlayson, you see.'

'Very little you can expect me to do about him, I'm afraid.' Woolley smiled a gentle smile which included everybody.

'No, but . . . Well, I need to go ahead, just the same.' He waited for Woolley to suggest something, or tell him to come back tomorrow, or forget the whole damn thing. 'Corps has promised the French their pound of flesh, you see. That's the only reason why . . . I mean, you know how the battle is going, we're in Queer Street . . . I agree, it's scandalous, but

211

Corps say we must have a scapegoat. Pure politics, you see. My hands are tied. Absolutely tied.'

Woolley let him finish. He chewed his lip while he thought about it, glancing cautiously at Rogers, Richards, Gabriel, Lambert and Beattie in turn.

Woodruffe broke the silence: 'Let's face it, the whole damn nonsense is a complete . . . nonsense. I mean, it might as well be *Kitchener* on a charge as any one of us.'

'Captain Rogers,' Woolley said at last. 'This seems to be your day for fame.'

Rogers hunched his shoulders and stared at Woolley's feet. There was a profoundly unhappy silence.

'Right, then,' Gibbs said. 'I'll get the documents altered tonight.'

Lambert walked out and slammed the door. Woolley stood with an empty glass in his hand, and blinked at Gibbs' empty sleeve. Richards drank up and left. One by one the others followed, until only Woolley, Gibbs and the adjutant were left.

'Funny business,' Woolley said.

A telephone rang, and the barman answered it. 'Major Woolley?' he called out.

'That must be Kitchener,' Woolley said. 'I expect he wants to plead Not Guilty.'

The guardroom was warm and dim, and smelled of toast. Two corporals were guarding her. They saluted Woolley. 'No identification, sir,' one said. 'Found wanderin' over by the hangar, sir. Distressed condition, sir. Says you can identify her, sir.'

'My dear Margery,' Woolley said. 'What on earth . . .'

'It was dark and I fell over a rope.' Her voice shook. 'They ran up and captured me.'

'And about time, too. I've been trying to find you for ages.'

'No, you haven't.'

'Honestly.'

'How can you talk about honestly? Or honesty. Or whatever it is.'

'My dear Margery—'

'No I'm not, I'm *not*.' She jumped up and ran to the door, but he grabbed her and she stumbled and they ended up holding each other.

'I take it you can positively identify this lady, sir?' the corporal said.

'But where've you *been*?' Woolley asked her.

'Waiting. Bloody waiting.'

'Where?'

'Sign here, sir, please.' The corporal gave Woolley a pen and held out a form on a clip-board. He signed for her and took her outside.

'I called you three times at the hospital,' he said. '*Four* times. They said you weren't there.'

'I wasn't there, I was near you. Just outside Achiet. In the pub at Bihucourt . . . to be near you. I couldn't stand going back to that rotten hospital, miles away from you, and waiting for the rotten telephone. I couldn't stand it, so I didn't go back after last time, I stayed. I've been there for ten bloody days.'

'But I didn't *know*. I kept calling the hospital and they said—'

'No you didn't, because I told them where I was going and if you called they were going to telephone me at the pub and tell me and then I'd know. But you never called so I stayed at that rotten pub. You never called.'

'I *did* call. Four times. I gave up because they said you were never there. I thought—'

'Then they must have forgotten. Or something. Is that it?'

'I don't know. I don't care. What does it matter? Where are we going?' He stopped and brushed the hair from her eyes. 'I'd given up. I thought you'd gone off home, or something . . . Are you all right? You look—'

'I just couldn't keep going back and forth between you and

213

the hospital, I *couldn't*. I wanted to be near you, even if you
. . . I used to walk out to the airfield and watch the planes
landing. I wanted you to call . . .' The tears came.

'Oh God,' Woolley whispered. 'Oh God. I thought you had
gone. I really thought you had gone for good. Never do that
again. Never.'

Force 12: Hurricane

Only strongest structures can withstand

T he dawn was an overdone backdrop for an expensive opera when Woolley strolled in through the gates of the airfield. The sentry saluted; Woolley touched his forelock and said, 'Thank 'ee kindly.' Inside the hut the guard corporal turned, stared and reached for the telephone.

Woolley walked as far as the aircraft and stood looking at the extravagant pinks and creams flooding the eastern sky. From the horizon came the irregular, muffled noises of artillery, grunting like sleeping hounds. He stretched, and stood with his legs apart, hands clasped on his head.

'Thank God you're back,' Woodruffe called, hurrying over. 'Corps's been on the phone all night, they want you to do two patrols as soon as possible, both frightfully urgent, there's a counter-attack, it's all down here.' He pushed maps and papers into Woolley's hands, and stared anxiously.

'What a glorious day,' Woolley said, fanning himself with the documents. 'Look at that sky.'

'What? Listen, they're in a terrible state up at Corps, they seem to think if this counter-attack doesn't work it's the end of the world. I don't know, you'd think they'd have learnt better by now, but still . . . They wanted me to go out and *find* you, for God's sake . . .'

'I've been down at the inn, Woody, and it wouldn't have done you any good to come looking, either.' The adjutant was not listening; he was looking at his watch and peering anxiously about him. 'And back to the bloody old inn I shall go just as soon as I can,' Woolley added.

'Quite. Quite,' Woodruffe said. 'I just hope to God they're all up by now. I ordered breakfast for ten minutes ago. Corps was *furious* when I told them I couldn't guarantee anything until you got back. They wanted—'

'Breakfast,' Woolley said. 'Now I could do with some of that.' He set off for the mess, papers spilling from under his arm. Woodruffe rescued them and hurried after. 'You know the difference between men and women, Woody? I'll tell you, I've just found it out, and it's bloody significant, too: men find causes to die for, and women find causes to live for.'

'So I've heard. It's not exactly original, you know.'

'By Christ, it's original to me.'

'Corps wanted Rogers to take over. I had to tell them he was sick. They didn't go for *that*, either, I can tell you. Then they got on to Gibbs, wanted to know why he hadn't set up the court-martial yet. *That* did even less good.'

'Why?'

'Gibbs had been drinking. With Rogers. He told Corps that you were off your – that you were unreliable. I think Corps fired him, I'm not sure.'

'*Is* Rogers sick?'

'He's *been* sick. Several times. I should think he's horribly hung-over now. He and Gibbs got through a bottle of Scotch and decided to – to sort you out.'

'Sort me out? How?'

'Well . . . beat you up, if you must know. Anyway, you weren't there so they smashed up your room instead. Then they started on the gin. All the Scotch was gone. Every time Corps came on the phone, Rogers insisted on talking to them. He kept blowing his whistle and shouting, "Under the top! Under the top!" I've had the devil's own time, what with Corps wanting to know what the hell—'

Woolley stopped with his hand on the mess door. '*Under* the top?'

216

'Oh, don't ask me, some kind of a joke. Instead of over the top.'

'Oh.'

'Over the top was no good any more, he said. The chap was blind drunk. Potty.'

They went inside. Woolley said: 'Morning, gents. Drink up your slops, it's dragon-slaying time again.'

All conversation ceased. Richards pushed his plate away and sat hugging his stomach. Gabriel continued to eat heartily, buttering toast and sucking at a mug of tea while he chewed. Lambert slowly turned his back and stretched his legs. Beattie and Callaghan looked nervously at the others; Killion yawned. Rogers made no move, but sat holding his head in his hands. A bowl of porridge lay in front of him, and as Woolley walked past he squinted at it. 'Are you going to eat that, Dudley?' he asked. 'Or have you already?' Callaghan tittered, then flushed at the others' silence.

'Make me a bacon sandwich,' Woolley told the mess orderly. 'Make it nice and fatty. And put some Daddies Sauce on it.' He poured himself a mug of tea and stirred in a big spoonful of condensed milk. They watched or ignored him with hostility, apprehension or indifference.

'To your new commanding officer!' he said, raising the mug. 'A man of unquestionable honour, chivalry and patriotism, by whom you will find it a real pleasure to be misled!' He drank noisily. Killion raised his eyebrows at Woodruffe, who shrugged.

'Don't forget that Corps want me to call them as soon as possible about that patrol,' the adjutant said wearily.

'Eat! Eat!' Woolley shouted. He pointed at Richards' plate. 'Gallant sailors drowned to bring you that bit of fried bread, cully. Christ, just because you work in a knacker's yard you don't have to be squeamish about your grub. You do a bloody awful job, sewermen to the sky by royal appointment, but why make it worse?' He took the sandwich from the orderly's plate and waved it about. 'Why make the worst of it when you can make the best of it? Right? The condemned man ate a hearty breakfast, three cheers, everyone feels better for that. What about the poor old bloody executioner? Nobody comes over and asks him if his egg's too hard. Look after yourself, no other bugger will.' He bit into his sandwich and tore away a length of streaky bacon. 'Isn't that right, Gabriel?' he said through the food.

Gabriel put down his tea. 'For the indignation of the Lord is upon all nations,' he announced, 'and his fury upon all their armies: he hath utterly destroyed them, he hath delivered them to their slaughter.' He glanced around to make sure that they understood. 'Their slain also shall be cast out, and their stink shall come up out of their carcasses, and the mountains shall be melted with their blood.' He snapped his fingers to indicate the thoroughness of the destruction.

'Good,' Woolley said. 'I'm glad somebody's enjoying his war.'

The telephone rang. Woodruffe took it. '*Corps*,' he whispered savagely, although his palm covered the mouthpiece. 'They *must* know *now*. When can you send the first patrol? Target A.' He pointed to Woolley's documents. They could hear the angry crackle continuing to demand action.

Woolley picked up a piece of paper. 'Ten minutes,' he said. The paper was upside-down. 'A quarter of an hour,' Woodruffe told the telephone. It grated viciously in reply. 'Oh my God,' he said. The instrument delivered one final harshness, then clicked dead. He stared at it as if it had spat on his hand. 'They've sent a colonel to find out what's going on,' he said. 'Corps have sent a colonel. They say he'll raise hell. He left half an hour ago.'

'Always glad to welcome our chums from Corps,' Woolley said. He put his head on one side, trying to read the upside-down writing. 'Anybody here understand Hebrew?' he asked.

Someone knocked on the door. 'That can't be him already,' Killion said before he could stop himself.

It wasn't. It was two very young replacement pilots. 'Shut the door. I hope you last longer than the last two,' Woolley

218

told them. Abruptly, Rogers was sick into his porridge. 'Thank God for that, I thought he was dead,' Woolley said. 'Now that you're fit and well again, Captain Rogers, you can lead the first patrol. Gabriel and Killion will fly with you.' He turned the paper round and read it properly. 'You're to attack a big old house which Jerry is using for his HQ, or something. It's all down here.' He flicked the sheet across. 'Go in low, blast it, get out fast. Ta-ta.'

Killion pulled the flying-coat around Rogers' shoulders and fed the other trembling arm into a sleeve. 'You don't have to go, you know,' he said, trying to make it sound matter-of-fact. 'You can tell him you're sick. You *are* sick, anyone can see that.' He buttoned the collar under Rogers' stubbly chin. 'I'll tell him, if you like.'

Rogers looked up at him until the light hurt his eyes. 'I wouldn't give the fucking bastard that pleasure,' he said. 'Hold that flask.'

Killion held the whisky and let Rogers suck at it. The spirit ran down his chin. He coughed, and pushed the flask away, and spat untidily. Then he tugged the flask back and drank some more. He stopped, and lay back. 'Fucking G. W. Grace,' he said.

'Lambert, one,' Woolley said. He chalked the name on the wall. 'Richards, two. Me, three. Beattie, four. Callaghan, five.' He drew a line around them. 'Say five. Only it's three, because I'm not going to take Beattie or Callaghan. There's bound to be more flying later on. I'll save them.' He put down the chalk. 'Okay?'

He and Woodruffe were standing in Woolley's billet. All that was breakable had been smashed. His accordion lay huddled in a corner, ripped and battered.

Woodruffe looked at the names, and then rubbed his tired, unhappy face. 'Three won't be enough, will it?' He felt a hardness inside, as if his stomach contained stone. 'They'll never agree, it's too important. It's a *counter*-attack.'

'Yes, but Beattie . . .' Woolley put his head on one side and examined the name. He took back the chalk and tidied up the double-t. 'He hasn't the experience. They both need training. They've only been out here a couple of days.'

'Three days.'

Woolley wrote 3 on the wall and looked at it. 'No, no,' he said.

Woodruffe picked out a paper from the bundle of maps and documents. 'Corps order,' he said. 'Every available pilot flies, irrespective of experience. We're to send up seven machines on the second patrol or give a written explanation why. It's all down here.'

Woolley went over and picked broken glass from a window. 'Things seem to have been taken out of my hands,' he said.

'You see, they know that the replacements are here,' the adjutant told him. 'They sent them. And this colonel is coming over to make sure they all fly.'

'*Then he can bloody well tell them himself!*' Woolley shouted. He seized the remains of a crate of Guinness and hurled it into a corner. A broken bottle emptied black liquid on to the floor, choking on its own foam. He went to the door and looked at the sunshine. 'Dear God . . .' he said quietly. 'That wouldn't do any good, though, would it. Better send them over here and let me talk to them.'

Woodruffe went out and then turned back. 'What shall I tell Corps?' he asked. There were tears in his eyes.

'Tell them to keep the war going. We'll join in as soon as we can.'

Gabriel was waiting by his SE when Rogers and Killion came out. He watched them trail over to their machines, and on an impulse he hurried across. His long stride, his high shoulders, his bony forehead, his intent expression: Gabriel meant business. 'Oh Christ,' Rogers muttered.

Gabriel raised an arm, signalling for their attention. 'For it is the day of the Lord's vengeance,' he called, 'and the year of recompenses for the controversy of Zion.'

220

'For Christ's sake get rid of the silly bastard!' Rogers told Killion, but Gabriel's gaze was keen and his voice was firm.

'The sword of the Lord is filled with blood,' he proclaimed. He pointed to the east. 'The Lord hath a sacrifice in Bozrah, and a great slaughter in the land of Idumea.'

'Piss off, Gabriel,' Killion said. He gave Rogers a lift-up to help him climb on to the wing, and then boosted him into the cockpit. 'Piss off!' he repeated as Gabriel came closer.

'For behold, the Lord will come with fire, and with his chariots like a whirlwind—'

'Go to hell!' Rogers shouted. 'Go and run up your arse!' He coughed painfully, and spat, and the breeze carried some of his spittle on to Gabriel's sleeve.

Gabriel looked down at it, and looked up at Rogers. He was pale, and he frowned fiercely. 'Therefore will I number you to the sword!' he shouted. 'And ye shall all bow down to the slaughter: because when I called, ye did not answer; when I spake—'

The engine fired as a mechanic swung the propeller; the roar drowned out Gabriel's threats. Killion was already halfway to his own plane. Gabriel stood for a moment in the gusty slip-stream, blinking and glaring, then he turned away. He was close behind Rogers when they took off; uncomfortably close, thought Killion.

'Lovely day,' Woolley said. He stood in the doorway of his ruined billet and snuffled at the sunshine. 'You must be . . . uh . . . Mackenzie and . . . uh . . .' A yawn overtook him.

'Wallace and Cowie, sir. I'm Wallace.' The replacement spoke alertly but respectfully, and tried not to look at the stains on Woolley's breeches.

'Yes. I expect you're right. Had breakfast? Let's take a walk around the field.' They strolled away from the aircraft. Woolley walked lazily, hands in pockets, and blinked at the blue sky. Wallace and Cowie did an uncomfortably slow march and tried not to swing their arms. They covered a hundred yards without speaking. Once, Woolley stopped to

221

watch a bird. He yawned frequently. Finally Wallace lost patience. 'The adjutant says we'll be flying this morning, sir,' he said. 'Jolly lucky, that, isn't it?'

'Lucky?' Woolley thought about it, then gave up. 'Are either of you married?'

They construed this as a possible obstacle, and said no.

'There's a lot to be said for it, even out here. Maybe *especially* out here. When you think about it, it's obvious really.'

'Yes, sir.'

'A lot to be said for it . . . Done lots of flying, have you?'

'As much as we could, sir,' Wallace said. 'The weather hasn't been awfully good in England lately.'

'No. Still, I expect you're okay on turns.'

'Turns, sir? You mean . . . banking? We all did banking—'

'No, no. Turns. Tight turns.' He demonstrated with his hands. 'Chase-your-tail turns.'

'We haven't actually done those yet, sir,' said Cowie.

'Struth. Well you *should* have. What about . . . Immelmanns? Rolls? Spins?'

'Not much, sir, I'm afraid,' Wallace said. 'Hardly any, really.' He was afraid Woolley might take them off the morning patrol.

'They said we'd get all that when we got to France, sir,' Cowie explained. 'We did mainly banking. And take-offs and landings, of course.'

'But you've got to be able to turn,' Woolley said anxiously. 'I mean, that's what it's all about, turning.' He rubbed his eyes, and looked at them, searching for improvement.

'I can do the loop, sir,' Cowie said helpfully. Wallace was silent.

'Well, how many hours have you got, anyway?' Woolley asked.

'I've got eight, sir, and he's got ten,' Wallace said.

Woolley stopped. 'Solo?'

'No, sir. All told.'

Woolley turned away and looked at the countryside. The fields lay empty in the easy sunshine. *I could order them to go*, he thought. *I could command them to walk away from this place and never come back. And I could go too.* 'And how many hours in SEs?' he asked.

Each waited for the other to speak. 'Oh, for God's sake,' Woolley said. He began walking again. 'I don't suppose you've done any low-level flying either,' he said. 'Or any air-to-air firing. In fact I don't know what in God's bleeding name you're doing here at all.'

'We've fired machine guns in the butts, sir. We can—'

'Listen, listen. Just stay out of trouble. Don't go anywhere *near* a Hun. If anybody even looks at you, fly away. Just get back home, that's all that matters. You shouldn't be in this, understand? It's all a mistake, you're not ready for it.'

'I'm nineteen, sir,' Wallace said stiffly. 'Without disrespect, sir, I'm ready for anything.'

'Shut up. Do as you're told. Just get back here in one piece, never mind the heroics. Leave the war to itself.'

'I take it we can open fire if any enemy plane comes within range, though, can't we, sir?' Cowie asked courteously.

'God help you if the enemy ever gets within range. Oh, Christ, I don't want to talk about it. Just shut up about it. We're all bloody cannibals here, we eat bloody death for bloody breakfast, it's what keeps us going. I didn't ask you to come here. Do you *want* to die? Christ, I don't.'

They all stared: Woolley sick with disgust, Wallace and Cowie startled and embarrassed. After a moment, Woolley looked away. A staff car was bumping over the airfield. He blew his nose, and waited.

Woodruffe, Gibbs and Colonel Hawthorn got out.

'Why aren't you on patrol, Woolley?' Hawthorn demanded. 'I insist that you take off forthwith. It is imperative. Get your squadron in the air, man, and look lively.'

'Look . . . these two aren't ready to go,' Woolley said. 'They're not trained, they've got no experience, they won't be the slightest use to anyone. It's just throwing away lives and I won't do it.'

'Who are they?' Hawthorn asked the adjutant.

'Lieutenants Wallace and Cowie, sir,' Woodruffe said. 'New replacement pilots. Came in this morning.'

'They look perfectly fit to me. This is an important attack, that's what you Flying-Corps wallahs don't appreciate. The Corps commander requires full support. Every pilot must fly. And that is an order.'

'Oh, balls,' Woolley said weakly. Hawthorn smiled with delight. 'I expected that,' he said. 'Major Gibbs: you will arrange court-martial proceedings against this officer on a charge of refusing to obey an order.' He thwacked his breeches with his cane.

'Sorry, sir,' said Gibbs hoarsely. He was ashen, and his eyes were pink and puffy. 'Didn't quite follow . . . Is this for the French, or . . .' But Hawthorn was talking to Woolley. 'There's no room for eccentrics in this war, Woolley,' he said briskly. 'The whole Corps must move as one man. Like a machine. Irresistibly. Smashing forward. All striking at the same target, together.'

'That reminds me,' Woodruffe said. 'This just came from Corps HQ.'

Woolley tore the envelope open. 'The first patrol is cancelled,' he said. 'Change of plan.'

'Good,' Hawthorn said. 'All the more for the second patrol.'

'If they come back.'

'That's not your responsibility.'

'No? They're my pilots.'

'Oh yes, of course. You're the one who keeps court-martialling them.'

'I should have put that bullet through your bloody head, not your hat.' Woolley was too defeated to be angry.

'Are you going on patrol, or shall I have you replaced here and now?'

'Bastard,' Woolley said. He looked at Gibbs. 'B-A-S-T-A-R-D,' he said.

They got into the car.

*　　*　　*

224

Killion landed while the pilots were assembling to be briefed.

He flew in hurriedly, landed across wind, and taxied right up to the buildings before he got out. Hawthorn tapped Woolley with his cane. 'We can't wait for the others,' he said. 'This is extremely urgent.' Woolley ignored him and went to the door and shouted to Killion.

Even Hawthorn was silenced by the look on Killion's face. 'We never even got there,' he said. 'It was the most incredible thing.'

'The patrol was cancelled anyway,' Woolley said. 'It didn't matter.'

'We used that main road as a bearing. It runs dead straight, due east. It was full of our troops, packed with them, all moving up, packed solid. Anyway . . . we got halfway there, pretty low, about two hundred feet . . . Then Gabriel . . . for no reason at all . . . he went down after them.'

'Down after them?' Richards stared. 'After who?'

'*Our* blokes! He just went down and started strafing them! Just flew up and down the road and let fly. At the troops. He just cut them down, I mean he was slaughtering them. You see . . . they weren't expecting it, they were right out in the open, they didn't know what to do. I could see them standing looking up at him. They could see the roundels, they *knew* he was British.'

'Gabriel wouldn't do that,' Lambert said. He looked around. 'Why would Gabriel do that?'

'But he did, he did. I saw it, they were lying all over the place – dozens, he just kept on firing, he must've emptied a drum by the time we caught him. Rogers got there first and chased him away. We didn't know what to do, we couldn't . . .'

'He will be court-martialled,' Colonel Hawthorn said firmly.

'Where has he gone now?' Richards asked.

'You see . . . we were too stunned . . . we just chased him away and looked at him . . . I mean, I suppose we both thought he'd made a mistake.'

'It could happen,' Lambert said.

'No, no, impossible. He *knew*. We saw him reload, he was going to go *back down* . . . So Rogers had a go at him, you know . . . tried to force him to land. But then he tried to kill Rogers, and finally they had the devil of a fight.'

'And?' Woolley said.

'Rogers shot him down. Only it wasn't like that. Gabriel's plane came to pieces, it just fell apart. I saw him fall, I saw it all happen. Everything.'

'Where's Rogers now?'

'Crashed,' Killion said. 'I think he took a bullet and passed out. He must be dead, too.'

Woolley sat in his cockpit, tightening and loosening his straps. Engines roared around him; all except his own. His mechanic stood with both hands on the propeller, staring impassively at Woolley's face. They were all ready to go, all waiting for him to lead the squadron into the air. Only Killion stayed behind. Killion, who – Hawthorn had decided – was too valuable as a witness of Gabriel's massacre to be risked on patrol. Lucky Killion.

Surprisingly, here was Killion now, running across the airfield, still in his flying-clothes. Woolley waved him back but he came on. He reached the plane and stood panting, embarrassed but determined. 'Just wanted to say,' he gasped, 'sorry I'm not with you. And good luck. And so on. Sir.' His chest heaved; his cheeks were bright red.

Woolley tried to smile, but his face was the wrong shape for that. He pointed thankfully over Killion's shoulder. 'Somebody wants you, Killion,' he said. Killion looked back. Jane Ashton was standing beside the adjutant, in front of Rogers' limousine. Killion was upset. 'I didn't send for her, sir. Honest,' he said.

'I did. I sent Woody to pick her up. When I knew you wouldn't be flying.'

'Really? What for?' Killion looked between them in amazement.

'I don't know. Margery told me about her last night. Margery knows her. For Christ's sake, Killion. How many bloody reasons do you need?' He looked the other way, unable to face what he had done.

When he turned back, Killion was pounding across the field towards her. The girl walked forward. Woolley shouted at his mechanic. The engine fired first time, and he powered it savagely until the whole plane shuddered. When he looked again the two figures were standing together watching him.

Still Woolley waited. He searched the cockpit: this was home, more familiar than any tent or billet; he knew every scratch and dent, every stain and patch. It was home and he was trapped in it. He sat and hated the cockpit for its emptiness, hated himself for his indecision, hated Hawthorn for his war.

Woolley leaned his head back and looked at the sky. For the first time ever, he wanted not to go up there. The sky was for killing and he was sick of death. His brain stealthily surrendered to images of Margery. Margery waving from the wheel of an ambulance. Margery glistening with a sheen of sweat in the light of a pressure lamp. Margery weeping over what they would call their home. Margery stiff and angry outside the guardroom. Margery shivering and saying goodbye at dawn.

'*Take off immediately.*' It was Colonel Hawthorn, standing beside the cockpit, shouting over the din. '*That is a direct order from the Corps Commander.*' He waved a revolver at Woolley's head.

All the way to the Front, Woolley went through the routine of searching the sky, but the images of Margery persisted. The pleasure of her nagged at him, and the thought of them both, of being together, distracted his brain. Although his eyes looked they did not see, and his reactions were too slow when a flight of slim grey machines knifed down from the glare of the sun. The first burst wrecked his cockpit and the SE turned sharply on her back. Woolley fell out, and the last that Wallace and Cowie saw of him, before they sheered away in fright, was his long brown flying-coat opening in the wind and checking his fall. For a moment it billowed out and let his smoking plane fall away; and then the coat collapsed, and Woolley dropped too.

Afterword

In 1968, when the R.A.F. was fifty years old, I read one of the many articles written to celebrate that jubilee. It contained some remarks by a former R.F.C. pilot, Oliver Stewart. He said that, to be strictly honest about it, the objective of a fighter pilot in the First World War 'was to sneak in unobserved close behind his opponent and then shoot him in the back'.

I was startled. I had grown up on Biggles, and that didn't sound like Biggles. Stewart went on, 'Bar-room brawling, bicycle chains and broken bottles have a closer affinity to the early fighting in the air than the chivalrous, formalised, knightly encounters with lance and épée to which it has been likened'.

Much of that likening was first done by politicians, for purposes of propaganda. It was Lloyd George who called R.F.C. squadrons 'the cavalry of the clouds'. At that time it was customary to talk of knights of the air, of jousting circuses, of duels in the sky. All this was useful because trench warfare gave no such opportunity for images of glamour and chivalry. But the truth is that the air war was just as brutal, squalid and wasteful as the slaughter in the trenches. There is nothing romantic about getting shot in the back at ten thousand feet.

All this I discovered when I began reading the real history

of the 1914–18 air war – the story revealed by the diaries, letters and memoirs of the pilots themselves. *Goshawk Squadron* was based on those accounts. The characters were invented but their behaviour, their attitudes and their activities were not. The broad structure of the story is true to the way the war went in 1918, and everything within that structure – training, tactics, aircraft performance, losses, and so on – is as authentic as I could make it.

When it first came out, *Goshawk Squadron* angered some veterans of the R.F.C. They felt it insulted the memories of their dead friends. I was saddened but not surprised. We all tend to forget the bad and remember only the good; and it must be especially tempting for survivors to believe that all the dead were heroes and that in any case victory justified their sacrifice. In fact we know that much of the slaughter was pointless. Courage was wasted along with everything else.

Some ex-pilots found *Goshawk Squadron* convincing. One, who flew in the R.F.C. for two years and served in the R.A.F. throughout the Second World War wrote, 'A fair comment . . . If we are honest we must admit that this "all jolly good sports" legend about the R.F.C. pilots and their opposite numbers in the German Air Force was, and is, a lot of balls – one either shot down or was shot down oneself.'

War is not sport. War is not fair. War in the sky, as Oliver Stewart remembered it, had to be unusually callous and cold-blooded. 'To those who studied it closely enough,' he wrote, 'the limitless open sky became as good a place to lie in wait for an unsuspecting passer-by as a darkened alley off a sleazy street, and the sudden act of violence, when it came, could be as deadly.' That – and not the myth of the cavalry of the clouds – is what *Goshawk Squadron* is about.

D.R.